VITRUVIUS BRITANNICUS

THE CLASSIC OF EIGHTEENTH-CENTURY BRITISH ARCHITECTURE

COLEN CAMPBELL

DOVER PUBLICATIONS, INC.
MINEOLA, NEW YORK

Bibliographical Note

This Dover edition, first published in 2007, is an unabridged republication of the first three volumes of *Vitruvius Britannicus, or The British Architect*, which were originally published by the author in London—the first volume in 1715, the second in 1717, and the third in 1725.

International Standard Book Number

ISBN-13: 978-0-486-44799-5
ISBN-10: 0-486-44799-5

Manufactured in the United States by Courier Corporation
44799504   2013
www.doverpublications.com

VITRUVIUS BRITANNICUS,

or

The British Architect,

Containing

The Plans, ELEVATIONS, and Sections

of the Regular Buildings, *both*

PUBLICK and PRIVATE,

IN

GREAT BRITAIN,

With Variety of New Designs; *in* 200 *large* Folio Plates, *Engraven by the* best Hands; *and Drawn either from the* Buildings *themselves, or the* Original Designs *of the* Architects;

In II VOLUMES

VOL. I. *by* Colen Campbell Esqr

VITRUVIUS BRITANNICUS,

ou

L'Architecte Britannique,

Contenant

Les Plans, ELEVATIONS, & Sections

des Bâtimens Reguliers, *tant*

PARTICULIERS que PUBLICS

de la Grande Bretagne,

Compris en 200 *grandes* Planches *gravez en taille douce, par les* Meilleurs Maitres, *et tous ou deßinez des* Bâtimens *memes, ou copiez des* Deßeins Originaux *des* Architectes:

EN DEUX TOMES.

TOME I. *Par le Sieur Campbell.*

CUM PRIVILEGIO REGIS..

Sold by the Author over against Douglas Coffee-house *in* S.t Martins-lane. John Nicholson *in* Little Britain, Andrew Bell *at the* Cross-Keys *in* Cornhil, W. Taylor *in* Pater-Noster-Row, Henry Clements *in* S.t Pauls Church-yard, And Jof. Smith *in* Exeter-Change. LONDON MDCCXV.

J. Sturt sculp.

To his most Sacred Majesty

King George,

Vitruvius Britannicus,

OR THE

British Architect

Is most humbly Inscrib'd, By

May it Please your Majesty

Yor Majties most faithfull & Obedient Subject

Colen Campbell

R. Snow scr. G. Bickham sculp.

THE
INTRODUCTION.

HE general Esteem that Travellers have for Things that are Foreign, is in nothing more conspicuous than with Regard to Building. We travel, for the most part, at an Age more apt to be imposed upon by the Ignorance or Partiality of others, than to judge truly of the Merit of Things by the Strength of Reason. It's owing to this Mistake in Education, that so many of the British Quality have so mean an Opinion of what is performed in our own Country; tho', perhaps, in most we equal, and in some Things we surpass, our Neighbours.

I have therefore judged, it would not be improper to publish this Collection, which will admit of a fair Comparison with the best of the Moderns. As to the Antiques, they are out of the Question; and, indeed, the Italians themselves have now no better Claim to them than they have to the Purity of the Latin.

We must, in Justice, acknowledge very great Obligations to those Restorers of Architecture, which the Fifteenth and Sixteenth Centurys produced in Italy. Bramante, Barbaro, Sansovino, Sangallo, Michael Angelo, Raphael Urbin, Julio Romano, Serglio, Labaco, Scamozzi, and many others, who have greatly help'd to raise this Noble Art from the Ruins of Barbarity: But above all, the great Palladio, who has exceeded all that were gone before him, and surpass'd his Contemporaries, whose ingenious Labours will eclipse many, and rival most of the Ancients. And indeed, this excellent Architect seems to have arrived to a Ne plus ultra of his Art. With him the great Manner and exquisite Taste of Building is lost; for the Italians can no more now relish the Antique Simplicity, but are entirely employed in capricious Ornaments, which must at last end in the Gothick.

For Proof of this Assertion, I appeal to the Productions of the last Century: How affected and licentious are the Works of Bernini and Fontana? How wildly Extravagant are the Designs of Boromini, who has endeavoured to debauch Mankind with his odd and chimerical Beauties, where the Parts are without Proportion, Solids without their true Bearing, Heaps of Materials without Strength, excessive Ornaments without Grace, and the Whole without Symmetry? And what can be a stronger Argument, that this excellent Art is near lost in that Country, where such Absurdities meet with Applause?

It

INTRODUCTION.

It is then with the Renowned Palladio *we enter the Lifts, to whom we oppofe the Famous* Inigo Jones: *Let the Banquetting-houfe, thofe excellent Pieces at* Greenwich, *with many other Things of this great Mafter, be carefully examined, and I doubt not but an impartial Judge will find in them all the Regularity of the former, with an Addition of Beauty and Majefty, in which our Architect is efteemed to have out-done all that went before; and when thofe Defigns he gave for* White-hall, *are publifhed, which I intend in the Second Volume, I believe all Mankind will agree with me, that there is no Palace in the World to rival it.*

And here I cannot but reflect on the Happinefs of the Britifh Nation, that at prefent abounds with fo many learned and ingenious Gentlemen, as Sir Chriftopher Wren, *Sir* William Bruce, *Sir* John Vanbrugh, *Mr.* Archer, *Mr.* Wren, *Mr.* Wynne, *Mr.* Talman, *Mr.* Hawkfmore, *Mr.* James, &c. *who have all greatly contributed to adorn our Ifland with their curious Labours, and are daily embellifhing it more.*

I hope, therefore, the Reader will be agreeably entertained in viewing what I have collected with fo much Labour. All the Drawings are either taken from the Buildings themfelves, or the original Defigns of the Architects, who have very much affifted me in advancing this Work: And I can, with great Sincerity, affure the Publick, That I have ufed the utmoft Care to render it acceptable; and that nothing might be Wanting, I have given the following Explanation to each Figure.

A N

P L A T E S
I N
The First Volume.

S. Paul's *Church*, London, *p.* 3, 4.

THIS Noble Fabrick was begun by Sir *Chriftopher Wren, Anno* 1672, and happily finifhed by him, 1710. I have made two Plates, the Plan and Weft Front; and did intend the Se-ction, but was prevented by the Ar-chitect, who propofed to publifh it himfelf. I have omitted the Rufticks and fluting the Columns in both Orders, to avoid the Confufion of fo many Lines in fo fmall a Scale. Here is a Ruftick Bafe-ment that carries two entire Orders, the firft is *Corin-thian,* 4 Foot in Diameter, with a plain Entablature; there is an Arcade all round the Building, that ferves for Lights: The fecond Order is Compofite, proportion-ably diminifhed with regard to the Inferior; here a very rich Tabernacle reigns throughout the whole Inter-Columnations, very like that excellent Mo-del in the *Rotundo* at *Rome,* but with this difference, that in this the Pedeftal is pierced, to give Light. A more particular Account is to be taken from the Defign by the Scale and Compafs, which would be too tedious in this Introduction. The whole Fabrick is performed in Stone, by thofe excellent and judicious Artifts, Mr. *Edward Strong, Senior* and *Junior,* whofe confummate Knowledge in their Profeffion, has greatly contributed to adorn the Kingdom; and it's beyond Exception, that this is the fecond Church in the World.

S. Peter's *at* Rome, *p.* 5, 6, 7.

I Thought it would not be improper to prefent the Curious with the Plan, Elevation, and Section of this Majeftick Building; and the more that I dare fafe-ly aver, that it's the moft correct, with refpect to the Truth of Architecture, or Cleannefs of Engraving, that was ever publifhed; and the Reader may have the Sa-tisfaction to view both, reduced to *Britifh* Meafure. The Criticks generally condemn the exceffive Height of the *Attick,* which they confine to a third of the infe-riour Column. That the Pediment, fupported by a Tetraftyle, is mean for fo great a Front, which at leaft would demand an Hexaftyle; that the Breaks are tri-fling, and the Parts without any Proportion; that the great Body of the Church, projected by *Carlo Maderno,* has extreamly injured the Auguft Appearance of the *Cupola,* which is very much loft by being removed fo

far from the Eaft Front, contrary to *Michael Angelo's* Defign, who conformed the whole Plan to a Square, wherein he defcribed a *Grecian* Crofs. But all agree, that the Width is noble, and the *Cupola* admirable: It was begun *Anno* 1513, and finifhed 1640.

A new *Defign for a Church in* Lincolns-Inn Fields, *p.* 8, 9.

THIS Defign I made, at the Defire of fome Per-fons of Quality and Diftinction, when it was propofed to have a Church in the Noble Square. The Plan is reduced to a Square and Circle in the Middle, which, in my weak Opinion, are the moft perfect Figures. In the Front I have removed the Angular Towers, at fuch a diftance, that the great *Cupola* is without any Ambarafs: Here is a regular Hexaftyle that commands the Front, which, with the other Parts, are all in certain Meafures of Proportion. I have introduced but one fingle *Corinthian* Order, fup-ported by a full Bafement, and finifhed with an At-tick and Balluftrade. The *Cupola* is adorned with a fingle Colonade of detached Columns; the whole is drefs'd very plain, as moft proper for the fulphurous Air of the City, and, indeed, moft conformable to the Simplicity of the Ancients. Done *Anno* 1712.

S. Philip's *Church at* Birmingham, *p.* 10, 11.

THIS Church is defigned by the ingenious Mr. *Archer;* and is juftly efteemed a very beauti-ful Structure. *Anno* 1710.

The Banquetting Houfe *at* Whitehall, *p.* 12, 13.

THIS incomparable Piece was defigned by the immortal *Jones,* as one Pavilion for that admi-rable Model he gave for a Royal Palace; and if this Specimen has juftly commanded the Admiration of Mankind, what muft the finifhed Pile have produced? I hope *Britain* will ftill have the Glory to acomplifh it, which will as far exceed all the Palaces of the Uni-verfe, as the Valour of our Troops and Conduct of our Generals have furpaffed all others. Here our ex-cellent Architect has introduced Strength with Polite-nefs, Ornament with Simplicity, Beauty with Maje-fty: It is, without Difpure, the firft Room in the World, and was built *Anno* 1616.

The

The Queen's *House at* Greenwich, *p.* 14, 15.

THIS is by the fame Architect, and was a Place of Retirement for the Queen-Mother. I have made two Plates: The Plan is near a Square, being 116 Foot by 120; the Proportion of the Rooms are extream juft; and the great Hall is admirable, making an exact Cube of 40 Foot. In the Front is a noble Ruftick Bafement, which fupports a beautiful and regular Loggio of the *Ionick* Order, finifhed with a juft Entablature and Balluftrade round the whole Building, which was executed *Anno* 1639.

The Great Gallery *in* Somerfet Gardens, *p.* 16.

THIS Noble Arcade was taken from a Defign of *Inigo Jones*, but conducted by another Hand: Some object, that the great Cornice is too camufe, and that the Drefs of the Windows have not Relief enough, which is only chargeable upon the Execution; but all agree, that the Proportions are juft, and the Defign excellent. I have neglected the Plan, being of little Ufe on this Occafion. It was built *Anno* 1662.

Gunnersbury Houfe, *near* Brentford, *p.* 17, 18.

THIS Houfe was executed by Mr. *Webb*, Difciple to *Jones*, from a Defign of his great Mafter. I have made two Plates; the firft is the Plan of the firft and fecond Floor; the Apartments are noble, regular, and commodious, the Rooms well-proportioned; the fecond is the Front, which contains a large plain Bafement, fupporting a handfome *Corinthian* Loggio. Some find the Inter-Columnation in this Hexaftyle too open, and that to leave out the Freeze and Architrave of each fide the Pediment, is a Licenfe not to be introduced without great neceffity. It was built *Anno* 1663.

A new Defign for the Duke of Argyle, *p.* 19, 20.

I Have infcrib'd this Defign to this illuftrious Name, whofe great Actions have filled the World with Surprize and Admiration; *Ramellies* and *Tanniers* are immortal. And as it's my greateft Honour to receive my Blood from his Auguft Houfe, I thought I could no where fo properly confecrate the firft Effay of my Invention, as an eternal Monument of the deepeft Refpect and Gratitude. I have given two Plates: In the firft are two Plans in a Square of 112 Foot; the Apartments of State are below, raifed from the Court by 6 Steps which leads into the great Hall, making a Cube of 50 Foot, and has a Poggio within dividing the two Stories; from the Hall you enter the Salon, attended with two noble Apartments of State fronting the Gardens; all the Rooms are either upon the Square, the Diagonal, or other Proportions univerfally received: In the fecond Story is a large Library, an Antichamber of each fide, with double Apartments; over which are *Mezonins*, for accommodating the Family, illuminated by low Lanterns from the Leads, whereby the Majefty of the Front is preferved from the ill Effect of crowded Apertures. The fecond is the Front, raifed from the Plinth which fupports the Rufticks, adorned with a Compofite Order of ¼ Columns, with a regular Entablature and Balluftrade; the Windows are drefs'd in the *Palladian* manner: And I have endeavoured to reconcile the Beauty of an Arcade in the ancient Buildings with the Conveniency of the Moderns, but muft leave it to others to judge of the Succefs. *Anno* 1714.

The firft Defign for Sir Richard Child, *Bar. p.* 21, 22.

THIS was intended for *Wanfted*, the Seat of Sir *Richard Child*, in a moft charming Situation, where are the nobleft Gardens now in the Kingdom: In this I was a little confined as to the Drefs of the

Windows, which are without Pediments, and feveral other Conveniences being wanting, the following Defign was preferred.

The fecond Defign for Sir Richard Child, *p.* 23, *to p.* 27. *inclufive.*

THE firft Plate contains the Plan of the principal Story, extended 260 Foot, raifed from the Court by a large Ruftick Bafement 15 Foot in Height: The Situation requiring this Height, to afford the State-Apartments a Profpect to thefe excellent Gardens. You afcend from the Court by double Stairs of each fide, which land in the Portico; and from thence into the great Hall, 51 Foot long, and 36 wide, and in Height the fame: This leads into the Salon, being an exact Cube of 30 Foot, attended with two noble Apartments of State, all fronting the Gardens. To the great Court are excellent Apartments for Sir *Richard* and my Lady, with great Conveniencies: And the whole Plan is clofed with a decent Chappel in one End, and a handfome Library in the other: The Offices are below, equal to the Court, and *Mezonins* above. The fecond is the Front, adorned with a juft Hexaftyle, the firft yet practifed in this manner in the Kingdom: The Order is *Corinthian*, and the Diameter 3 Foot, with its proper Entablature and Balluftrade, adorned with Figures, and a *Cupola*. The third is the Section, and the fifth a Green-Houfe, but defign'd by another Hand.

A new Defign infcrib'd to the Earl of Hallifax, *p.* 28, 29, 30.

AS this Noble Lord is the diftinguifhed Patron of the Mufes, the great *Mæcenas* of our Age, I have prefumed to honour this Defign with the Patronage of fo great a Name, as a fmall Evidence of my Gratitude, who have been honoured very early with his Lordfhip's Countenance, by encouraging my Labours. Of this I have made two Plates; the firft is the Plan of the principal Story, extending 300 Foot, and 150 deep, raifed from the Court by 6 Steps, which leads into a noble Hall, Tribune and Salon, with double Apartments of State to the Gardens: The fame Apartments are repeated to the great Court; and the whole Plan is clofed with a large Gallery in one End, and a Chappel, Library, and great Stair-Cafe in the other: What is of Diftinction in this Difpofition, is, that the Bed-chambers are removed from interrupting the grand Vifto, and ftill the State is preferved in entring them when neceffary; which I have not yet obferved in any former Defign. The fecond is the Front where a large Ruftico fupports a Loggio with ¼ Columns of the *Corinthian* Order: Here the Windows are placed at due Diftance, and free from that bad Effect we fo frequently fee when they are crowded, which deftroys that Repofe and Appearance of Strength, fo neceffary in Architecture. Done *Anno* 1715.

Burlington Houfe *in* Pickadilly, *with the Duke of* Kent's *Pavillion, p.* 31, 32, 33.

THE firft Plate contains the two Plans of the following Fronts: The fecond is the Front of *Burlington Houfe*: The third is the faid Pavilion in his Grace's Gardens in *Bedfordfhire*. Defign'd by Mr. *Archer, Anno* 1709.

Montague Houfe, London, *p.* 34, 35, 36.

THIS great Houfe was built by the late Duke of *Montague*, in the *French* manner; the Apartments are very noble, and richly adorned. Here Monfieur *la Fauffe*, Mr. *Rouffeau*, and Mr. *Baptift*, have exprefs'd the Excellence of their Art. The Architecture was conducted by Monfieur *Pouget*, 1678.

Drumlenrig Castle *in* Scotland, *p.* 37, 38.

IS the ancient Seat of his Grace the Duke of *Queenf-bury*, in the Shire of *Dumfries* : It was greatly a-dorned by the two preceding Dukes, with noble Gar-dens, and many other expenfive Decorations.

Marlborough Houfe, *St.* James's, *p.* 39, 40.

IS the Refidence of his Grace in *London* ; where are fine Gardens, and Profpeᵏt over St. *James's* Park. The Defign was given by Mr. *Wren, Anno* 1709.

Powis's Houfe, London, *p.* 41, 42.

THIS Houfe is built with the beft *Portland* Stone, well executed ; enriched with a *Corinthian* Pilaftrade, befides a confiderable Attick and Baluftrade, fupported with a ruftick Bafement ; and was finifh'd *Anno* 1714.

Buckingham Houfe, *p.* 43, 44.

THIS is the Seat of his Grace the Duke of *Buck-ingham*, in a moft admirable Situation, having the nobleft Avenue in *Europe*, the Mall, and com-mands an entire Profpeᵏt over St. *James's* Park. I have made two Plates: The firft is the general Plan, where the Apartments are extreamly noble, richly fur-nifhed ; here is a great Stair-Cafe, auguft and lofty ; here is a curious Colleᵏtion of the beft Painting, an ad-mirable Piece of Statuary of *Cain* and *Abel*, by the fa-mous *Jean de Boulogn*, with many other Rarities of great Value. In the fecond is the Front, adorned with a Pilaftrade of a *Corinthian* Tetraftyle. The whole was conduᵏted by the learned and ingenious Capt. *Wynne, Anno* 1705.

Stoke, *in the County of* Hereford, *p.* 45, 46.

IS the Seat of Mr. Auditor *Foley*, defign'd and built by himfelf, attended with fine Gardens. Here Mr. *Thornhill* has exprefs'd his excellent Genius in Paint-ing the Cieling of the great Hall, and many other no-ble Decorations. *Anno* 1710.

Kings-Wefton, *in* Gloucefterfhire, *p.* 47, 48.

IS the Seat of the Right Honourable *Edward South-well*, Efq; who is the *Angaranno* of our Age, to whom my Obligations are fo deep, that to repeat the leaft Part of them, would offend the Modefty of my Benfaᵏtor. I have made two Plates: The firft contains the Plans of the firft and fecond Floor ; the Apartments of State are raifed from the great Court by 12 Steps, which lead in-to a very lofty and fpacious Hall, that rifeth the full Height of both Stories ; from this you enter into the Apartments of State, very handfome and commodious ; above is the Lodging-Story, with an Attick for the reft of the Family: The fecond Plate is the Front, adorned with an Hexaftyle of a *Corinthian* Pilaftrade ; the Archi-teᵏture is great, and Mafculine ; the Windows at pro-per Diftance ; and the whole Defign fufficiently de-monftrates the great Genius of the Architeᵏt, which was given by Sir *John Vanbrugh*, and finifhed *Anno* 1713.

Lindfey Houfe *in* Lincolns-Inn Fields, London, *p.* 49, 50.

BElongs to the Right Honourable the Marquis of *Lindfey*, Lord Great Chamberlain of *England*, and is another Piece of *Inigo Jones*. I have made two Plates: In the firft are the Plans of the firft and fecond Stories, which contain as much State and Conveniency as can be expeᵏted in a Line of 62 Foot: The fecond is the Front, which has a good ruftick Bafement ; from which rifeth a regular *Ionick* Pilaftrade, including the principal, and an Attick Story: The Windows are well-

proportion'd, gracefully drefs'd, without Affeᵏtation. The Fabrick is cover'd with a handfome Baluftrade ; and, in a word, the whole is conduᵏted with that Harmony that fhines in all the Produᵏtions of this great Mafter, who defign'd it *Anno* 1640.

Willbery *in* Wiltfhire, *p.* 51. 52.

IS the Seat of *William Benfon*, Efq; invented and built by himfelf in the Stile of *Inigo Jones*, who, by this excellent Choice, difcovers the Politenefs of his Tafte : And as he is Mafter of the moft refined Parts of Litera-ture, has here exprefs'd a particular Regard to the no-bleft Manner of Architeᵏture in this beautiful and regu-lar Defign, which was executed *Anno* 1710.

A new Defign for the Earl of Iflay, *p.* 53, 54.

AS this Noble Lord is Brother to his Grace the Duke of *Argyle*, who poffeffeth all the great Qualities of the Family, adorned with the brighteft Endowments of Nature and Acquifition, I have prefumed to fkreen this Defign with his Lordfhip's Name. Here are two Plates: The firft contains the two Plans, in a Square of 76 Foot ; the principal Story is raifed from the Court by 6 Steps, which leads unto the great Hall 30 in Front, 40 deep, and 30 Foot high ; behind this Hall is the Salon 30 by 24 Foot, attended with double Apartments of State; the Salon is 20 Foot high, and the reft 18 ; here are no Bed-Chambers, this entire Floor being devoted to State: In the next Floor are two double Apartments, *viz.* Anti-Chamber, Bed-Chamber, &c. with a large Library over the Salon ; above the other Apartments are *Mezonins*, for accom-modating the Family, illuminated from the Leads. The fecond Plate contains the Front, which has a large Ru-ftico that fupports a regular *Ionick* Colonade of Co-lumns, though exprefs'd in the Plan as Pilafters: Here I have omitted to continue the Rufticks, to entertain the Eye with fome Repofe ; the Windows are propor-tion'd and drefs'd in the *Palladian* Stile. *Anno* 1715.

Blenheim, *from p.* 55, *to p.* 62, *inclufive.*

THIS Noble Fabrick is the Seat of his Grace the Duke of *Marlborough*, in *Oxfordfhire*. In this Colle-ᵏtion I prefent the Curious with all the Plans and Ele-vations, by the particular Direᵏtion of Sir *John Van-brugh*, who gave the Defigns of this Magnificent Palace. Here I am at a Lofs, how to exprefs my Obligations to this worthy Gentleman for promoting my Labours, in moft generoufly affifting me with his Original Draw-ings, and moft carefully correᵏting all the Plates as they advanced. All I can fay, falls infinitely fhort of what I owe ; and yet am afraid, what is already faid is much more than he will approve. The Manner is Grand, the Parts Noble, and the Air Majeftick of this Palace, adapted to the Martial Genius of the Patron. The firft Plate contains the Ground-Story, or Vaults: The fe-cond the Principal, or Floor of State ; where the Reader may, with great Eafe, enter into a full Detail of the Whole by the Scale: The third is the general Front as you enter, making a Line of 490 Foot: The fourth is the Garden-Front: The fifth is the Elevation of one End; the other being anfwerable to it : The laft is the general Plan. Here are noble Gardens; a ftately Bridge, with an Arch 100 Foot in Diameter ; with many other excellent Embellifhments: But above all, the intended Paintings by Mr. *Thornhill*, the Modern *Apelles*, whofe bright Pencil is only capable to tranfmit to Pofterity the Glory of the *Britifh* Arms, whereof the Models are already made. It was built *Anno* 1715.

Caftle Howard, *from p.* 63, *to p.* 71, *inclufive.*

IS the Noble Seat of the Right Honourable the Earl of *Carlifle*, in *Yorkfhire* : The Plans, Elevations, and Seᵏtions, are all drawn from the Originals of the Archi-teᵏt, tect, Sir *John Vanbrugh*, and by him moſt carefully re-viſed. The firſt Plate is the general Plan, making a Line of 660 Foot, wherein all the Offices are expreſs'd. The ſecond is the Plan of the principal Floor, the Por-tico, Great Hall, and Salon, are extream Magnificent, richly adorn'd with Sculpture ; the Painting by Signor *Pilligrini* ; in the *Dome* is expreſs'd the Fall of *Phaeton* : The Apartments of State are very Noble, fronting the Gardens, with a Line of 300 Foot ; the reſt is ſuited to Conveniency. The third Plate is the general Front. The fifth is the Front to the great Court. The fifth is the Garden Front ; and the laſt is the Section. Here are excellent Gardens, Parks of great Extent, lofty Obeliſks. And in fine, this Seat is truly worthy of ſo great and ſo liberal a Patron, which was built *Anno* 1714.

Chatſworth, *from p.* 72, *to p.* 76, *incluſive*.

IS the magnificent Palace of his Grace the Duke of *Devonſhire*, in *Derbyſhire* ; which, for the Quality of Materials, Neatneſs of Execution, rich Furniture, and all proper Decorations, is ſecond to none in the Kingdom, and perhaps in *Europe*. I have given three Plans, and two Elevations : The firſt is the Plan of the Offices, with a ſpacious Court, a-dorned with two noble Arcades : Here is a Chap-pel, great Hall, and Stair-Caſe, extreme Magnifi-cent. The ſecond is the Plan of his Grace's proper Apartment, very rich, where State is joined with great Conveniency ; here is a noble Gallery, a Library, with a Collection of the moſt valuable Authors, and many excellent Original Paintings of the moſt celebrated Ma-ſters. The third is the Plan of the principal Floor ; containing the Apartments of State, which, indeed, are extreme Noble. The fourth is the Weſt Front, a very rich Piece of Architecture ; the Terraſs is dreſs'd with Froſt-Work ; from which is raiſed a large ruſtick Baſe-ment, that ſupports an *Ionick* Order ; and in the Mid-dle a beautiful Tetraſtyle, covered with an enriched Pe-diment : The whole Front is dreſs'd with excellent Sculpture, and finiſhed with a regular Baluſtrade, a-dorned with Vaſes of an exquiſite Choice. The laſt Plate is the South Front, which is very fine, but not ſo rich as the former. The whole is performed in the beſt Stone, deſerving of the beſt of Patrons ; and is the Invention of Mr. *Talman*, *Anno* 1681.

Mr. Johnſton's Houſe *at* Twickenham, *p.* 77.

THIS is the Seat of the Right Honourable *James Johnſton*, Eſq ; which is regular, and commodi-ous. The principal Floor is raiſed by 8 Steps from the Court, where you find a very handſome Hall that leads into the great Apartments. Here is an admirable Pro-ſpect of the moſt charming Part of the *Thames*, where the Eye is entertain'd with a Thouſand Beauties, not to be conceived but from this Situation. The Gardens are extreme curious, the Plantations moſt artfully di-ſpoſed ; and every thing contributes to expreſs the re-fined Taſte, and great Politeneſs of the Maſter. De-ſign'd by Mr. *James*, 1710.

Sir Walter Yonge's Houſe, *p.* 78, 79.

THIS is the Seat of Sir *Walter Yonge*, Bar. in *De-vonſhire*. I have made two Plates : The firſt contains the two Plans of the firſt and ſecond Story ; in the firſt is the Floor of State, raiſed from the Court by 12 Steps, where you find very handſome Apart-ments well furniſhed. In the ſecond Story is the Cham-ber Floor, with proper Conveniencies. The ſecond Plate is the Front, which was executed *Anno* 1690.

Mr. Cary's Houſe *at* Rowhampton, *p.* 80, 81.

THIS is the Seat of *Thomas Cary*, Eſq ; in *Surrey* ; in a moſt agreeable Situation : The Apart-ments are well diſpoſed for State and Conveniency. The Salon is very Noble, and has an excellent Ciel-

ing, by Mr. *Thornhill*. But above all, the Humanity and Liberality of the Maſter deſerves to be tranſmit-ted to Poſterity. The Deſign was given by Mr. *Archer*, *Anno* 1710.

Greenwich Hoſpital, *from p.* 82, *to p.* 89, *incluſive*.

THIS Royal Hoſpital was at firſt intended by King *Charles* II. for a Royal Palace ; but was given by King *William* and Queen *Mary* for the Relief of decay'd and diſabled Seamen, who had ſpent their Blood and Strength in the Naval Service. It is ſitua-ted on the Bank of the *Thames*, 4 Miles below the Bridge of *London*, and is for Magnificence, Extent, and Conveniency, the firſt Hoſpital in the World. I have given four large Plates : The firſt is the general Plan of this ſtupendous Structure, which contains the State-Apartments, with great variety of Accommodation : The ſecond is the general Front, that commands a charming Proſpect of the River and adjacent Country : The third is a double Pavilion at large, which makes a Part of the preceding Front : And the laſt is the Re-turn of the ſame Pavilion, flanking the firſt great Court as you aſcend from the Water. The Stile of Architecture is Great and Noble, executed by Mr. *Webb*, from a Deſign of his great Maſter *Inigo Jones*. Some are of Opinion, that the Attick over the great *Corin-thian* Order is too high by the great Plinth, being juſt ſo much more than One third of the Column, which, probably, was changed from the Original Drawing. In the beſt Remains of Antiquity, we find great Varie-ty in their Proportions : In the Triumphal Arch of *Titus*, the Attick has a full Third of the en-tire Ordonnance ; in that at *Benevento* near the ſame ; at *Ancona* a fourth ; in that of *Conſtantine* the Attick has 4. 9. Parts of the Column ; that of *Severus* is pre-ciſely one Third : I ſhall leave it to better Judges to determine the Preference. But to return to the pre-ſent Subject : Here the Ruſticks are introduced with ſo much Art, the Ornaments with ſo much Grace, the whole Diſpoſition is ſo Noble and Lofty, that, in the Opinion of many, it's one of the beſt Lines of Building in the World. There is ſo much to be ſaid on this co-pious Subject, that, indeed, it requires an entire Vo-lume ; and poſſibly I may, one Day, entertain the Pub-lick with it. But here I can't neglect mentioning that excellent Cieling in the great Hall, by Mr. *Thornhill*, to his eternal Honour, and his Country : Here Fo-reigners may view with Amaze, our Countrymen with Pleaſure, and all with Admiration, the Beauty, the Force, the Majeſty of a *Britiſh* Pencil ! rich in Invention, cor-rect in Deſign, noble in Diſpoſition, in Execution ad-mirable. 1715.

Thorsby Houſe, *p.* 90, 91.

IS the Seat of the Right Honourable the Marquis of *Dorcheſter*, in *Nottinghamſhire*. I have made two Plates : The firſt is a Plan, which entertains you with a noble Hall, a fine Chappel, a large Court, Apart-ments of State, and all other Conveniencies : The ſe-cond is the Front, extreme rich ; performed by the ſame Hand that afterwards built *Chatſworth*. Here are beau-tiful Gardens ; and all is worthy of ſo noble and great a Patron. It was built *Anno* 1671.

Stainborough, *p.* 92, 93, 94.

THIS is the magnificent Seat of the Right Ho-nourable the Earl of *Strafford*, &c. in *Yorkſhire*. Of which I have made two Plates : In the firſt are the Plans of the firſt and ſecond Stories ; the firſt is raiſed above the great Court by 12 Steps, which leads into a ſpacious Hall, and very large Apartments of State and Conveniency : The ſecond Plan preſents you with a noble Gallery, that takes up the entire Front in a Line of 180 Foot, and has the Height of the Principal and Attick Story ; here the noble Patron is preparing a curious Collection of Painting, Sculpture, and other

excellent

excellent Decorations. The second Plate is the Front of this sumptuous Fabrick, raised with a large Basement, where the Coins are bound with Rusticks, which support a rich *Corinthian* Pilastrade, that carries the Principal and Attick Story; the Order has a regular Entablature, a handsome Balustrade, adorned with Figures and Vases; the Windows are richly dress'd : The whole Architecture is after the *Venetian* Manner, performed in Stone; and all is agreeable to the Politeness, Quality, and Distinction of the Patron. *Anno* 1715.

A new Design for the Lord Percival, *p.* 95, 96, 97.

I Have inscrib'd this Design of my Invention to this Noble Lord, who has universally encouraged all Arts and Sciences, and that of Architecture in a most particular manner. Here are two Plates: The first is the general Plan; the two covered Arches that join the Offices to the House, are disposed to receive Coaches, for Conveniency in wet Weather; the chief Floor is above, having a noble Salon in Front, and two fine Apartments behind. The second is the general Front, making a Line of 245 Foot; the Body of the House contains 120, which I have dress'd with the two most ancient Orders, the *Dorick* and *Ionick*, in a double Hexastyle; the first has 2¼ in Diameter, the second has 2 Foot; the first advanceth ¾ from the Wall, and

has but 8 Diameters in Height, which I thought the best Proportion to support the Superiour Order, to which I give 9. The Arcade is equal to one half of the Hexastyle; the Pavilion extends 36, and has 30 in Height, including the Balustrade. I have left out all manner of Rusticks and other Ornaments generally practised, purely to shew the Harmony of Proportion in the greatest Simplicity. 1715.

The Lord Leimpster's House, *p.* 98, 99, 100.

THIS is the Seat of the Lord *Leimpster*, in *Northamptonshire*. Of which I have made two Plates: The first is the general Plan, including all the Offices, great Court, and Plan of the principal Floor; where are very noble Apartments, with great Conveniency. The second is the general Front, with a rustick Basement, which supports a *Corinthian* Pilastrade that carries two Stories: The Fabrick is finished with an Attick, and all is performed in very good Stone; and is the ingenious Invention of Mr. *Hawksmore*, to whom I am indebted for the Original Drawings of this House, and many other valuable Pieces, for enriching this Work, which I could not in Gratitude conceal from the Publick: The Building was finish'd *Anno* 1713; with which I conclude this First Volume.

A LIST *of what is contain'd in the First Volume.*

GEORGE R.

 HEREAS Our Trufty and Well-beloved *COLEN CAMPBELL*, Efq; Author of the Work, *John Nicholfon*, *Andrew Bell*, *Wiliam Taylor*, *Henry Clements*, Bookfellers, and *Jofeph Smith*, Mapfeller, of our City of *London*, have humbly reprefented to Us, That they have, with great Labour and Expence, prepared for the Prefs a Book, Entituled, *Vitruvius Britannicus*, or the *Britifh* Architect; containing the exact Plans, Elevations, and Sections of the Regular Buildings, both Publick and Private, in *Great Britain*; with variety of New Defigns. In Two Volumes. And have, therefore, humbly befought Us, to grant them our Royal Privilege and Licenfe for the fole Printing and Publifhing thereof, for the Term of Fourteen Years. We being willing to give all due Encouragement to Works of this Nature, are gracioufly pleafed to condefcend to their Requeft: And We do, therefore, by thefe Prefents, grant unto them, the faid *Colen Campbell*, *John Nicholfon*, *Andrew Bell*, *William Taylor*, *Henry Clements*, and *Jofeph Smith*, their Executors, Adminiftrators, and Affigns, Our Royal Licenfe for the fole Printing and Publifhing the aforefaid Book, Entituled, *Vitruvius Britannicus*, or the *Britifh* Architect, for the Term of Fourteen Years from the Date hereof: Strictly forbidding all Our Subjects within Our Kingdom, and Dominions, to reprint the fame, either in the like, or in any other Volume or Volumes whatfoever; or to import, buy, vend, utter, or diftribute any Copies thereof, reprinted beyond the Seas during the Term of Fourteen Years, without the Confent or Approbation of the faid *Colen Campbell*, *John Nicholfon*, *Andrew Bell*, *William Taylor*, *Henry Clements*, and *Jofeph Smith*, their Heirs, Executors, and Affigns, under their Hands and Seals firft had and obtain'd, as they will anfwer the contrary at their Peril: Whereof the Commiffioners, and other Officers of our Cuftoms, the Mafter, Wardens, and Company of *Stationers* are to take Notice, that the fame may be entred in the Regifter of the faid Company; and that due Obedience be rendred thereunto.

Given at Our Court at St. James's, *the Eighth Day of* April, 1715, *in the Firft Year of Our Reign.*

By His MAJESTY's Command,

Ja. Stanhope.

N. B. In the Second Volume, what remains of INIGO JONES will be moft carefully collected over the Kingdom, with the incomparable Defigns he gave for *WHITE-HALL*; all taken from the invaluable Original Drawings of that Great Mafter; with the other moft Regular Edifices.

A

A LIST *of those who have already subscribed before the 25th of March, 1715.*

A.

Settt.

DUKE of *Argyle*, Groom of the Stole to his Royal Highnefs the Prince 2
The Marquis of *Annandale* 2
Earl of *Albemarle* 2
Earl of *Arran* 1
The Lord *Afhburnham* 1
Sir *John Anftruther*, Bar. 1
Sir *Jacob Aftley*, Bar. 1
Sir *Robert Adair*, Knt. 1
John Arthbuthnott, M. D. 2
David Anderfon, S. T. D. 1
James Anderfon, D. V. M. 1
James Anderfon, Gent. Waiter to the Signet in *Edinborough* 1
The Honourable *John Aiftabie*, Efq; 1
Thomas Archer, Efq; 1
Francis Annefley, Efq; 1
Alexander Abercrombie, Efq; 1
Mr. *James Ayres* 1
Mr. *Francis Anderton* 1

B.

DUke of *Beaufort* 2
Duke of *Buckingham* 2
Duke of *Bolton* 2
Duchefs of *Buccleugh* 2
Earl of *Bridgewater*, Lord Chamberlain to her Royal Highnefs 2
Earl of *Burlington* 2
Earl of *Brodalbin* 1
Earl of *Buchan* 1
Earl of *Bute* 1
Lord Vifcount *Bolingbroke* 1
Lord *Balmerinoch* 1
Lord *Bruce* 1
Lord *Bathurft* 1
Lord *Berkeley* of *Stratton* 1
Lord *Bingly* 1
Sir *Juftus Beck*, Bar. 1
Sir *Jacob Banks*, Knt. 1
Sir *James Bateman* 1
The Honourable *George Baily*, Efq; Commiffioner of the Admiralty 1
The Right Hon. *William Bromley*, Efq; 1
The Right Hon. *William Blathwayt*, Efq; 1
William Benfon, Efq; 1
J. Barington Shute, Efq; 1
John Boulter, Efq; 1
Nathanael Blackerby, Efq; 1
William Burnet, Efq; 1
John Basket, Efq; Printer to the King's moft Excellent Majefty 2
Mr. *Richard Brown* 1
Mr. *James Bateman* 1
Mr. *James Blacket*, Joiner 1
Mr. *Francis Bird*, Statuary 1

C.

William Lord *Cowper*, Lord High Chancellor of *Great Britain* 2
Earl of *Carlifle* 2
Earl of *Carnavan* 2
Earl of *Cholmondeley*, Treaf. of the Houfhold 2
Earl of *Clare* 2
Lord *Craven* 1
Lord *Colerane* 1
Lord *Coningsby* 1
Lord *Conway* 1
Lady *Cairnes* 1
The Lady *Cary* 1
The Right Honourable *Tho. Coke*, Efq; Vice-Chamberlain 1
Sir *Archibald Campbell*, Knt. 1
Sir *Duncan Campbell*, Bar. 1
Sir *Hugh Campbell* of *Calder*, Bar. 1
Sir *James Campbell* of *Ardkinglafs*, Bar. 1
Sir *James Campbell* of *Achinbrake*, Bar. 1
Sir *James Campbell* of *Abruchill*, Bar. 1
The Honourable *John Campbell*, Efq; 1
The Hon. Coll. *James Campbell*, Efq; 1

Setts.

The Hon. Coll. *John Campbell*, Efq; Gentleman of the Bed-Chamber to his Royal Highnefs 1
Archibald Campbell, Efq; 1
Daniel Campbell, Efq; 1
Duncan Campbell, Efq; 1
Capt. *Matthew Campbell*, Efq; 1
Baily *John Campbell* of *Edinburgh*, Efq; 1
Colen Campbell, Efq; 1
Sir *Richard Child*, Bar. 3
Sir *James Carmichel*, Bar. 1
Sir *James Cuningham*, Bar. 1
Sir *Thomas Cofs*, Bar. 1
Sir *Robert Child*, Knt. 1
Sir *Alexander Cummins*, Knt. 1
The Honourable *George Clark*, Efq; 1
George Lockhart of *Carnwath*, Efq; 1
R. Crefwell, Efq; 1
George Culworth, Efq; 1
Thomas Cary, Efq; 1
Henry Cuningham, Efq; 1
Mr. *Cranenburgh*, late Refident for His Majefty 1
Mr. *Chetwynd* 1
Mr. *John Churchill*, Mafter Carpenter to His Majefty 1
John Corbet, LL. D. 1

D.

DUke of *Devonfhire*, Lord Steward of the King's Houfhold 2
Duke of *Douglafs* 1
Marquis of *Dorchefter* 2
Earl of *Dorfet* 2
Earl of *Denbigh* 1
Earl of *Dundonald* 1
Sir *David Dalrymple*, Bar. 1
The Honourable *George Dodington*, Efq; one of the Lords of the Admiralty 1
Montague Gerrard Drake, Efq; 1
William Dafhwood, Efq; 1
William Dun of *Liveyeard*, Efq; 1
Archibald Douglafs of *Cavers*, Efq; 1
Thomas Dawfon, D. D. 1
Capt. *N. Duboife* 6
Mr. *Dodd* of *Lincolns-Inn* 1
Mr. *William Dickinfon* 1
Mrs. *Dolben* 1

E.

RIght Hon. Lieut. General *Earl* 1
Sir *John Evelyn* 1
Sir *Gilbert Elliot* of *Munto*, Bar. one of the Senators of the College of Juftice 1
R. Edgecomb, Efq; 1

F.

EArl of *Findlator* and *Seafield* 1
Lord *Foley* 1
Lord *Forrefter* 1
Sir *Robert Furnefe*, Bar. 1
Sir *Thomas Frankland*, Bar. 1
Richard Fuller, LL. D. 1
Mr. Auditor *Foley* 1
Thomas Frankland, Efq; 1
James Fury, Efq; 1
John Forbes of *Colloden*, Efq; 1
William Freeman, Efq; 1

G.

DUke of *Grafton* 2
The Earl of *Godolphin* 2
Lord *Guilford* 1
His Excellency the Lord Baron *Goerts,&c.* 1
Sir *Richard Grofvenar*, Bar. 1
Sir *Robert Gordon*, Bar. 1
Sir *William Gordon*, Bar. 1

Settt.

Alexander Gordon of *Pitburg*, Efq; 1
Alexander Grant, Efq; Brigadier General 1
Francis Gwynn, Efq; 1
William Le Grand, Efq; 1
Richard Golph, Efq; 1
Sir *Samuel Garth*, M. D. 1
Robert Gray, M. D. 1
Mr. *Tho. Granger* of the *Eaft-India Houfe* 1
Mr. *Andrew Gelph* 1

H.

DUchefs of *Hamilton* and *Brandon* 2
Earl of *Hallifax*, firft Lord Commiffioner of the Treafury 2
Earl of *Hopeton* 2
Earl of *Haddington* 1
Lord *Harley* 1
Lord *Haverfham* 1
Sir *Thomas Hanmer*, Bar. 1
Sir *Roger Hill*, Bar. 1
Sir *Jof. Hodges*, Bar. 1
Sir *David Hamilton*, Knt. 1
John Henley of *Briftol*, Efq; 1
Richard Hill of *Richmond*, Efq; 1
William Herbert, Efq; 1
William Hedworth, Efq; 1
John Huggins, Efq; 1
Nicholas Hawkfmoor, Efq; Clerk of His Majefty's Works 1
Mr. *John Hare* 1
Mr. *Thomas Hinton* 1
Mr. *Robert Hynd* 1

I.

EArl of *Iflay*, Lord Regifter, and Juftice General for *North Britain* 2
Sir *Theodore Janfen*, Knt. and Bar. 1
Sir *Henry Innes*, Bar. 1
Sir *William Johnfton*, Bar. 1
The Right Hon. *James Johnfton*, Efq; 1
Tobiah Jenkyns, Efq; 1
Thomas Jett, Efq; 1
Mr. *John James* of *Greenwich* 1
Mr. *William Jones* 1
Mr. *Henry Joines* of *Woodftock* 1
Mr. *Edward James* 1
Mr. *William Jones*, F. R. S. 1

K.

DUke of *Kent* 2
Earl of *Kinnoul* 2
Lord Vifcount *Kilfyth* 1
Lord Chief Juftice *King* 1
Robert Keck, Efq; 1

L.

DUke of *Leeds* 2
Marquis of *Linfey*, Lord Great Chamberlain of *England* 2
Earl of *Loudoun* 2
Lord *Lanfdown* 1
Lord *Leimpfter* 1
Lord *Langfdale* 1
Lord Bifhop of *London* 1
Nicolas Lechmere, Efq; Solicit. General 1
Samuel Lynn, Efq; 1
Benjamin Lacy, Efq; 1
Mr. *Lockman*, St. *James's* 1
Mr. *John Leggat* 1
Mr. *William Law* 1

M.

DUke of *Marlborough*, Captain General of all His Majefty's Forces 2

D Duchefs

	Setts.
Duchefs of *Marlborough*	2
Duke of *Montague*	2
Duchefs of *Montague*	2
Duke of *Montrofe*, principal Secretary of State	2
Earl of *Marefhall*	2
Earl of *Marr*	2
Lord *Manfell*	1
Lord *Middleton*	1
Sir *William Manfell*, Bar.	2
Sir *Chriftopher Mufgrave*, Bar.	1
Sr *Nicolas Morice*, Bar.	1
George Maddifon, Efq;	1
Abraham Meure, Efq;	1
Capt. *Mandell*	1
Doctor *Mede*, M. D.	1
Doctor *John Milbourne*, M. D.	1
Mr. *John Mum Moor*	1
Mr. *Arthur Manley*	1
Mr. *George Montgomery*	1
Mr. *Ifaac Mars*	1

N.

Earl of *Nottingham*, Lord Prefident of the Council	2
Grey Neville, Efq;	1
Edward Nicolas, Efq;	1

O.

Duke of *Ormond*	2
Earl of *Orford*, firft Lord of the Admiralty	2
Earl of *Orrery*	2
Earl of *Orkney*	2
Earl of *Oxford*	2

P.

Duke of *Powis*	2
Earl of *Portland*	2
Lord *Polworth*	1
Lord *Percival*	1
Lord Chief Juftice *Parker*	1
Sir *Robert Pollock*, Bar.	1
William Pulteney, Efq; Secretary of War	1
Robert Pringle, Efq; Under-Secretary	1
Blackwell Perkins, Efq;	1
John Pringle of *Haining*, Efq;	1
Silvefter Pettyt of *Bernard's Inn*, Gent.	1

	Setts.
Mr. *John Price*, Jun.	1
Mr. *Francis Price*	1
Mr. *Alexander Prichard*, Mafon	1
Mr. *Andrew Peters*, Painter	1
Mr. *Bart. Peifley* of *Oxon*, Mafon	1

Q.

Duke of *Queensbury*	2

R.

Duke of *Richmond*	2
Duke of *Roxburgh*	2
Duke of *Rutland*	2
Earl of *Rochefter*	1
Earl of *Rothes*	1
Earl of *Rofeberry*	1
Sir *William Robinfon*, Bar.	1
Richard Rooth, Efq;	1
Hugh Rofe of *Kilravock*, Efq;	1
Benjamin Robinfon, Efq;	1
Samuel Ravenel, Efq;	1
John Rudy, Efq;	1
Mr. *John Richards*	1

S.

Duke of *Somerfet*, Mafter of Horfe to the King	2
Duke of *Shrewsbury*, Lord Chamberlain	2
Marquis of *Seaforth*	2
Earl of *Sunderland*, Lord Lieut. of *Ireland*	2
Earl of *Scarborough*	2
Earl of *Strafford*	2
Earl of *Sutherland*	1
Earl of *Stairs*	2
Lord *Somers*	2
Bord *Shelburne*	1
Sir *Fulworth Skipwith*, Bar.	1
Sir *William Stewart*, Bar.	1
Sir *John Smith*, Bar.	1
The Right Hon *Edward Southwell*, Efq;	1
Mrs. *Eliz. Southwell*	1
Thomas Strangewayes, Efq;	1
James Sadler, Efq;	1
Hans Sloane, M. D.	1
Mr. *Edward Strong*, Jun.	4
Mr. *John Sturges*	1
Mr. *Andrew Smith*	1
Mr. *Thomas Sadler*	1

	Setts.
Mr. *Richard Sanders*, Joiner	1
John Sturt, Engraver	1

T.

Marquis of *Tweeddale*	1
Earl of *Thanet*	1
Lord Vifcount *Townfhend*, Principal Secretary of State	1
Lord *Thomond*	1
James Taylor, Efq;	1
Cholmondeley Turner, Efq;	1
John Talbot, Efq;	1
William Tomlins, Efq;	1
John Talman, Efq;	1
Capt. *Tufnel* of *Weftminfter*	1
Mr. *James Thornhill*, Painter	1

V.

Sir *John Vanbrugh*, Knt. Comptroller of His Majefty's Works	1
James Vernon, Efq;	1
Mr. *Vanhuls*	1

W.

Marquis of *Wharton*, Lord Privy Seal	1
Earl of *Warwick*	1
Earl of *Weymife*	1
Lord Bifhop of *Winchefter*	1
Sir *William Wyndham*, Bar.	1
Sir *John Walter*, Bar.	1
Sir *Tho. Webfter*, Bar.	1
Sir *Chriftopher Wrenn*, Knt. Surveyor-General of His Majefty's Works	1
The Honourable *Robert Walpole*, Efq; Paymafter General	1
Chriftopher Wren, Efq;	1
Thomas Woodcock, Efq;	1
Doctor *Welwood*, M. D.	1
Mr. Serjeant *Wynne*	1
Mr. *Sam. Waters* of the *Eaft-India Houfe*	2
Mr. *Robert Wood*	1
Mr. *James Williams*, Mafon	1

Y.

Sir *Walter Yonge*, Bar.	1

NB. If any Subfcribers are omitted in the above Catalogue, their Names fhall be inferted in the Second Volume, and likewife all thofe who fhall hereafter fubfcribe, before the Work is finifh'd.

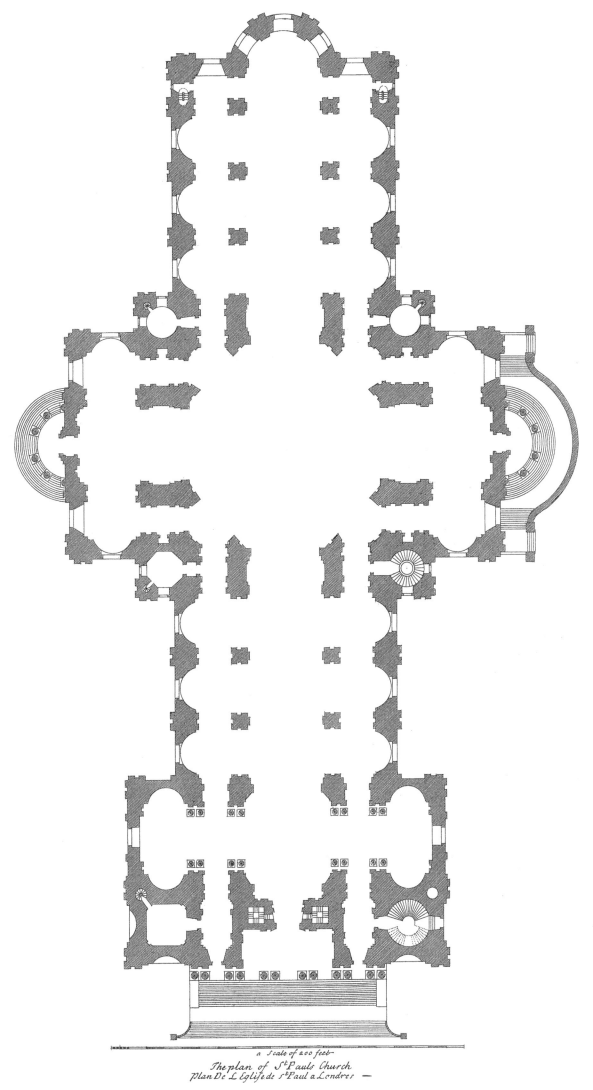

a Scale of 200 feet

The plan of St Pauls Church

Plan De L Eglise de St Paul a Londres

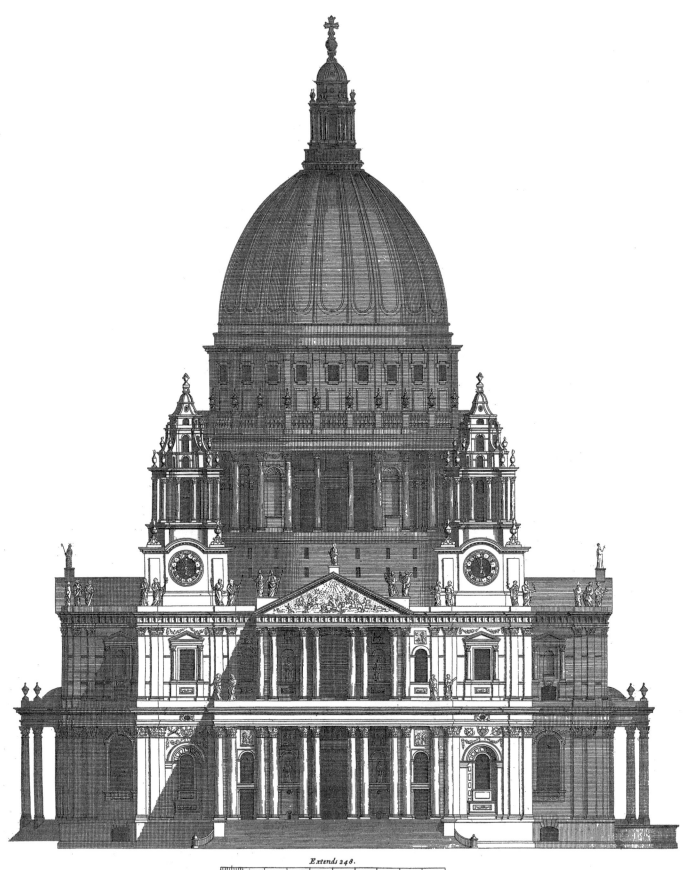

Extends 248.

a Scale of 100 Feet

The West Prospect of St. PAUL'S CHURCH, begun Anno 1672 and finish'd 1710, by
St. Christopher Wren Kt.
Is most humbly Inscribed to the Rt. Revd: Father in God IOHN Lord BISHOP of LONDON, Dean of all Her MAJESTYS Chapels. and one
of Her MAJESTYS most Honorable privy Council.

Elevation Occidental Del' EGLISE de St. PAUL a LONDRE Commencée 1672 et achevée 1710 par Christophre Wren Chevallier.

Ca Campbell Delin

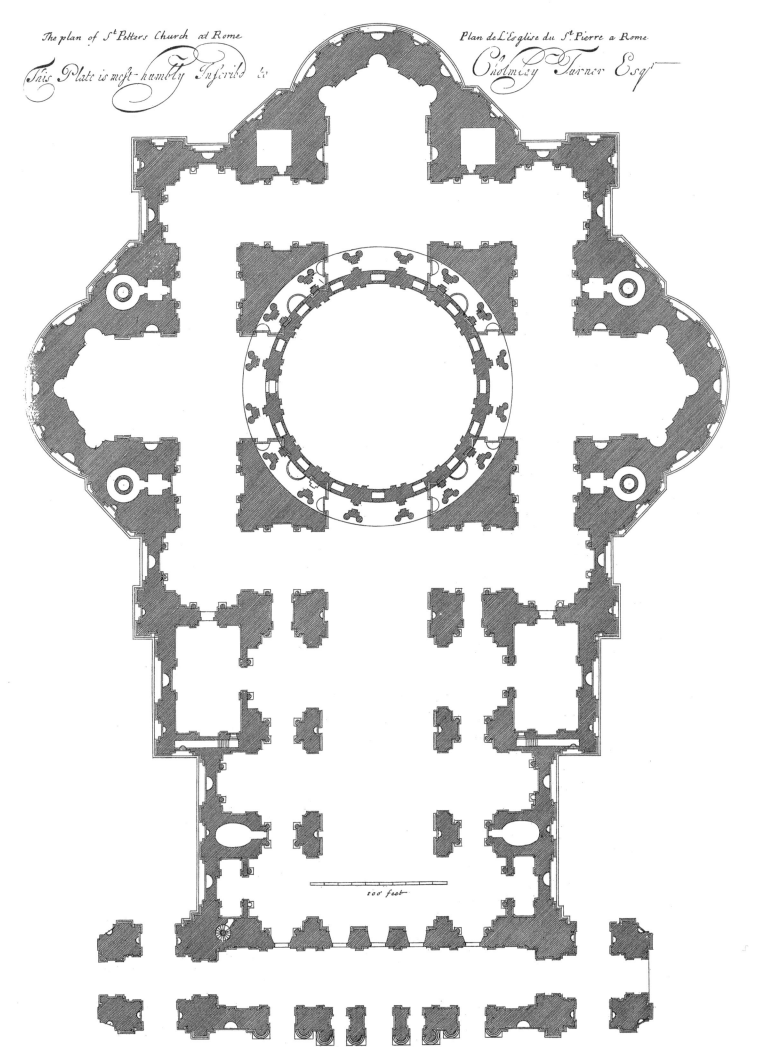

The plan of St Petters Church at Rome

Plan de L'Esglise du St Pierre a Rome

This Plate is most humbly Inscribd to

Cholmley Turner Esqr

100 feet

Extends 400.

a Scale of 200 Feet

The Elevation of St PETERS CHURCH at ROME Founded by CONSTANTIN the Great Anno 310. The present Fabrick was begun by
POPE IULIUS the II conducted by BRAMANTE Anno 1513 to whom SANGALLO and the Famous MICHEL ANGELO BONAROTI Succeeded.
The Frontispiece and Body of the CHURCH was Erected by P. PAUL the V. under the direction of CARLO MADERNO 1613. and the Balustrade and
other Ornaments were added by CAVALIER BERNINI 1640.

L'Eglise De St PIERRE a ROME

C. 1, PL. 6

Ca Campbell Delin:

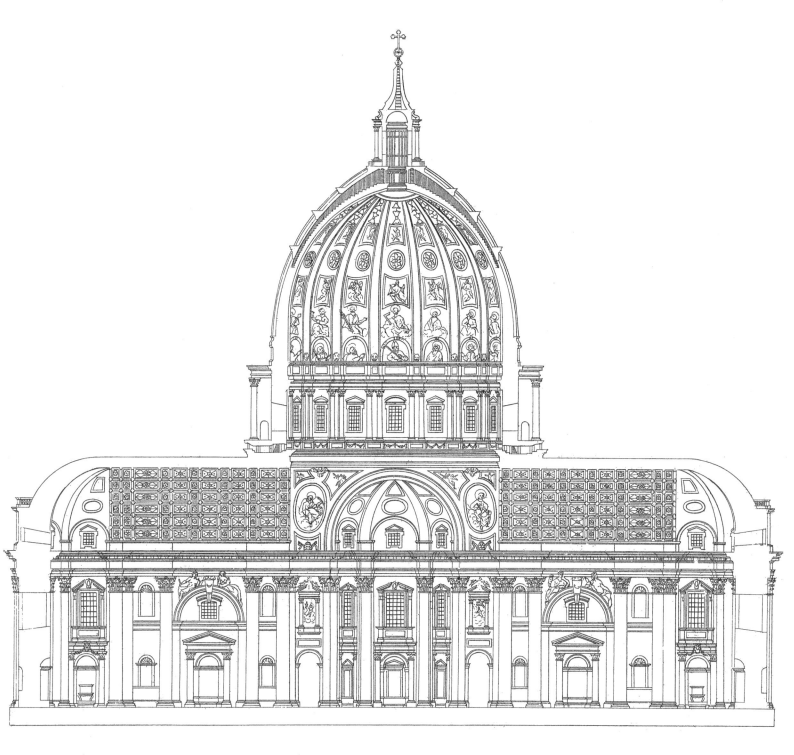

The Section of St Peters Church in Rome.

Le Profil de l'Eglise du St Pierre a Rome.

This plate is most humbly inscrib'd to James Tayler Esqr

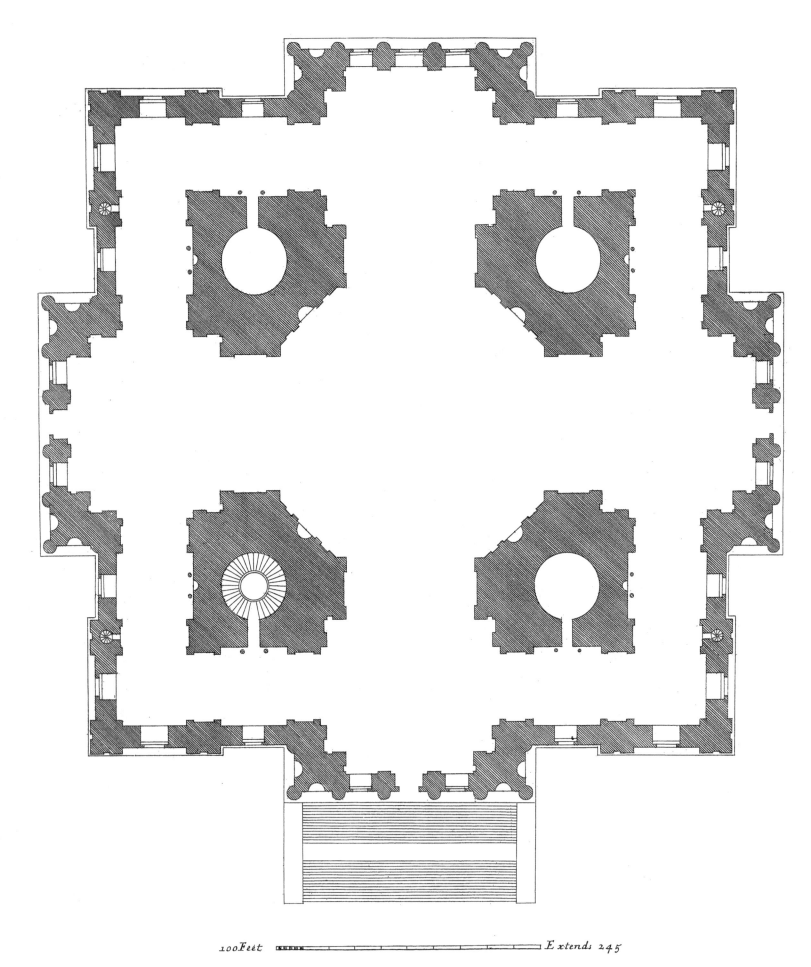

100 Feet   Extends 245

Plan of a new Deſſign of a Church of my Invention for Lincolns inn Fields.

Plan D'un Nouveau Deſſin de mon Invention pour une Eſgliſe dans la place de Lincolns inFields aLondres.

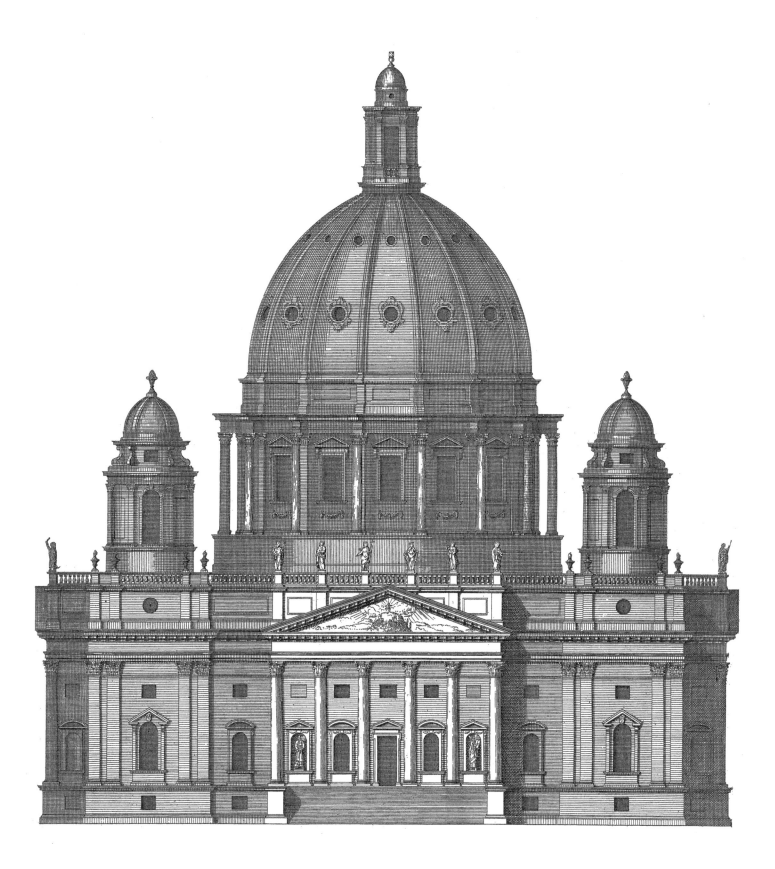

100 Feet |⊞⊞⊞⊞⊞⊞⊞⊞⊞⊞⊞⊞⊞⊞⊞⊞⊞⊞⊞⊞⊞⊞⊞⊞⊞⊞⊞| Extends 280.

*This new Design of my Invention for a Church in Lincolns in Fields is most
humbly Inscribed to the Revd Dr Lancaster, Vicar of St Martins in the Fields
Arch=Deacon of Midlesex, and Provost of Queens Colledge Oxon .*

*Elevation d'un Nouveau Desin de mon Invention pour une Eglise dans la place de
Lincolns in Fields a Londres .*

Ca: Campbell Inv.^t et Delin:

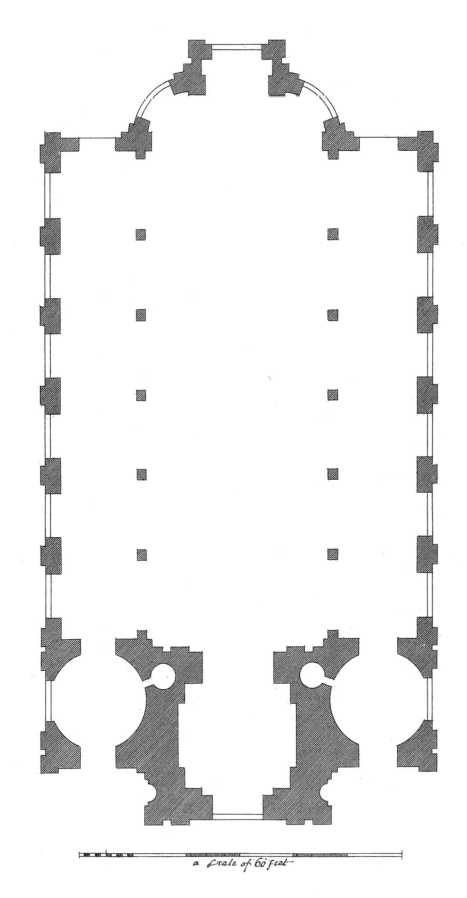

a scale of 60 feet

The plan of Birmingham Church
Plan de L'Esglise a Birmingham

a Scale of 40 Feet.   Extends 75.

The East Prospect of St. PHILIP'S CHURCH at BIRMINGHAM in WARWICKSHYRE. Invented by Tho: Archer Esq.

Elevation Oriental Del ESGLISE Du St. PHILIP a BIRMINGHAM dans La COMTÉ de WARWICK.

This plate is most humbly inscrib'd to the Honble William Pultney Esqr. Principall Secretary of War &c.t

Ca. Campbell Delin:

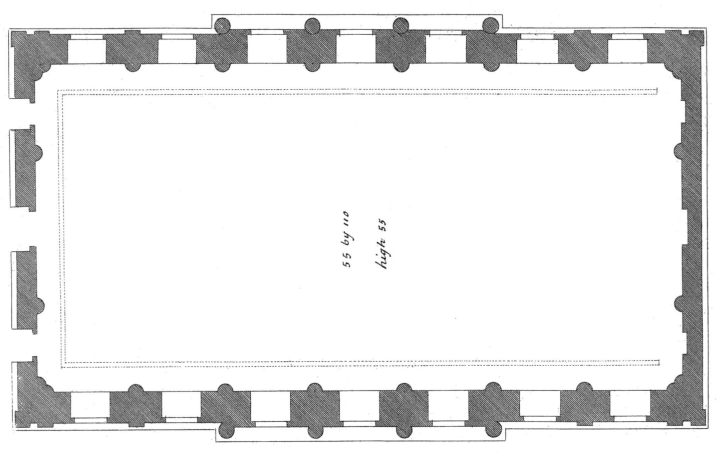

55 by 110

high 55

The plan of y^t Bankelting house.
Plan de la Grande Chambre D'Audience

a Scale of 40 feet

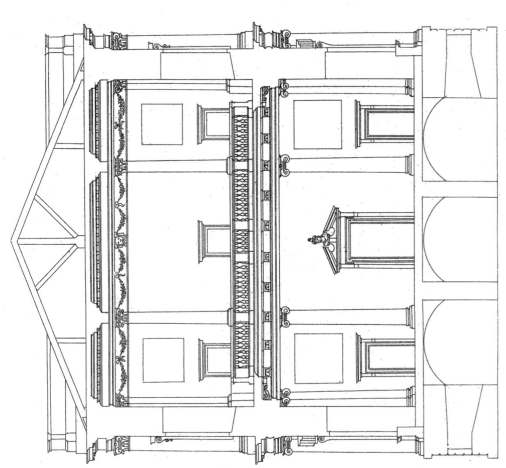

The Section

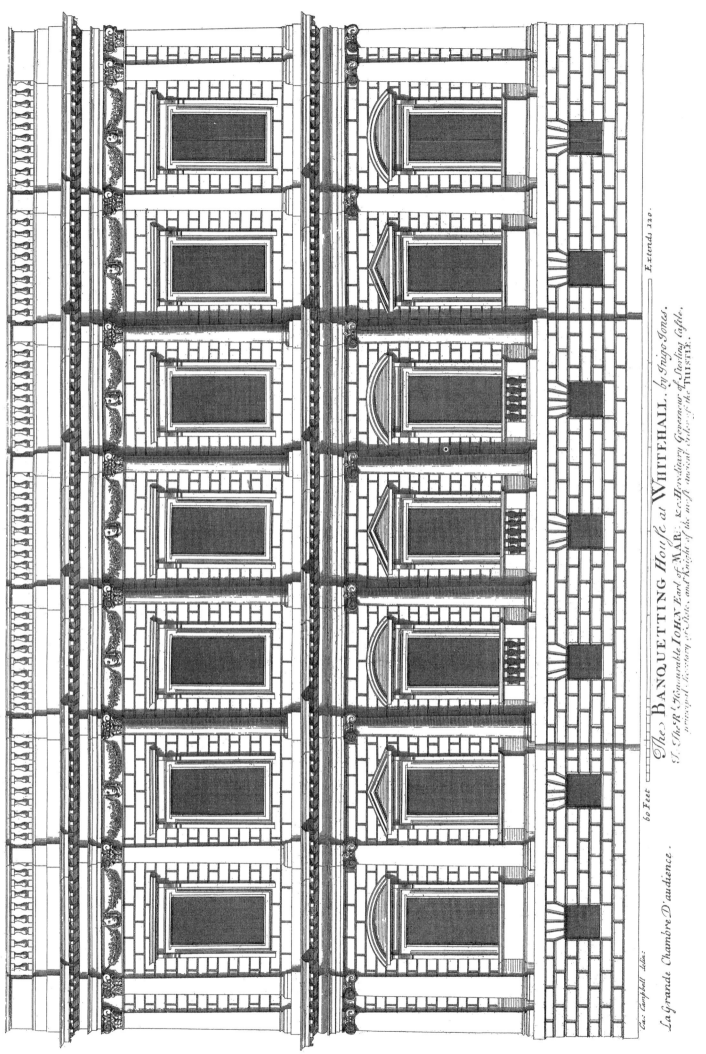

La Grande Chambre D'audience.

The BANQUETTING *House at* WHITEHALL, *by Inigo Jones.*

T. *The* R*t.* *Honourable* IOHN *Earl of* MAR, &c. *Hereditary Governour of Sterling Castle.*
principal Secretary of State, and Knight of the most ancient Order of the THISTLE.

Col. Campbell delin.

60 Feet   Extends 120.

C. 1, PL. 13

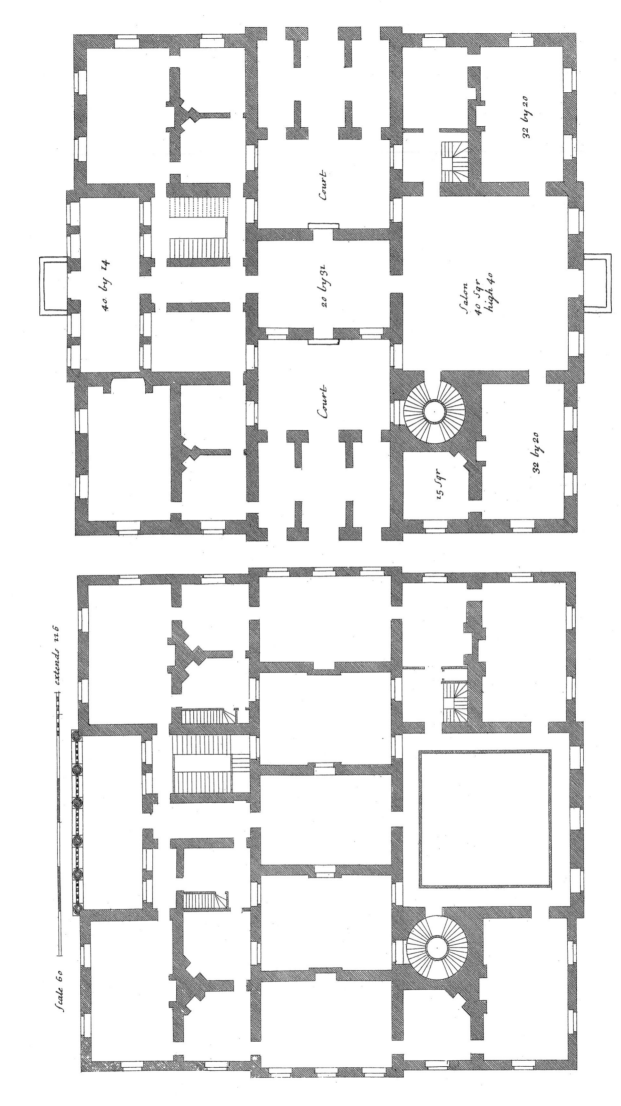

Court

40 by 14

20 by 32

Court

Salon
40 Sqr
high 40

32 by 20

15 Sqr

32 by 20

The plan of the first Story of yᵉ Kings Houſe att Greenwich
is most humbly inſcribd to Sʳ Wᵐ Gyfford Kᵗ Governor of yᵉ Hoſpitall

extends 116

scale 60

Plan of yᵉ Second floor
Plan du Second Etage

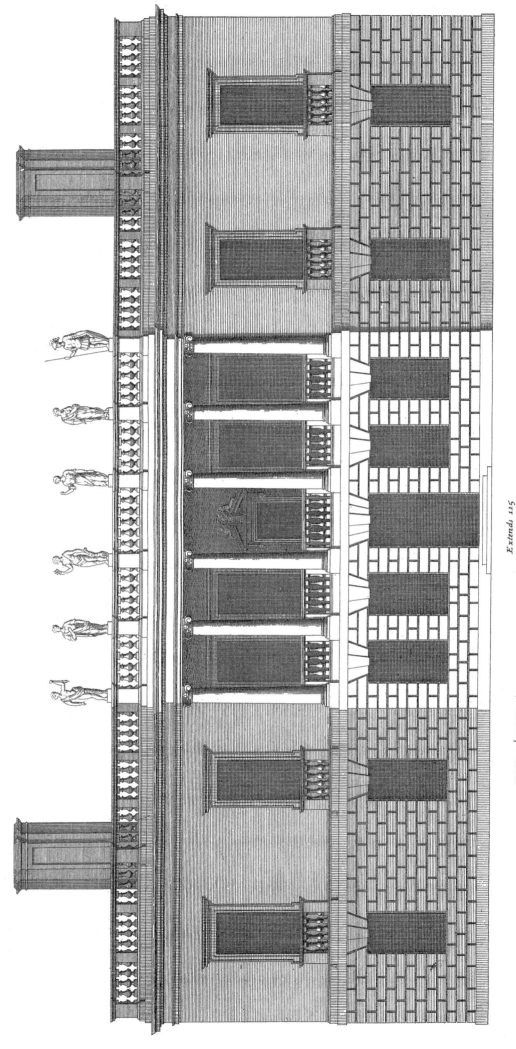

The Elevation of the QUEENS House to the Park at GREENWICH Invented by Inigo Iones 1639. is most humbly Inscribed to the Hon.ble GEORGE CLARKE Esqr One of the Lords of the Admiralty: &c.

Elevation D'une Maison appartenante a La REINE. Du Cofté Du Parc a GREENWICH tres humblement Dedié a Monsieur Mr. CLERC. &c.

Extends 115

a Scale of 60 Feet.

C.a Campbell Delin.

Extends 131.

a Scale of 60 Feet.

The Elevation of the Great Gallery in SOMERSET House to the River.

Is most humbly Inscribed to the Right Hon:ble the Earl of OXFORD &c. My Lord High Treasurer of Great BRITAIN, Knight of the most Noble Order of the Garter &c:

Elevation de La Grande Gallerie De l'Hostel de SOMERSET du costé de la Riviere, est tres humblement Dedié a Monseigneur Le Cont D'OXFORD &c.

Ca: Campbell Delin:

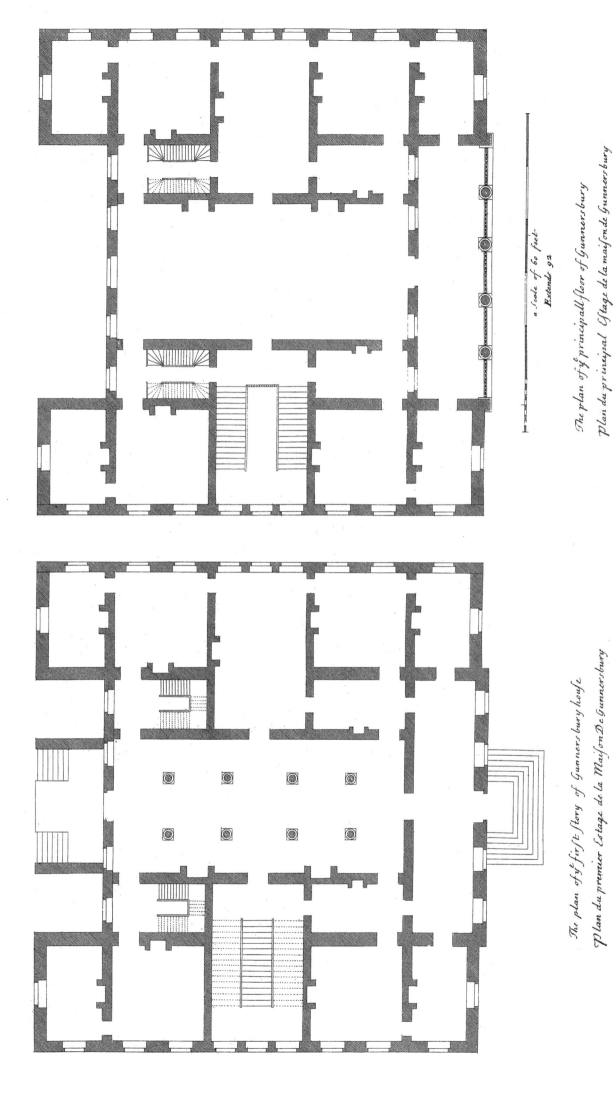

The plan of ye principall floor of Gunnersbury
Plan du principal Estage de la maison de Gunnersbury

a scale of 60 feet
Extends 92

The plan of ye first story of Gunnersbury house
Plan du premier Estage de la Maison De Gunnersbury

C. 1, PL. 17

The Elevation of GUNNERSBURY House near BRANTFORD in the County of MIDDLESEX. by Inigo Iones.

Elevation de La Maison de GUNNERSBURY une Demie Lieue du BRANTFORD dans la Comte de MIDLESEX

i. a. Campbell Delin.

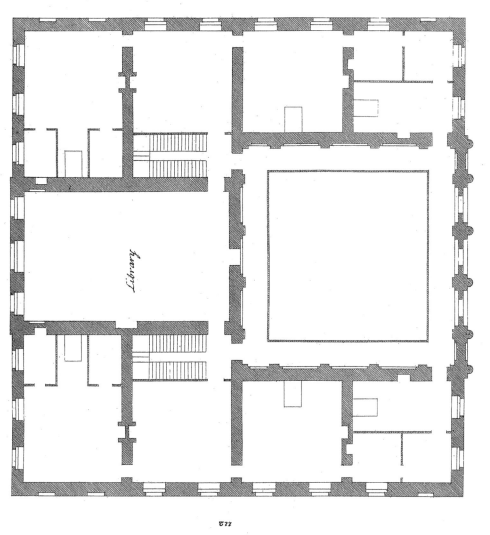

Extends 112

a Scale 60 feet

The plan of ỹ Chamber floor
Plan du Second Etage.

The plan of the principall Story of a New design for His Grace ỹ Duke of Argile
Plan du principal Etage.

Library

30 by 50

50 Sqr

34 by 24

24 Sqr

high 21

24

21

The Elevation of a New Design of my own Invention in the Style of Inigo Iones.
Is most humbly Inscribed to his Grace the Duke of ARGYLE &c Knight of the most Noble Order of the Garter.
Elevation D'un nouveau Dessein De mon Invention. tres humblement Dedié a Monseigneur Le Duc D'ARGILE.

a Scale of 60 Feet.

Extends 112.

Ca: Campbell Inv: et Delin:

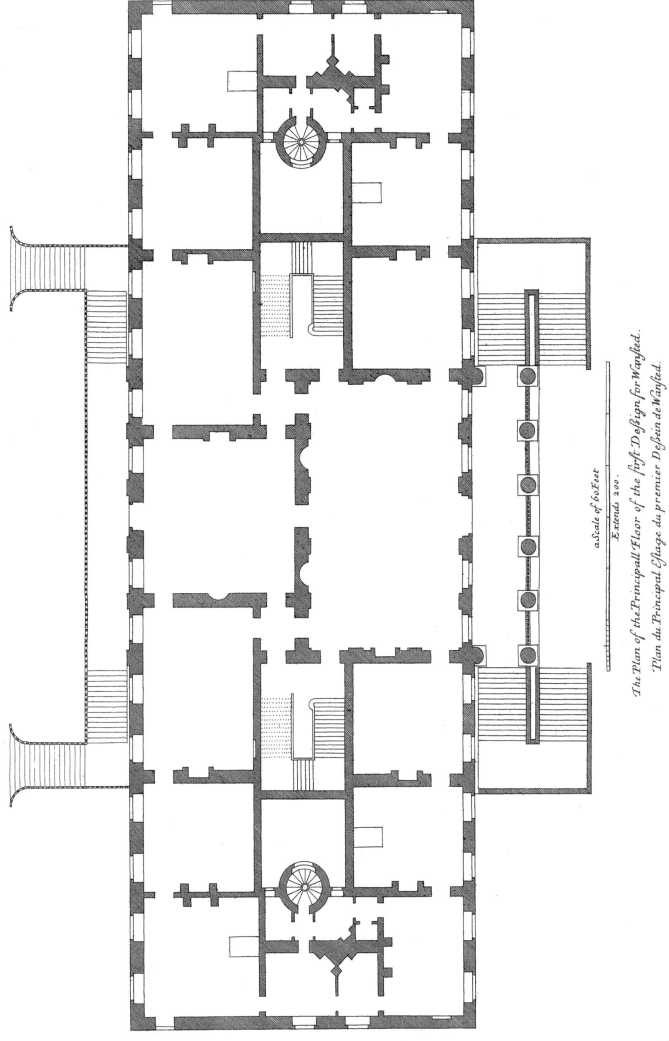

a Scale of 60 Feet.

Extends 200.

The Plan of the Principall Floor of the first Deßign for Wanßted.

Plan du Principal Eßtage du premier Deßein de Wanßted.

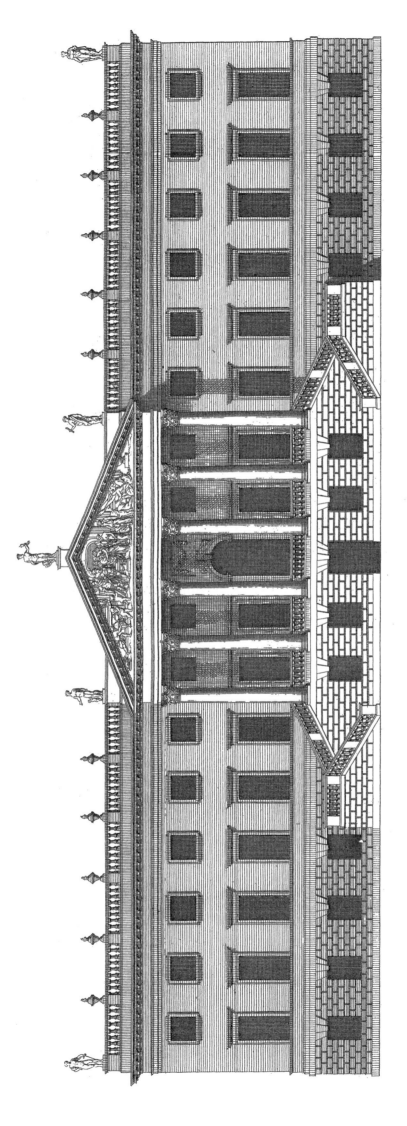

Extends 200.

a Scale of 100 Feet.

The first Design of the West Front of Wansted as intended by Sr. Richard Child Bart.

Is most humbly Dedicated to my Lady Child

Elevation de la Maison de Wansted comme esté la Premiere pensé de L'Architecte.

Ca: Campbell Inv: et Delin.

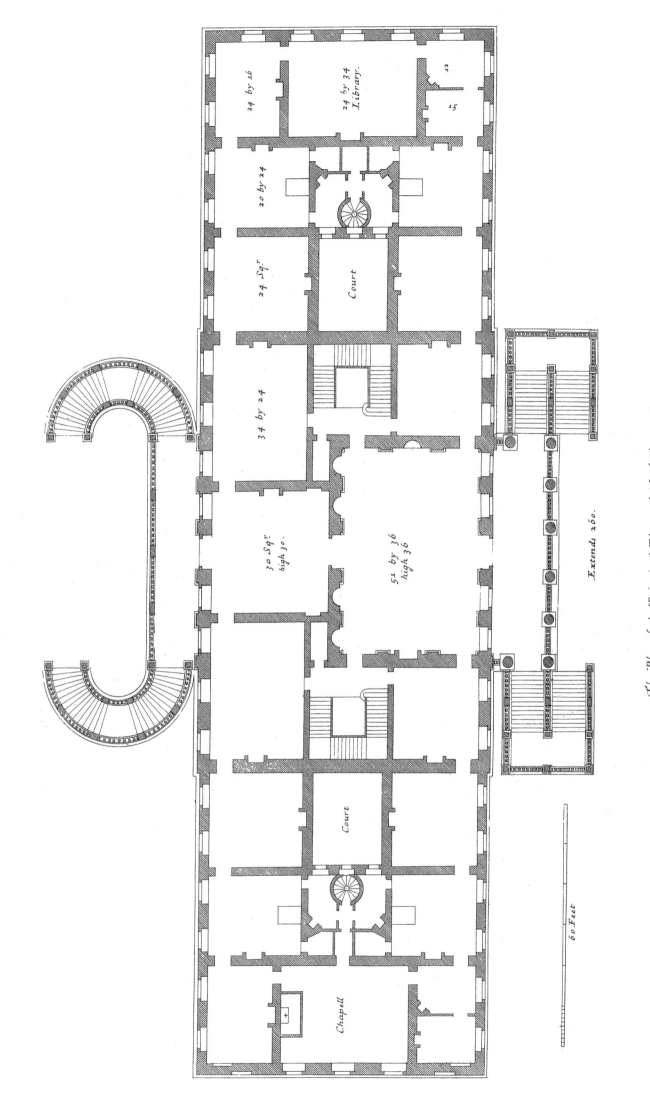

24 by 16

24 by 34
Library.

15

20 by 24

24 Sqr.

Court

34 by 24

30 Sqr.
high 30.

52 by 36
high 36

Court

Chapell

Extends 260.

The Plan of the Principal Floor of Wansted.

Plan du Premier Etage.

60 Feet

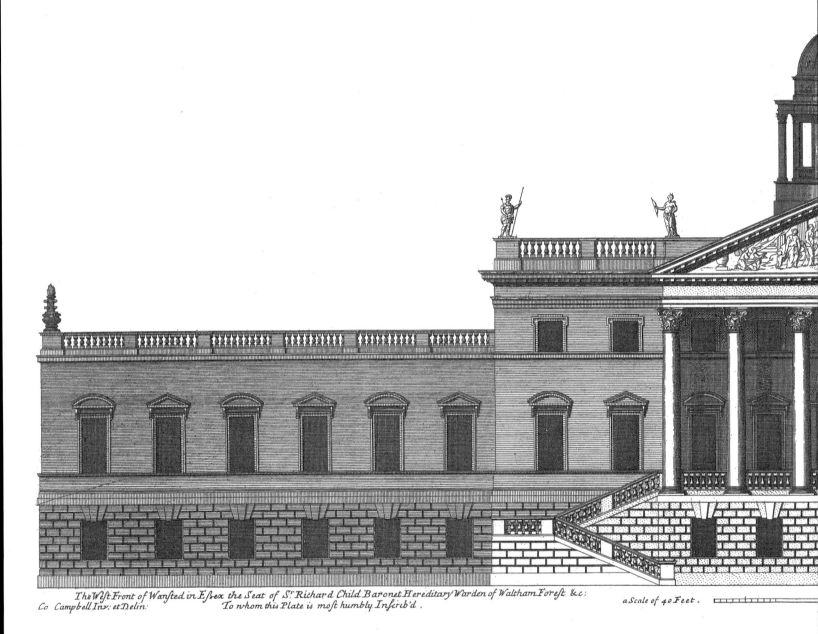

The West Front of Wansted in Essex the Seat of Sᵗ Richard Child Baronet Hereditary Warden of Waltham Forest &c:

Co Campbell Inv: et Delin: To whom this Plate is most humbly Inscrib'd .

a Scale of 40 Feet .

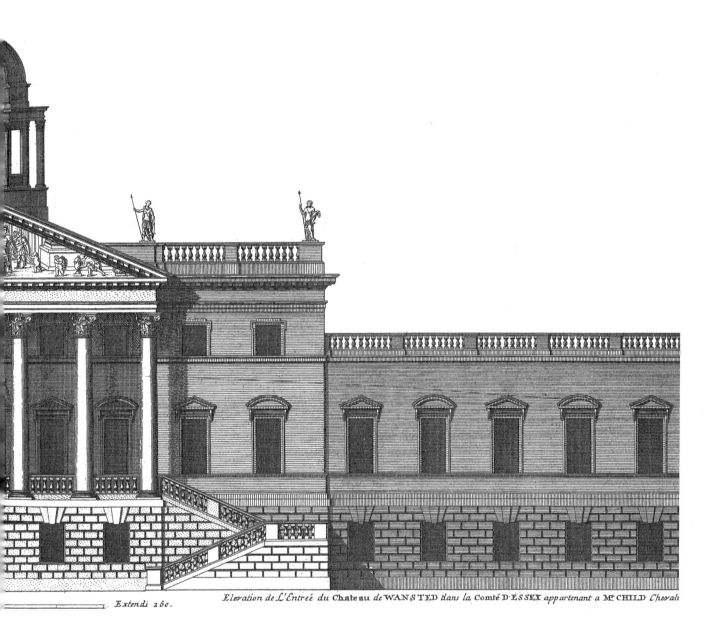

. *Extendi 260.*   *Elevation de L'Entreé du Chateau de* WANSTED *dans la Comté* D·ESSEX *appartenant a* M.r CHILD *Chevali*

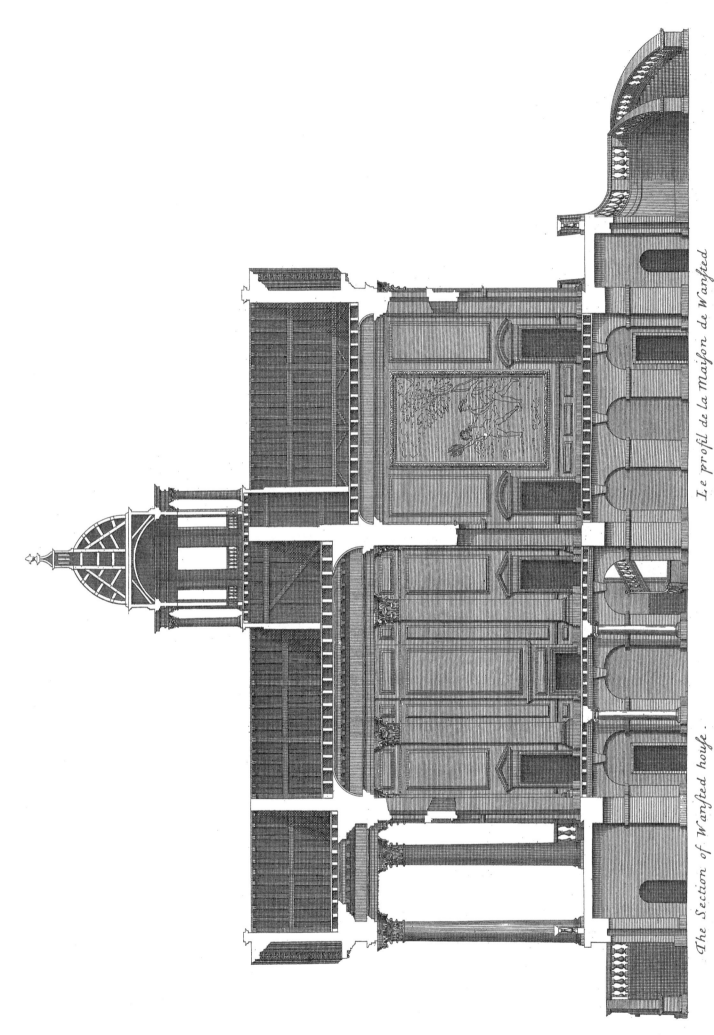

The Section of Wanstead house.

Le profil de la Maison de Wanstead

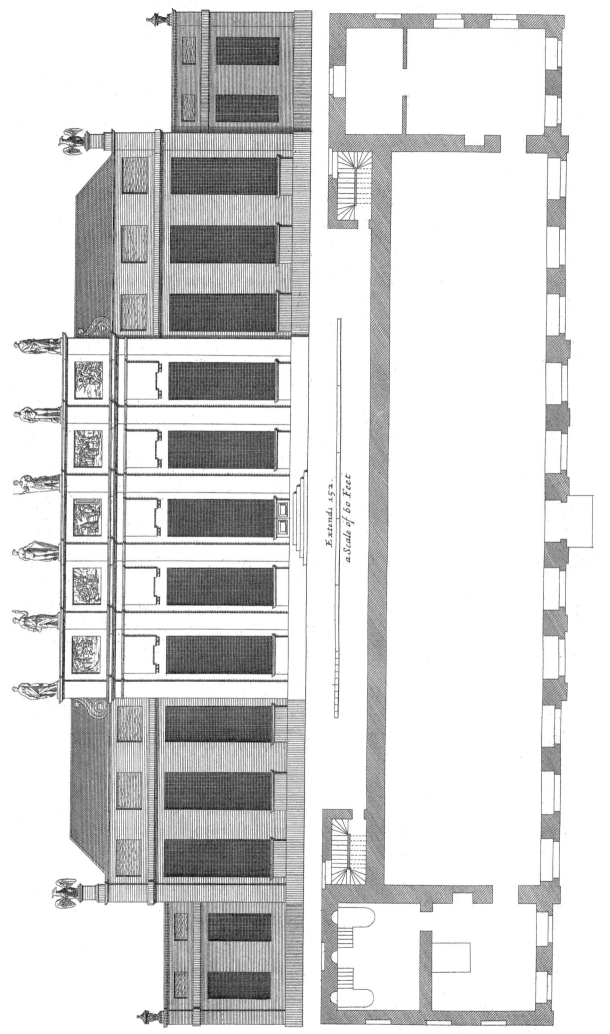

Extends 152.

a Scale of 60 Feet

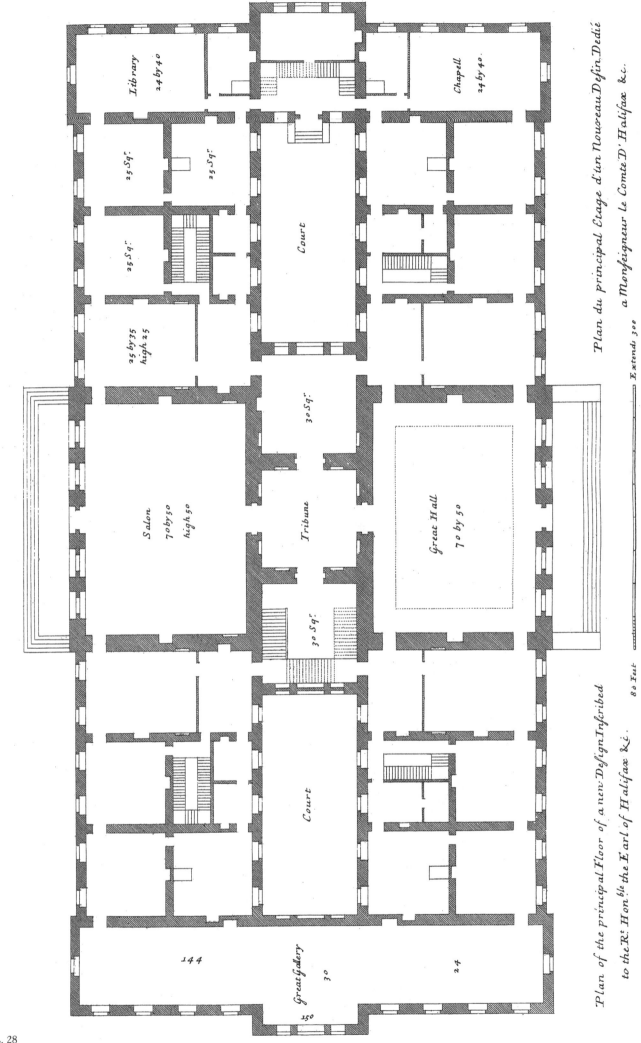

Library
24 by 40

Chapell
24 by 40

25 Sqr.

25 Sqr.

25 Sqr.

Court

25 by 35
high 25

Salon
70 by 50
high 50

30 Sqr.

Tribune

Great Hall
70 by 50

30 Sqr.

Court

Great Gallery
30

144

24

150

Plan du principal Etage d'un Nouveau Defin. Dedié
a Monfeigneur le Comte D' Halifax &c.

Extends 300

Plan of the principal Floor of a new Defign Infcribed
to the Rt. Honble. the Earl of Halifax &c.

80 Feet

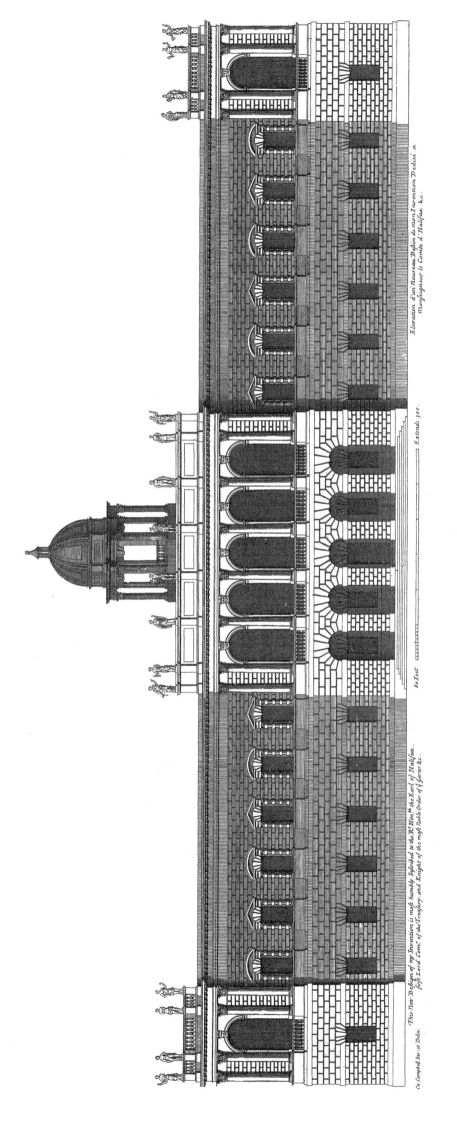

This New Design of my Invention is most humbly Inscribed to the R.t Hon.ble the Earl of Halifax, first Lord Com.r of the Treasury, and Knight of the most Noble Order of y.e Garter &c.

Co: Campbell Inv: et Delin:

Elevation d'un Nouveau Design de mon Invention Dedieé a Monseigneur le Comte d'Halifax &c.

Extends 300.

60 Feet.

C. 1, PL. 29–30

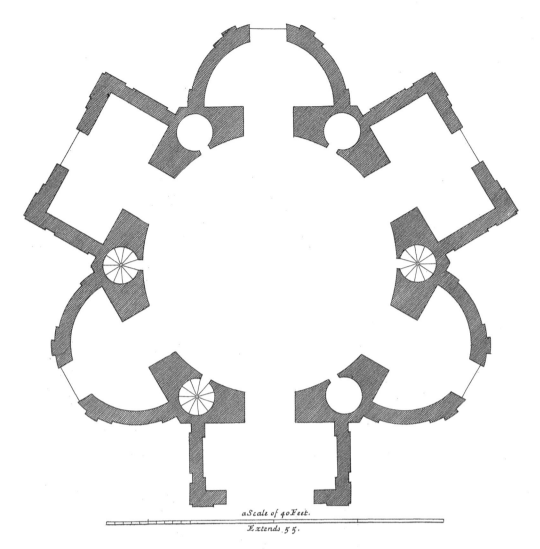

a Scale of 40 Feet.

Extends 55.

The Plan of his Grace the Duke of Kent's Garden Pavilion.

Plan D'un Nouveau Batiment au Iardin du Monseigneur le Duc de Kent.

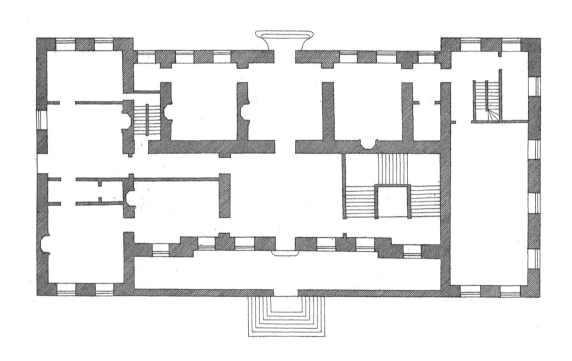

a Scale of 80 Feet.

Extends 130.

The Plan of Burlington house in Pickadilly

Plan de L'Hostel de Burlington.

Burlington house in Piccadilly London

To the Right Hon.ble the Richard Boyle Earl of Burlington and Cork &c.
Hereditary Lord High Treasurer of the Kingdom of Ireland

Extends 55
a Scale of 30 Feet

A New Building at y̔ end of his Grace y̔ Duke of KENTS *Gardens in* BEDFORDSHIRE. *Invented by Tho: Archer Esq*

To the most Potent Prince HENRY *Duke of* KENT *&c. Knight of y̔ most Noble Order of y̔* Garter. *this New Building at y̔ end of his*
Graces Gardens in BEDFORDSHIRE *is most humbly Inscribed.*
Un Nouveau Batiment a bout des Iardins Du Duc De Kent dans Le Comté de BEDFORD

Colenus Campbell Delin:

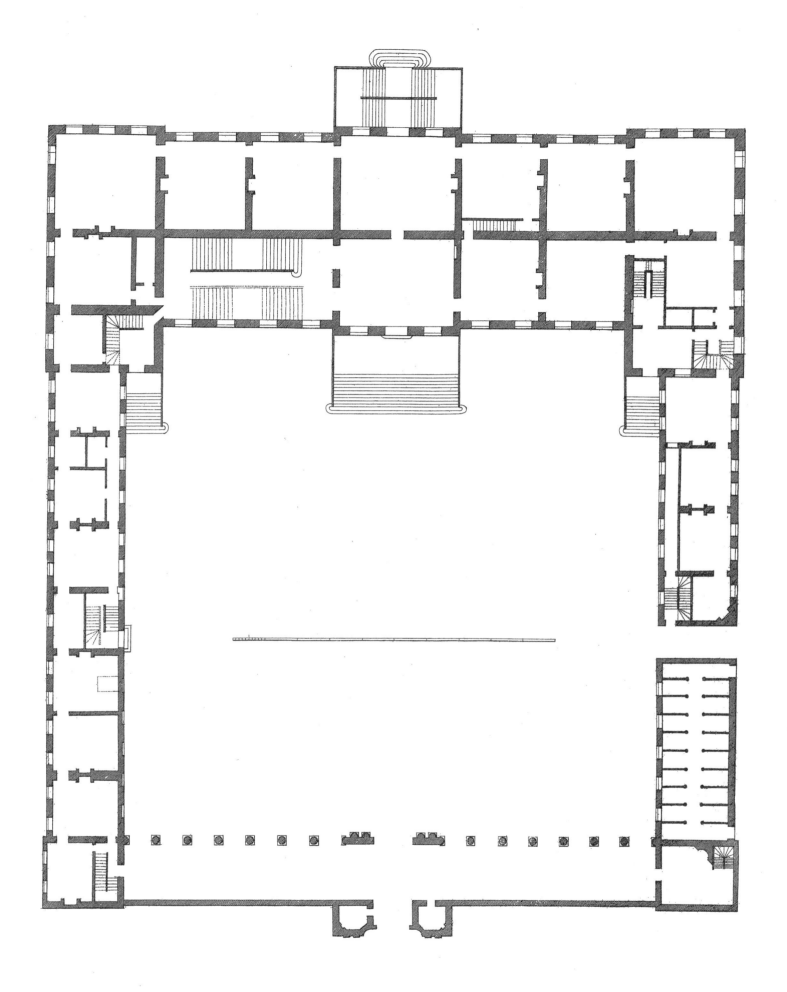

The Plan of y *Principal Floor of Montague House is most humbly dedicated to her Grace y* **Dutches of Montague,** *&c.*

Plan du   premier Estage de L'Hostel de Montague.

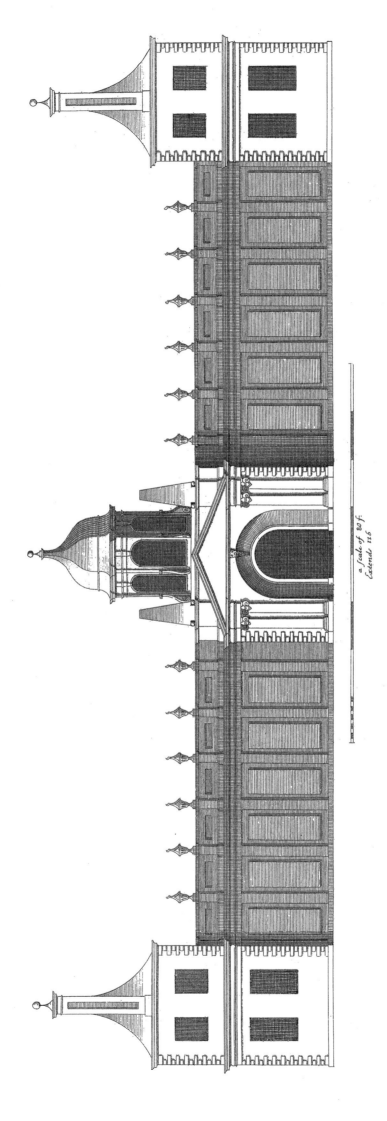

The prospect of Montague house to the street London

Elevation de L'Entree de L'Hostel de Montague a Londres

a scale of 80 f.
Extent 126

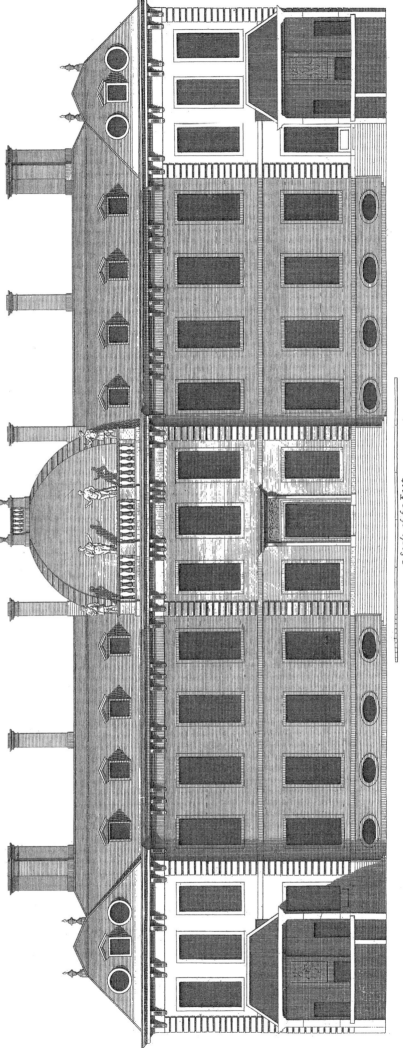

The Elevation of MONTAGUE House to the Court in Great Russell Street LONDON.
Is most humbly Inscribed to his Grace the Duke of MONTAGUE &c:

Elevation Del Hostel De MONTAGUE, du costé de La Cour a LONDRES Inven: par Mr. Pouget.

a Scale of 6 o Feet.
Extend 216.

Ca: Campbell Delin:

C. 1, PL. 36

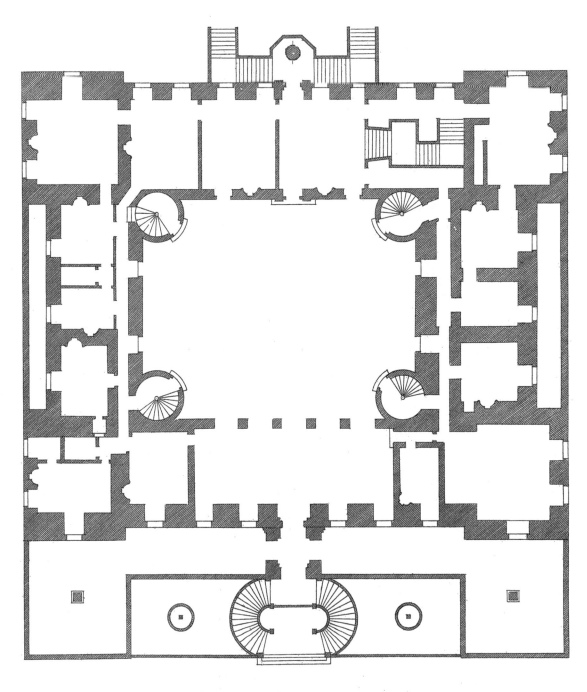

a Scale of 60 feet
Extends 145

The Plan of Drumlenrig Castle in Scotland

Plan du Chateau de Drumlenrig

The Elevation of DRUMLENRIG Castle the Seat of His Graces Duke of Queensberry
and Dover &c.t
Elevation Du Chateau de Drumlenrig apartement a Duc De Queensberry à Dover &c.t

a Scale of 40 Feet

Ca. Campbell delin.

C. 1, PL. 38

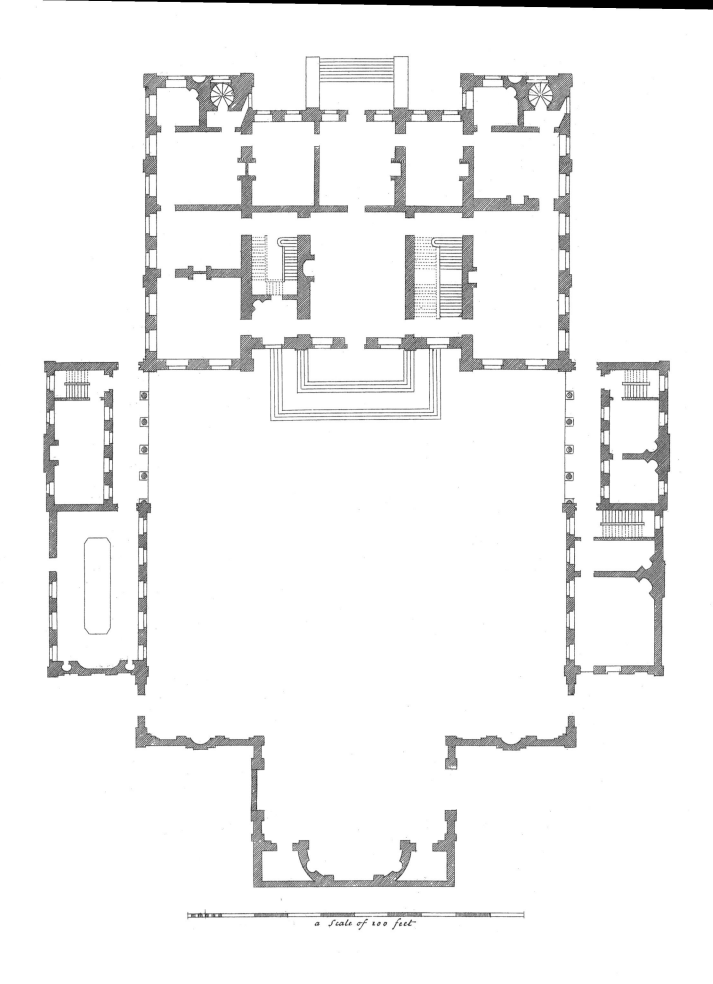

a Scale of 100 feet

The plan of Marlborough house St James.s
Plan de L'Hostel de Marlborough a Londres

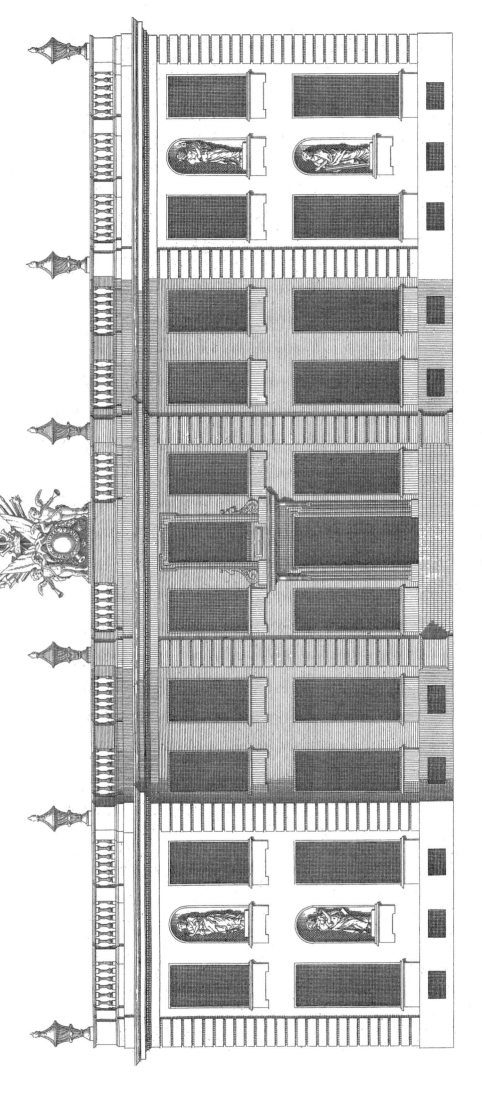

The Elevation of MARLBOROUGH Houfe to St IAMES' PARK. Invented by Chriftopher Wren Efqr. 1709.
Is moft humbly Dedicated to her Grace the Dutchefs of MARLBOROUGH Princefs of MENDELHEIM &c.

Elevation Del Hoftel De MARLBOROUGH du cofté du PARC Du St IACQUES a LONDRES.

Extends 125.

a Scale of 60 Feet.

Ca: Campbell Delin:

C. 1, PL. 40

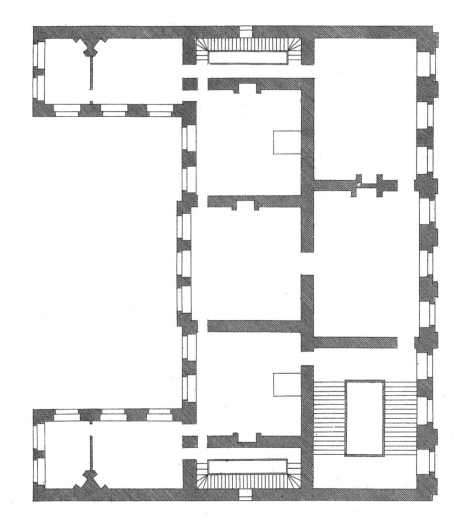

The plan of ye Second Story
plan du Second Estage

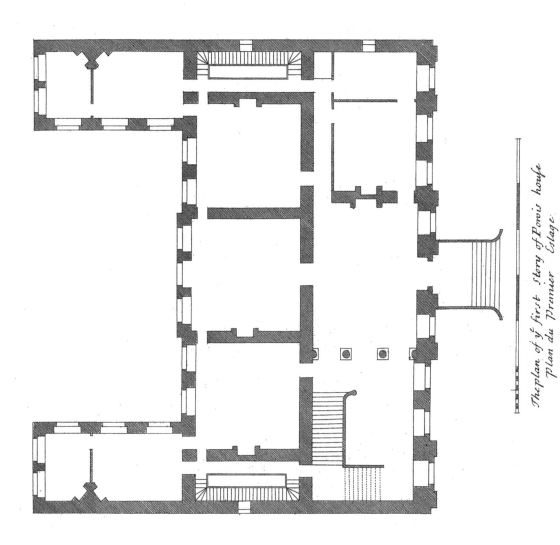

The plan of ye First Story of Powis house
plan du Premier Estage.

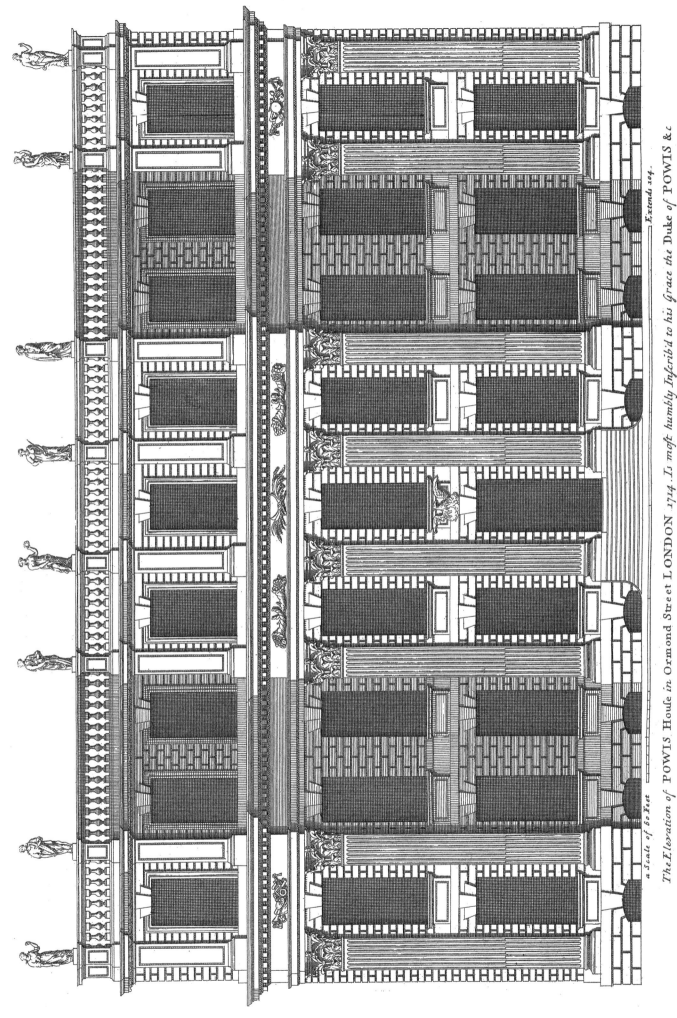

a Scale of 60 Feet   Extends 104.

The Elevation of POWIS House in Ormond Street LONDON 1714. Is most humbly Inscrib'd to his Grace the Duke of POWIS &c.

Elevation Del Hostel De POWIS a LONDRES Bati 1714.

Ca: Campbell Delin:

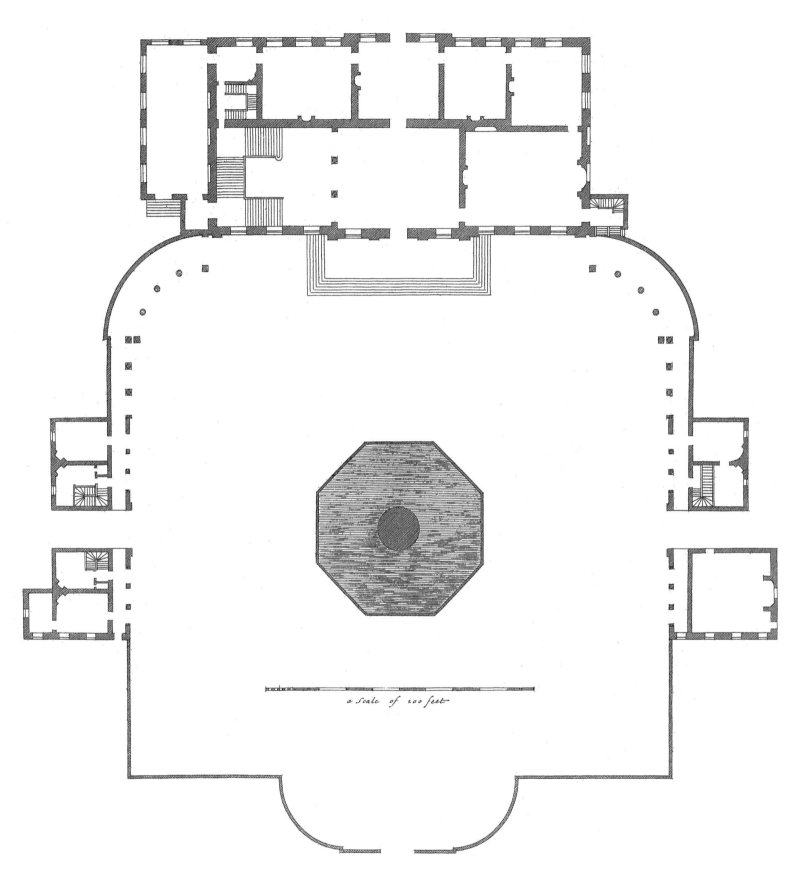

a Scale of 100 feet

The Plan of Buckingham house in St James's Park

Plan De L'Hostel De Buckingham

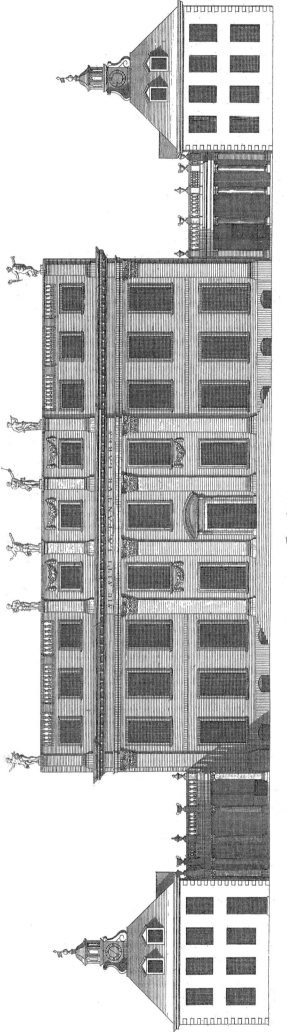

The Elevation of BUCKINGHAM House in St IAMES's PARK.

Is most humbly Inscrib'd to his Grace the Duke of BUCKINGHAM Lord President of Council.
and Knight of the most Noble Order of the Garter &c:

Elevation Del'Hostel De BUCKINGHAM du costé Du PARC de St IACQUES a LONDRES.
est tres humblement Dedié a Monseigneur le Duc De BUCKINGHAM &c:

Extends 140.

a Scale of 60 Feet

Ca: Campbell Delin:

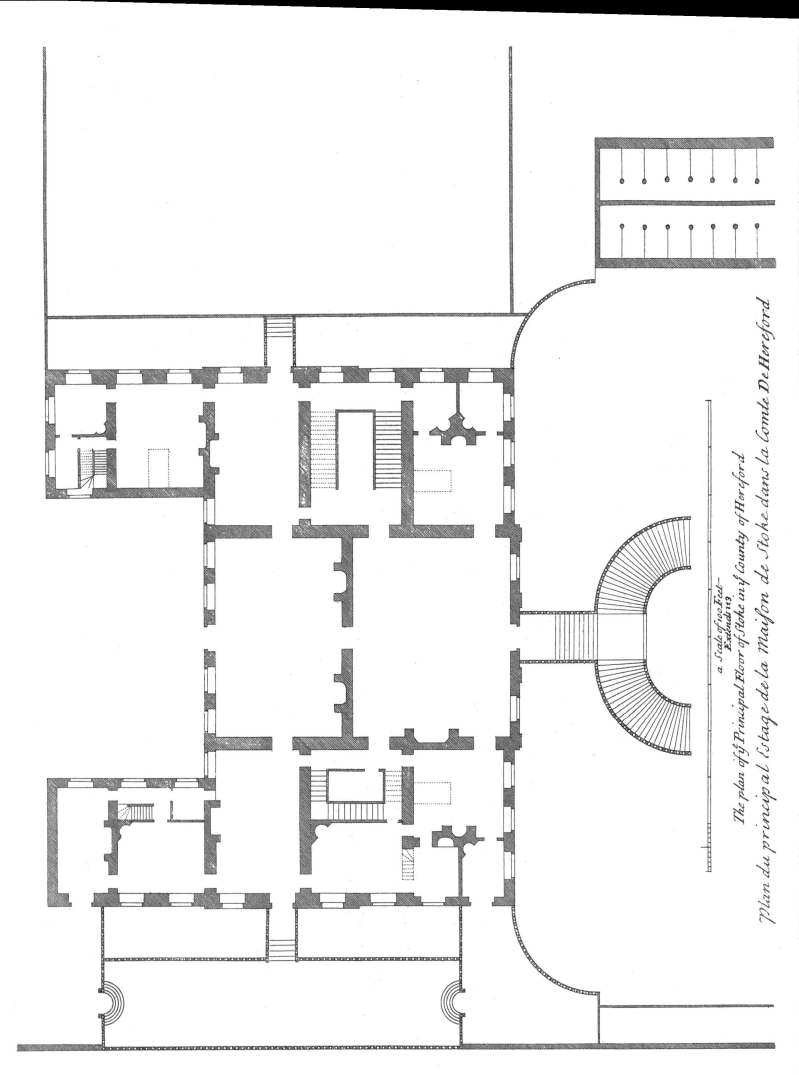

a Scale of 100 Feet —
Extendt 113.

The plan of y Principal Floor of Stoke in y County of Hereford

Plan du principal Estage de la Maison de Stoke dans la Comte De Hereford

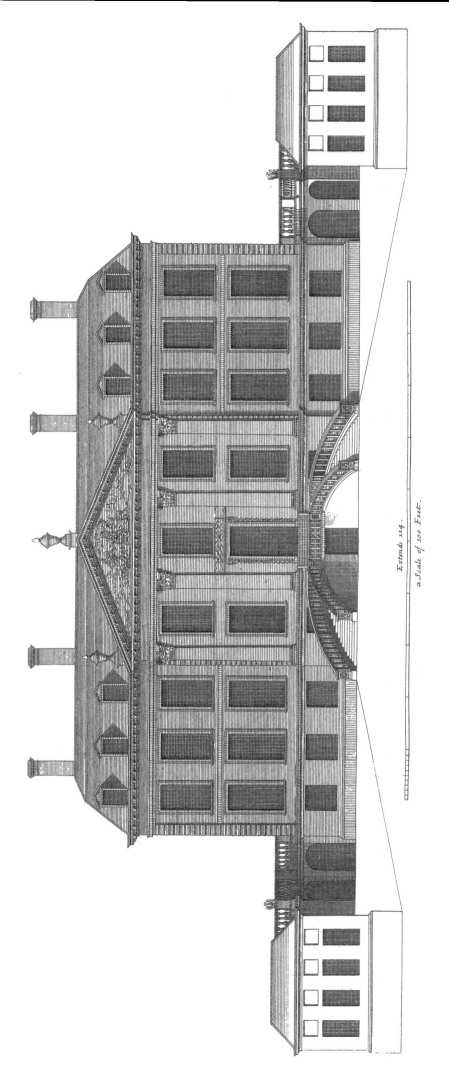

Extends 114.

a Scale of 100 Feet.

The Elevation of STOKE in the County of HEREFORD, the Seat of Mr. AUDITOR FOLEY,
to whom this Plate is most humbly Inscrib'd.

Elevation de La Maison de STOKE dans La Comté de HEREFORD appartenentz a Mr. FOLEY.

Ca. Campbell Delin:

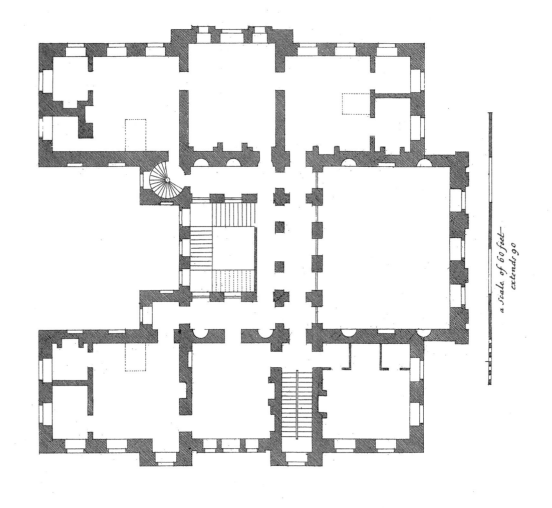

The Plan of y.ᵉ Chamber floor of Kings Weſton

Plan du Second Eſtage de Kings Weſton

The Plan of y.ᵉ Principal floor of Kings Weſton

Plan du Premier Eſtage de Kings Weſton

a Scale of 60 feet
extend.90

21 by 20

22 by 20

21 by 29

21 by 20

22 by 18

21 by 20

36 by 29
high 30

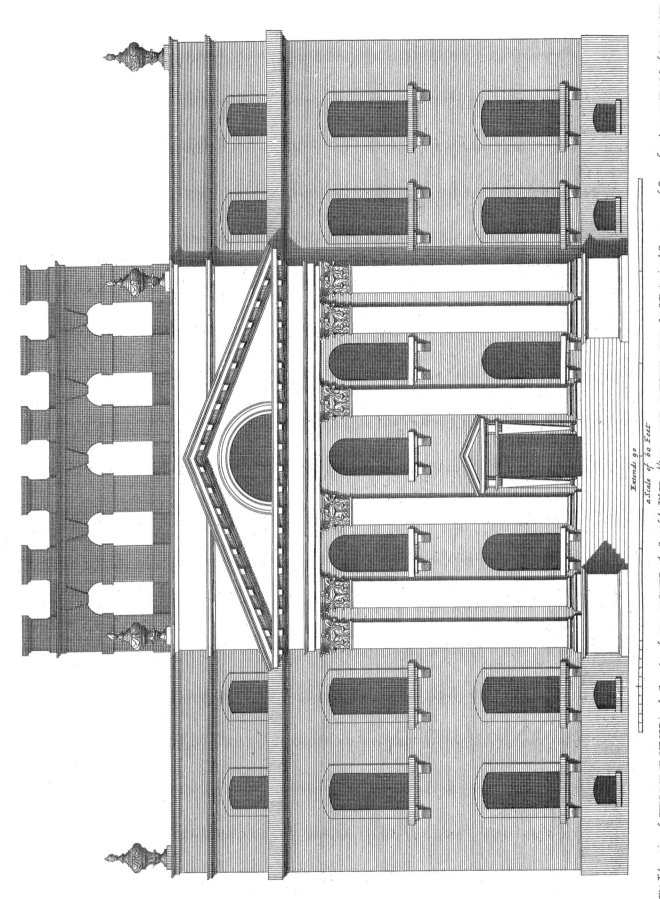

The Elevation of KINGSWESTON in the County of GLOCESTER the Seat of the R.t Hon.ble EDWARD SOUTHWELL Esq.r Principal Secretary of State for the KINGDOM of IRELAND

Deſigned by S.r Io: Vanbrugh K.t

Elevation de La Maiſon De KINGSWESTON dans La Comté de GLOCESTER.

Extends 90

a Scale of 60 Feet

Ca Campbell Delin:

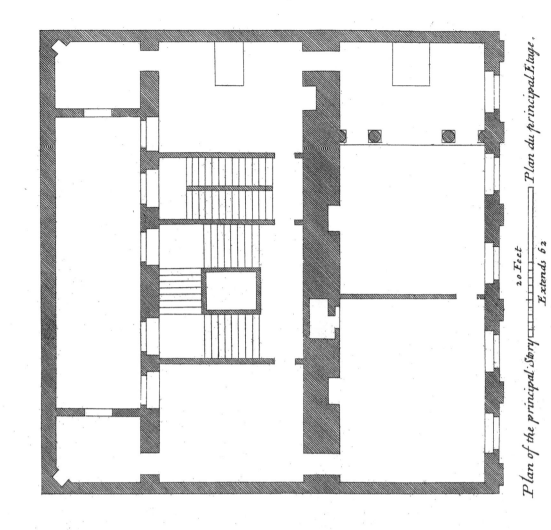

Plan of the principal Story   Plan du principal Etage

20 Feet

Extends 62

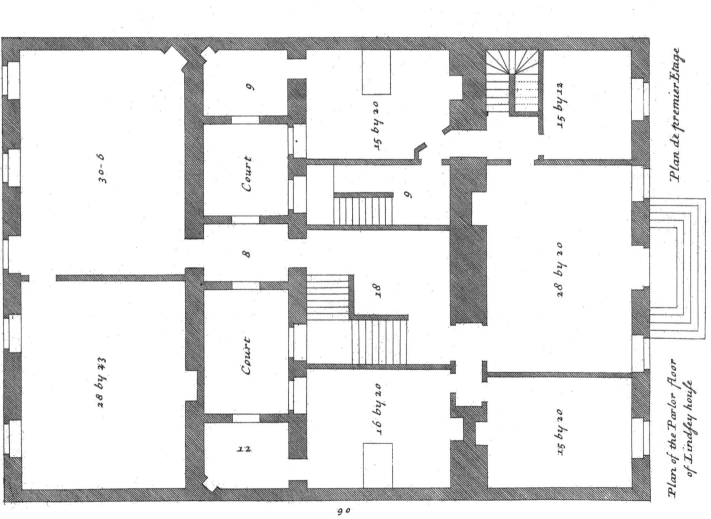

Plan of the Parlor floor   Plan de premier Etage
of Lindsey house

C. 1, PL. 49

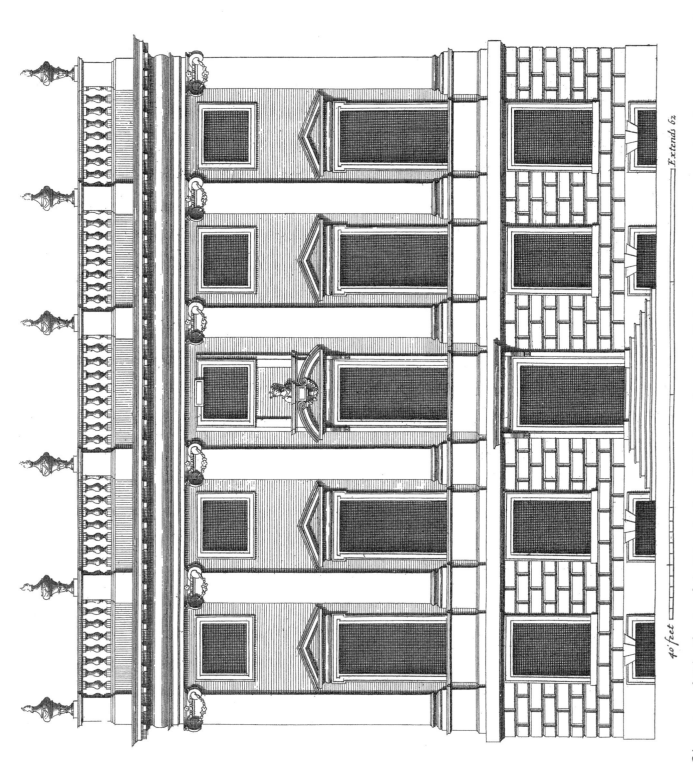

The Elevation of Lindfey houfe in Lincolns inn fields, is moft humbly Infcribed to the R.t Honorable the Marquifs of
Lindfey Lord Great Chamberlain of England &c.

Elevation de l'Hoftel de Lindfey dans la place de Lincolns innfields a Londres.

Ca: Campbell Delin:

Inigo Iones Inv:

40 feet

Extends 62

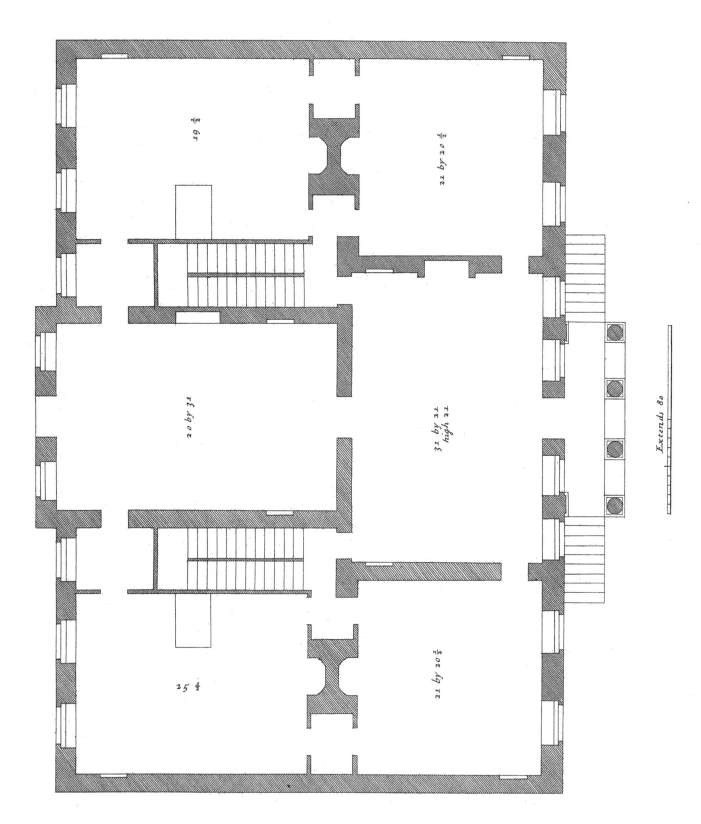

$19\frac{1}{2}$

21 by $20\frac{1}{2}$

20 by 31

31 by 21
high 21

$25\frac{1}{4}$

21 by $20\frac{1}{2}$

Extends 80

Plan of the principal Floor of Wilberry houfe

Plan du principal Etage de la Maifon de Wilberry

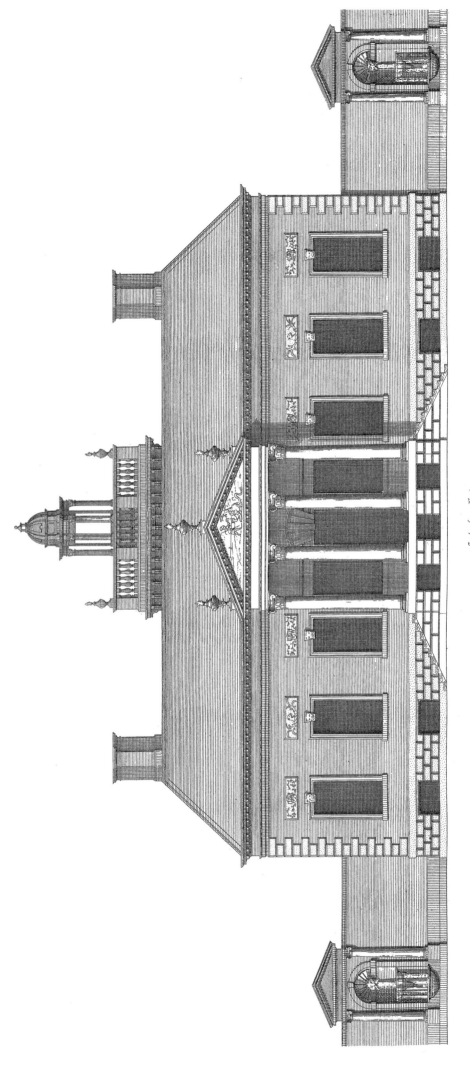

The Elevation of Wilberry houſe in the County of Wilt the Seat of William Benſon Eſq: Invented and built by himſelf
in the Stile of Inigo Iones to whom this Plate is moſt humbly Inſcribed.

Elevation de la Maiſon de Wilberry dans la Comté de Wilt.

a Scale of 30 Feet.

E. ſtends 81.

Ca: Campbell Delin:

C. 1, PL. 52

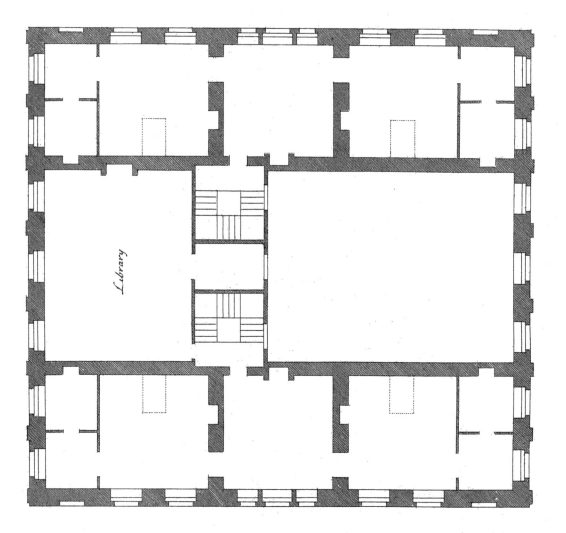

Library

Extends 76

The Plan of ye Chamber floor
Plan du Second Etage

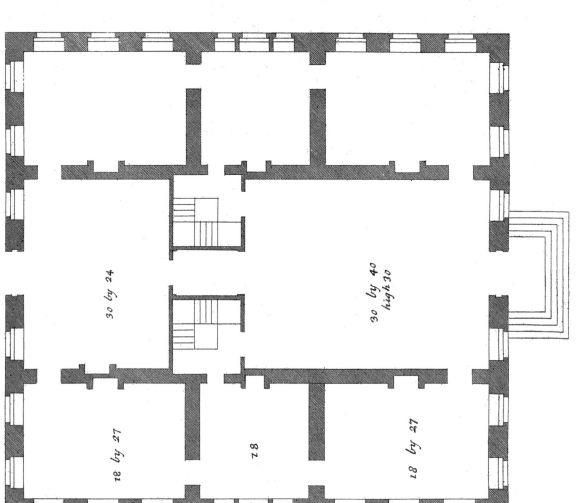

30 by 24

30 by 40
high 30

18 by 27

28

18 by 27

The plan of ye Principall Story of the Earl of Islay's new Design.
Plan du principal Etage

This new Design of my Invention is most humbly Inscrib'd to the Rt Honbl. The Earl of I∫lay &c. Justice General and Lord Register for North Brittain.

Elevation d'un nouveau De∫∫ein de mon Invention tres humblement Dedié a Mon∫eigneur le Comte D'I∫lay &c.

Extends 78

20 Feet

Ca: Campbell Inv: et Delin:

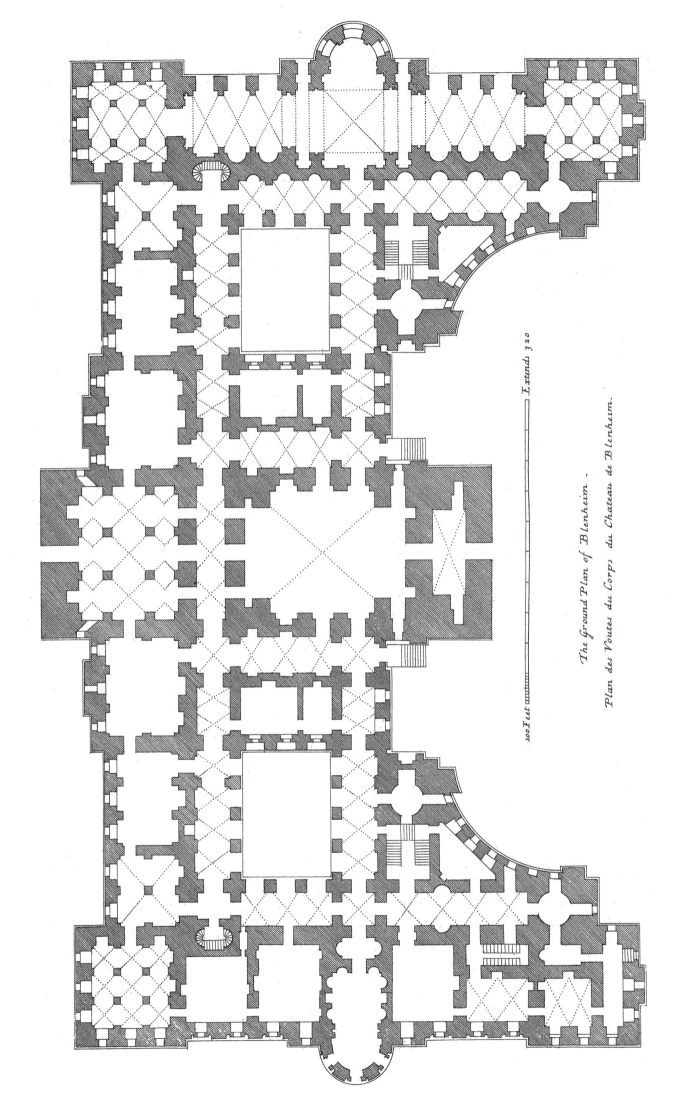

The Ground Plan of Blenheim .

Plan des Voutes du Corps du Chateau de Blenheim.

Extends 320

100 Feet

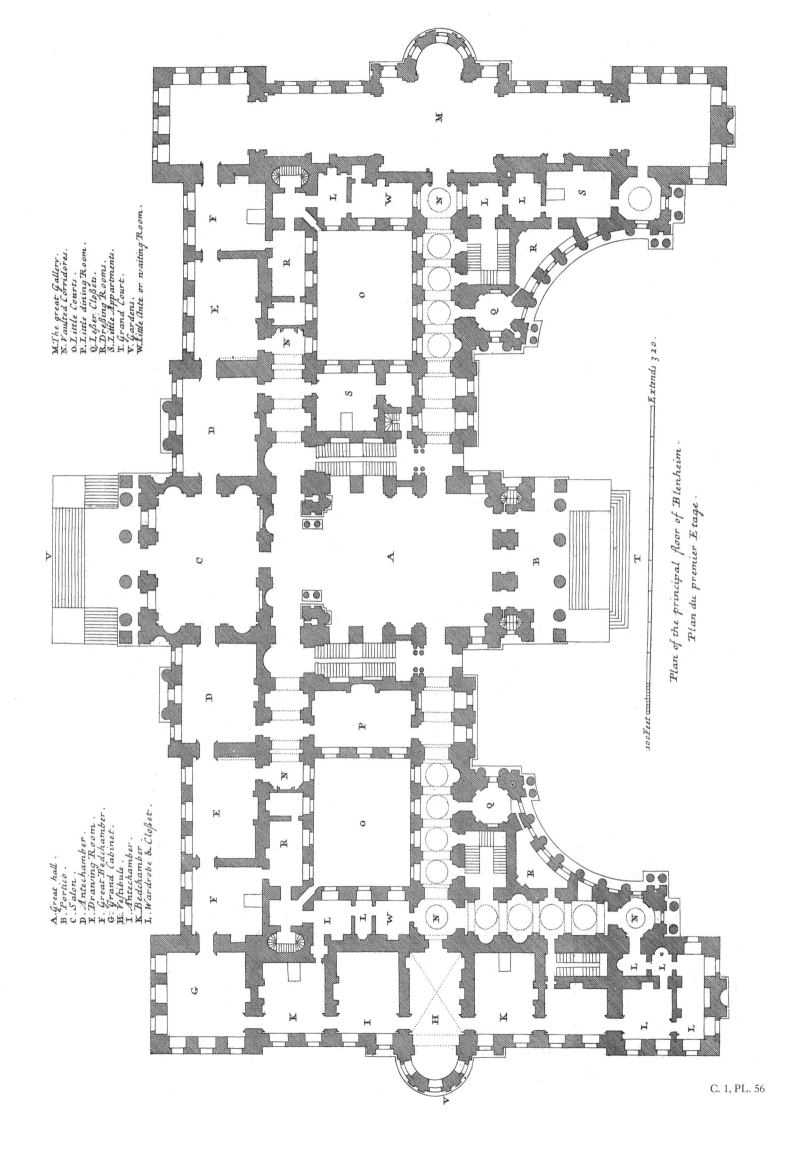

A. Great hall.
B. Portico.
C. Salon.
D. Antechamber.
E. Drawing Room.
F. Great Bedchamber.
G. Grand Cabinet.
H. Vestibule.
I. Antechamber.
K. Bedchamber.
L. Wardrobe & Closet.

M. The great Gallery.
N. Vaulted Corridores.
O. Little Courts.
P. Little dining Room.
Q. Lesser Closset.
R. Dressing Rooms.
S. Little Appartments.
T. Grand Court.
V. Gardens.
W. Little Ante or waiting Room.

Plan of the principal floor of Blenheim.
Plan du premier Etage.

100 Feet   Extends 320.

C. 1, PL. 56

100 Feet

The Generall Front of Blenheim Castle is most humbly Inscrib'd to his Grace Iohn Duke of Marlborough, Prince of the Holy Empire. C

Elevation General du

Ca: Campbell Delin:

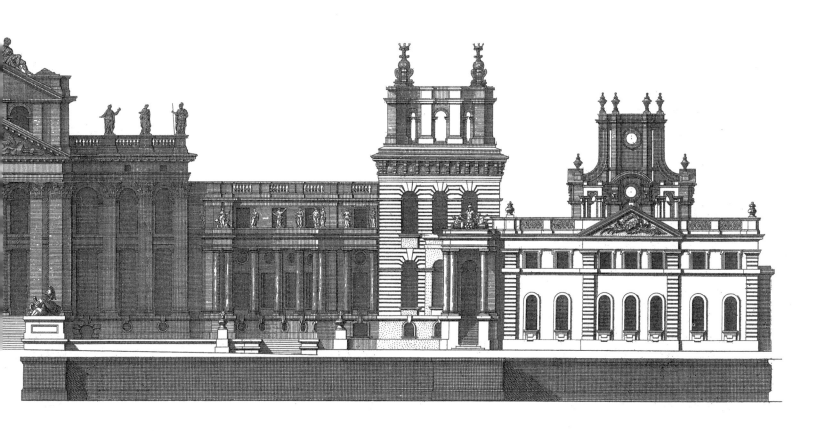

Extends 490

erall of all his Majesty's forces. and Knight of the most Noble Order of the Garter &c. Design'd by Sr. John Vanbrugh Kt.

au de Blenheim:

The Elevation of BLENHEIM Castle towards the Gardens. Is most humbly Inscrib'd to his Grace IOHN Duke of MARLBOROUGH Prince of the Holy EMPIRE, Capt: General of all his MAJE,STYES Forces, and Knight of the most Noble Order of the Garter &c. Invented by Sr. Io: Vanbrugh Kt.

Ca Campbell Delin:

a Scale
Exter

Elevation Du Chateau de BLENHEIM *du Cofté des Jardins.*

Inventeé par M. Io : Vanbrugh *Chevalier.*

Feet.

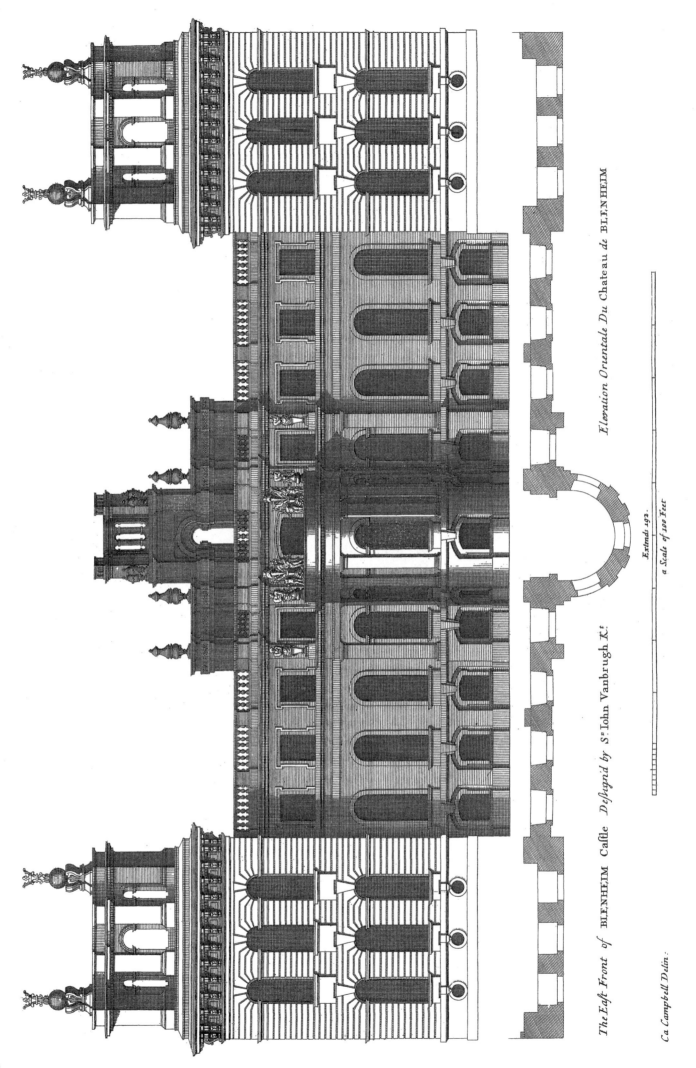

The East Front of BLENHEIM Castle Defign'd by Sʳ Iohn Vanbrugh Kᵗ.

Eleration Orientale Du Chateau de BLENHEIM

Extends 193.

a Scale of 100 Feet

Ca Campbell Delin.

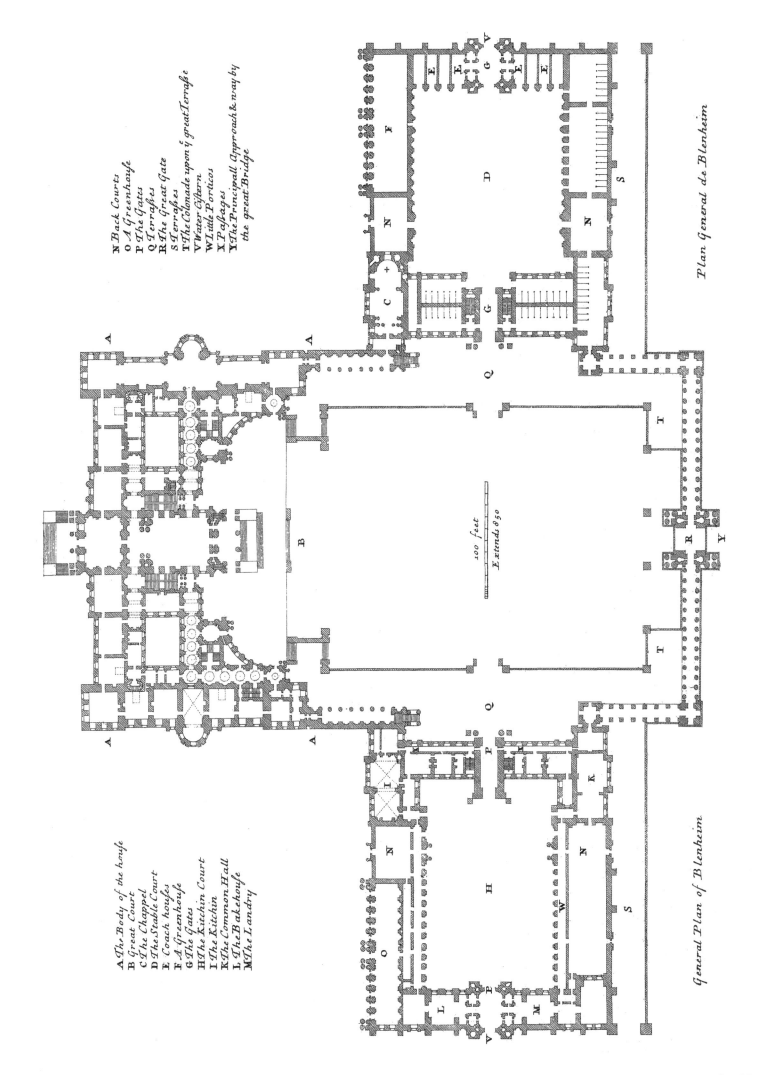

N Back Courts
O A Greenhouse
P The Gates
Q Terrasses
R The Great Gate
S Terrasses
T The Colonade upon ÿ great Terrasse
V Water Cistern
W Little Porticos
X Passages
Y The Principall Approach & way by
    the great Bridge

A The Body of the house
B Great Court
C The Chappel
D The Stable Court
E Coach houses
F A Greenhouse
G The Gates
H The Kitchin Court
I The Kitchin
K The Common Hall
L The Bakehouse
M The Landry

100 feet
Extends 850

Plan General de Blenheim

General Plan of Blenheim.

C. 1, PL. 62

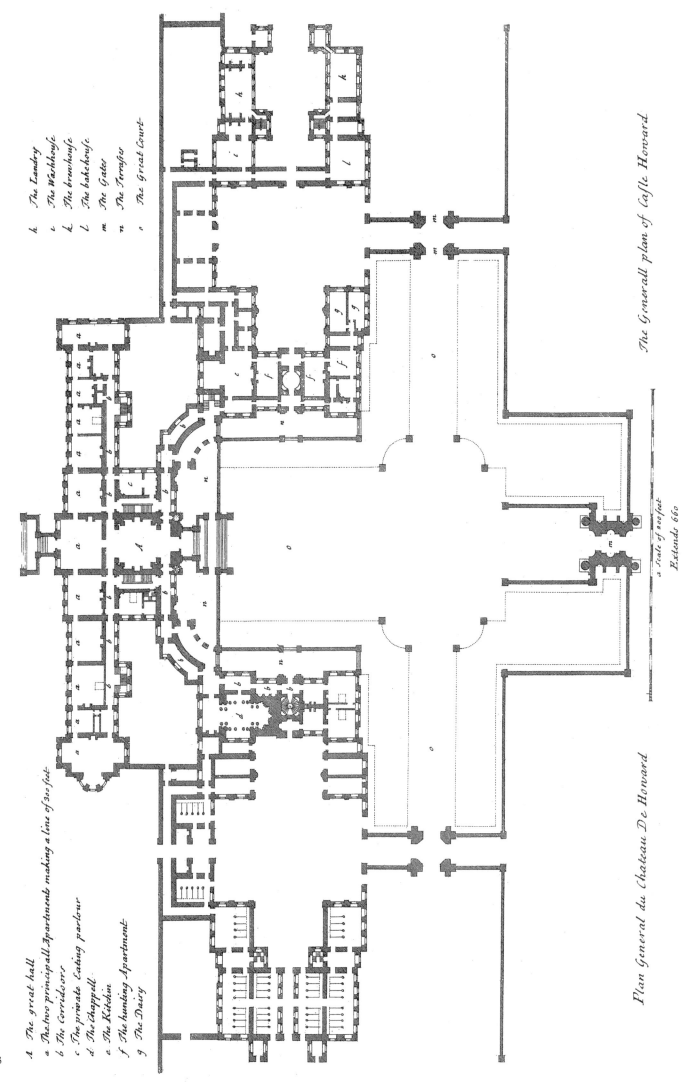

A   *The great hall*
a   *The two principall Apartments making a line of 300 feet*
b   *The Corridors*
c   *The private Eating parlour*
d   *The Chappell*
e   *The Kitchin*
f   *The hunting Apartment*
g   *The Dairy*

h   *The Landry*
i   *The Washhouse*
k   *The brewhouse*
l   *The bakehouse*
m   *The Gates*
n   *The Terrasses*
o   *The Great Court*

Plan General du Chateau De Howard

The Generall plan of Castle Howard

Scale of 200 feet

Extends 660

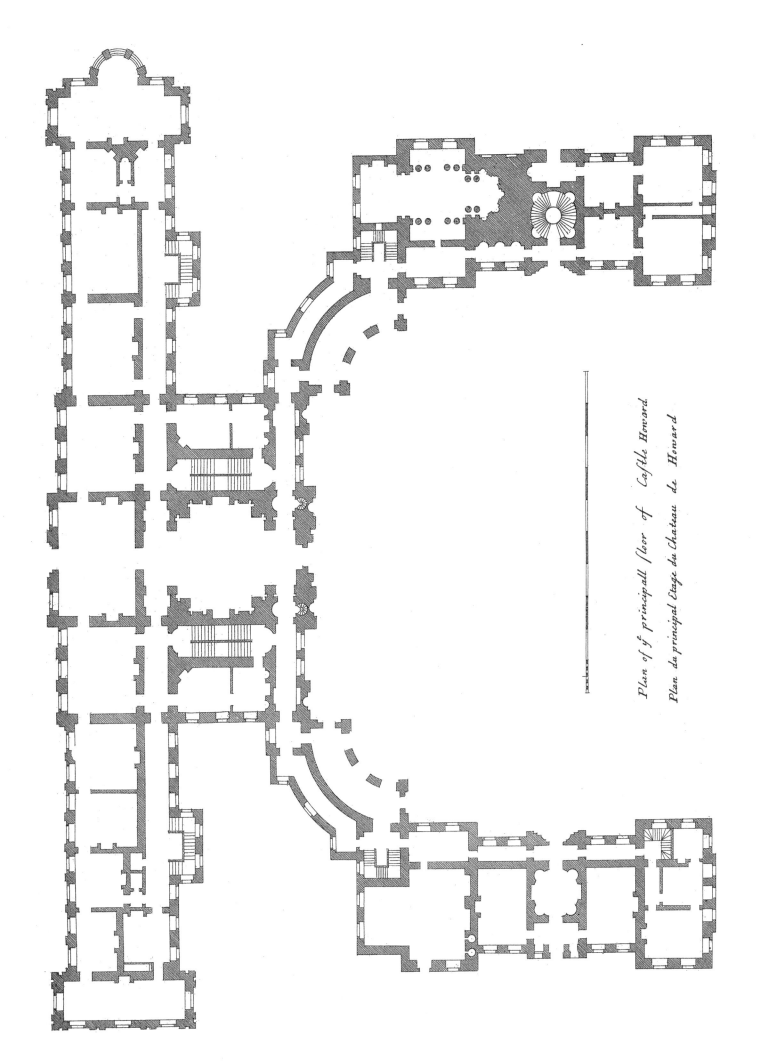

Plan of y.ᵉ principall floor of Castle Howard.

Plan du principal Etage du Chateau de Howard

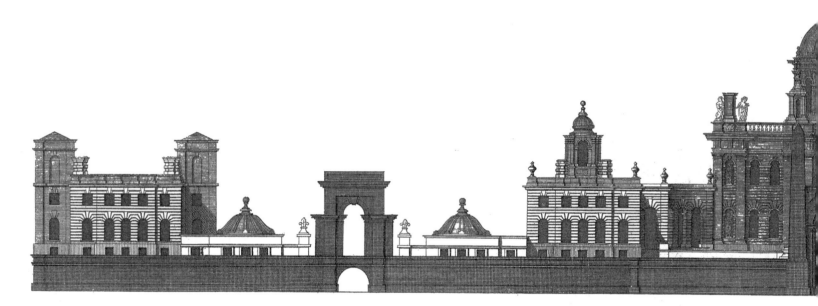

200 Feet

The Elevation of the General Front of Castle Howard in Yorkshire the Seat of the Rt. Honour

Elevation General du Chateau

Ca: Campbell Delin:

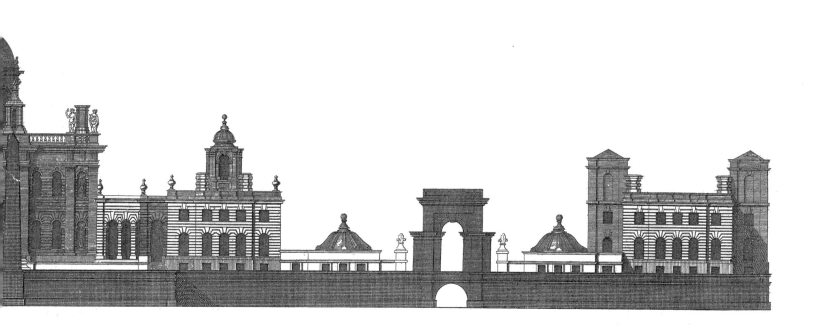

≡ *Extends 667*

E. arl of Carlisle. to whom this Plate is most humbly Inscribed. Design'd by Sr. I. Vanbrugh Kt.

·d dans la Comte de York.

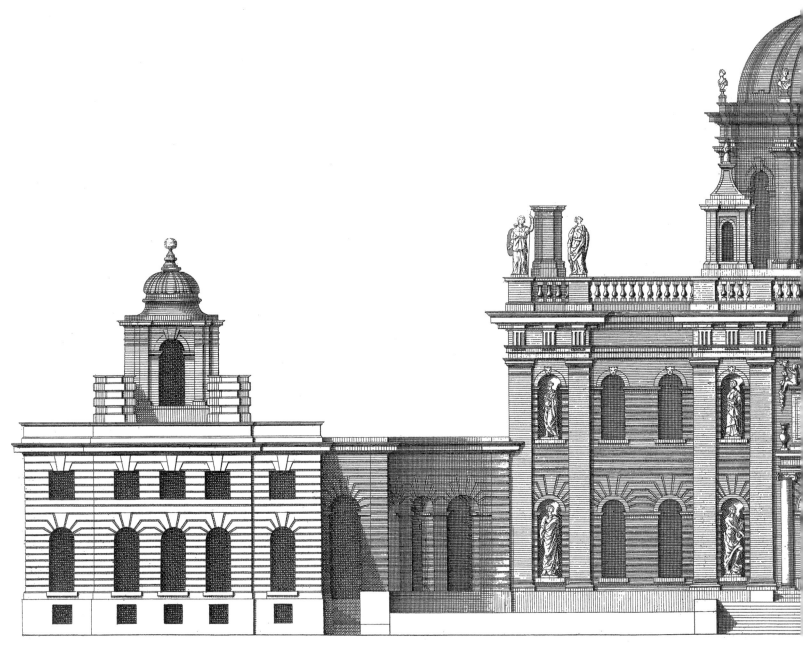

40 Feet

The Front to the Court of Castle I.

Elevation du Chateau D'Hor.

Ca: Campbell Delin:

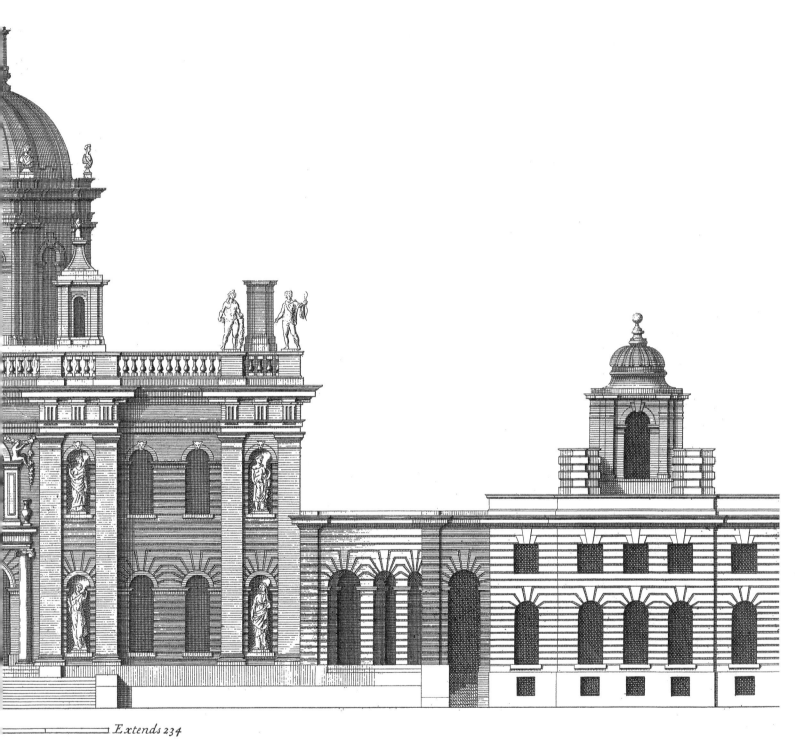

Extends 234

rd. Defignd by Sr I. Vanbrugh Kt.

du cofté de la Cour.

Elevation de la Maison de HOWARD Dans La Comté de YORK
appartenante a Son Excellence Le Comte De CARLISLE &c.
Deßeignez par M.r Le Chevalier Vanbrugh .

Extends 292

40 Feet ⊏⊓⊓⊓⊓⊓⊓⊓⊓⊓⊓⊓⊐⎯⎯⎯⎯⎯⎯⎯⎯⎯⎯⎯⊐ Extends 89

The Section of Castle Howard.
Profil du Chateau D'Howard.

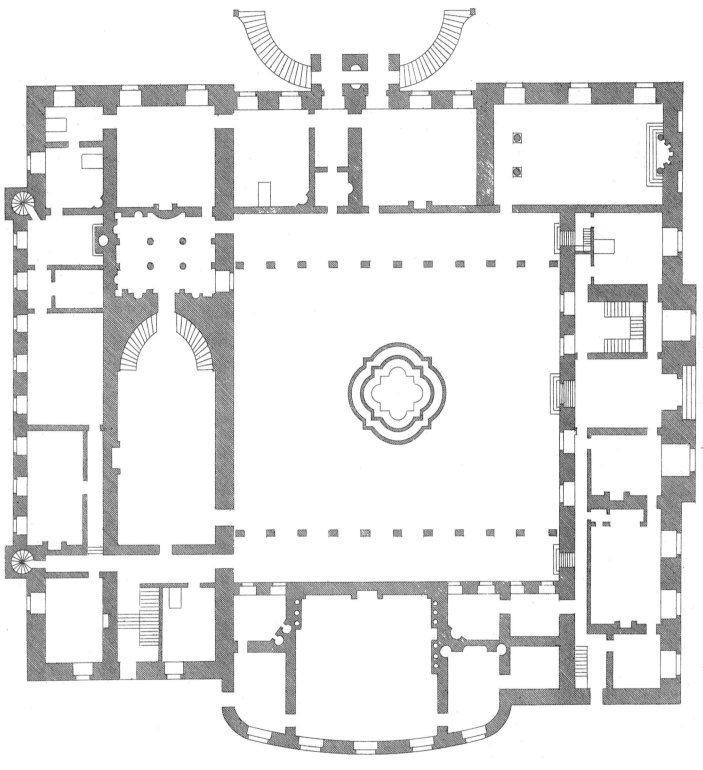

a Scale of 40 feet

The plan of ye first Story of Chatsworth

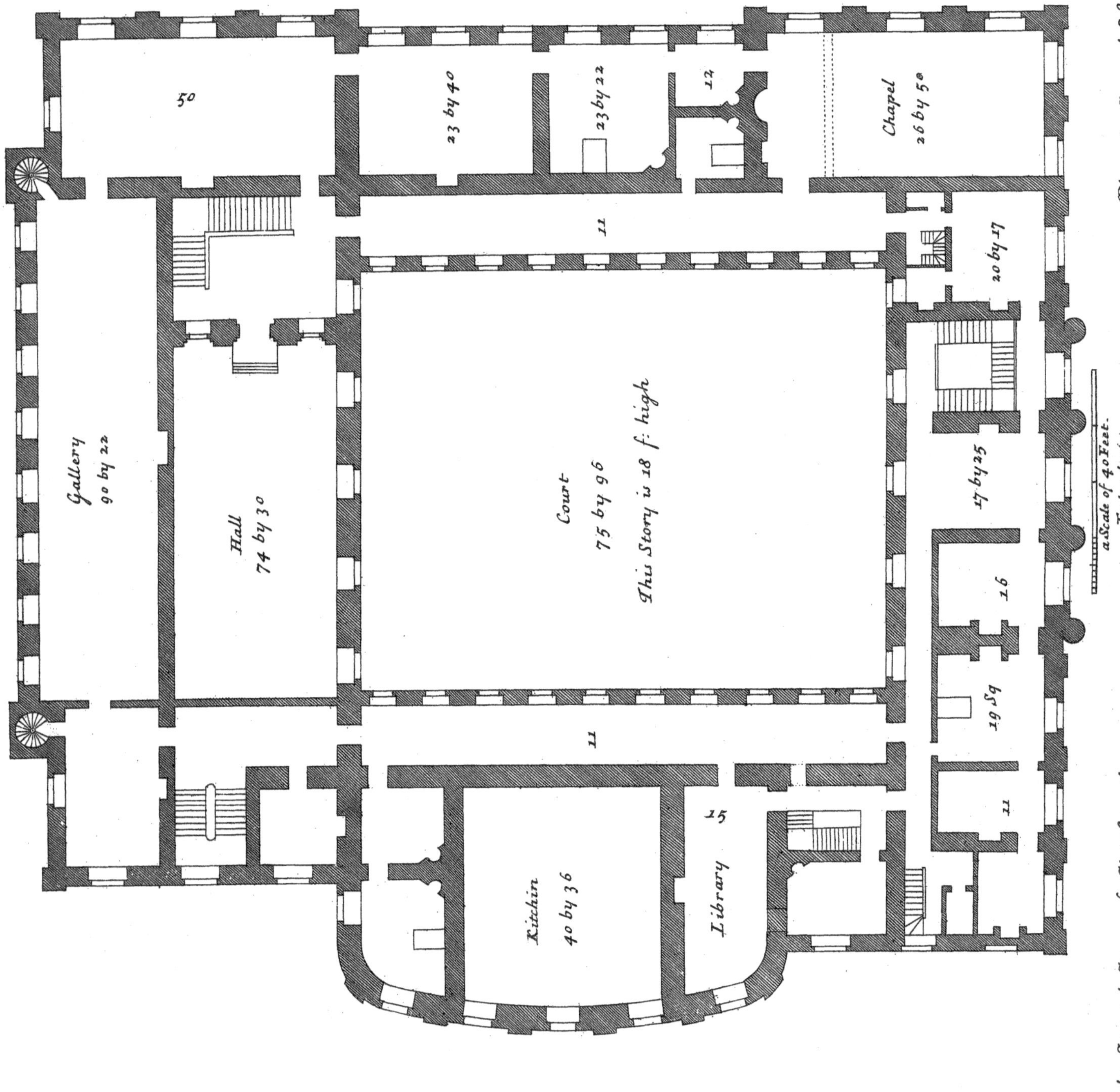

Gallery
90 by 22

50

Hall
74 by 30

23 by 40

23 by 22

12

Chapel
26 by 50

Court
75 by 96

This Story is 18 f: high

11

11

20 by 17

17 by 25

19

19 by 5

11

Kitchin
40 by 36

Library

15

a Scale of 40 Feet.
Extends 140.

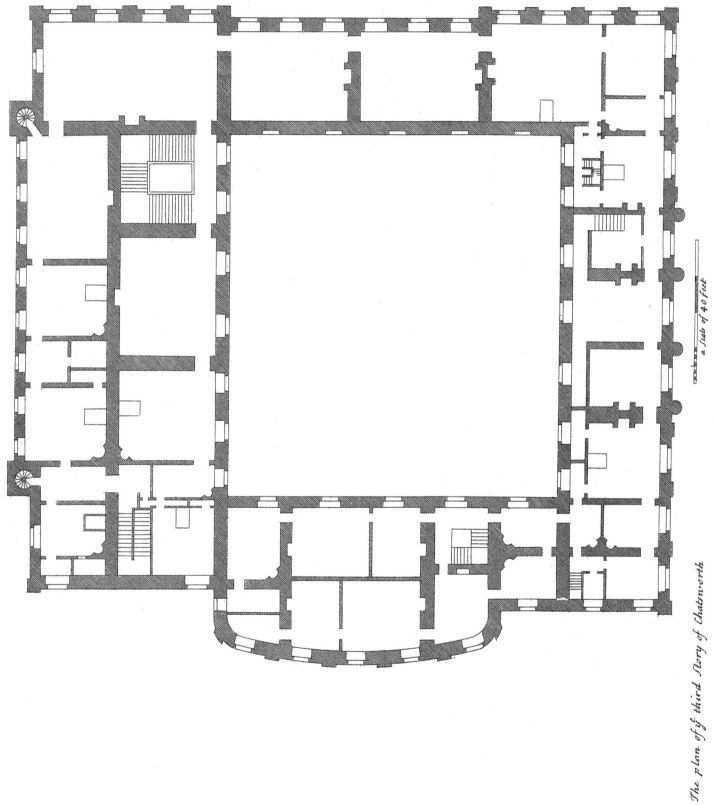

plan du troisième Etage.

a Scale of 40 feet

The plan of y third Story of Chatsworth.

The *West Prospect of* CHATSWORTH *in* DARBYSHIRE, *the Seat of his Grace the Duke of* DEVONSHIRE &c Lord Steward of his MAJESTY'S Houshold, and Knight of the most

Noble Order of the Garter. To whom this Plate is most humbly Inscrib'd.

Elevation Occidental du Chateau de CHATSWORTH dans la Comté de DERBIE. Invenit pr. Mr Talman.

a Scale of 100 Feet
Extendi 172.

Ex Authographo D.I.Thornill.

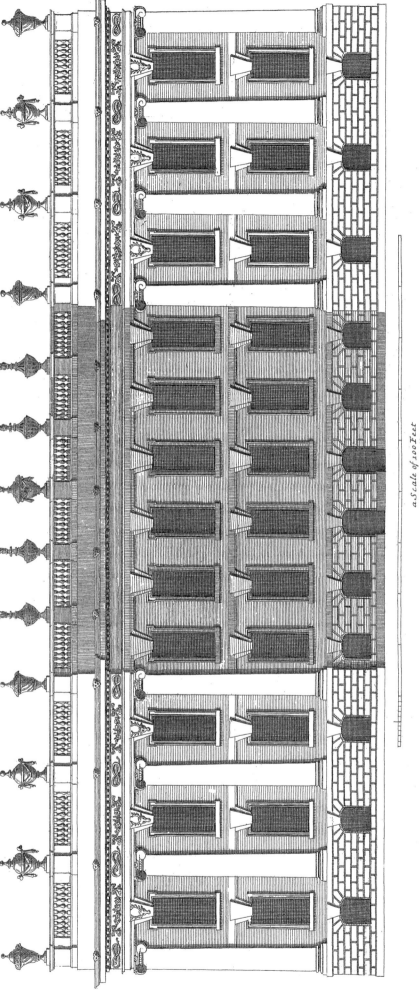

a Scale of 100 Feet
Extends 190 f.t

The South front of Chatsworth.
Elevation Meridional de Chatsworth.

Ca: Campbell Delin:

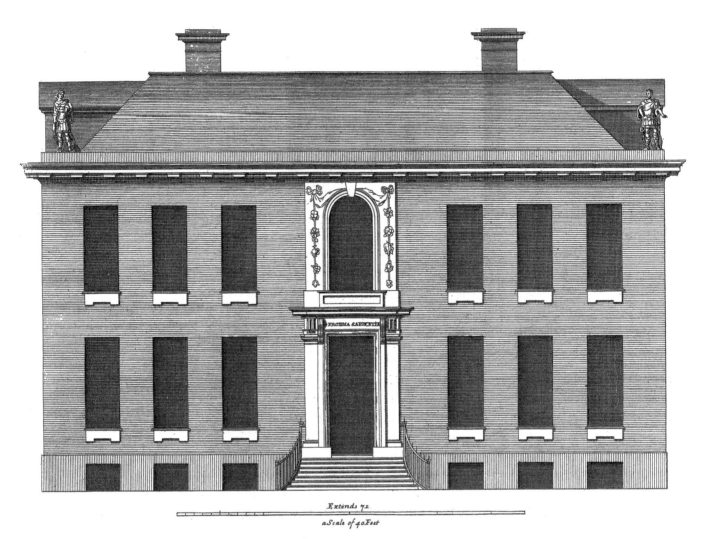

Extinds 71.

aScale of 40 Feet

The Prospect to the Gardens of the Hon.ble IAMES IOHNSTON Esq.r his House at TWITTENHAM in the County of MIDLESEX . 1710 .

Elevation Du costé Du Jardin De La Maison Du Monsieur Mons.r IOHNSTON a TWITTENHAM Dans La Comté De MIDLESEX .

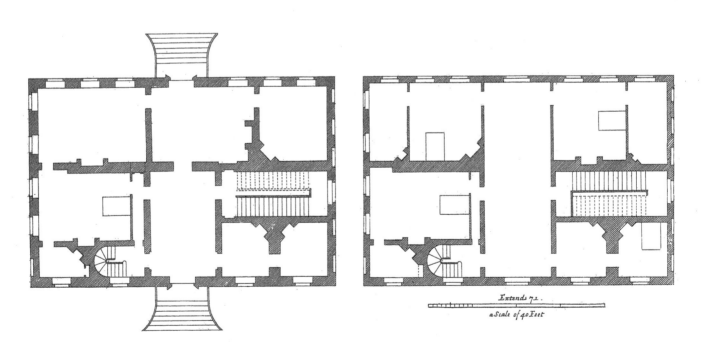

Extinds 71 .

aScale of 40 Feet

The Plan of the first Floor .

Plan de La premiere Estage .

The Plan of the Chamber Floor .

Plan de La Seconde Estage .

Ca Campbel Delin:

The plan of the principall story of St Walter Yonge Bart his House in Devonshire
Plan du premier Etage

The plan of yᵉ Chamber floor
plan du Second Etage

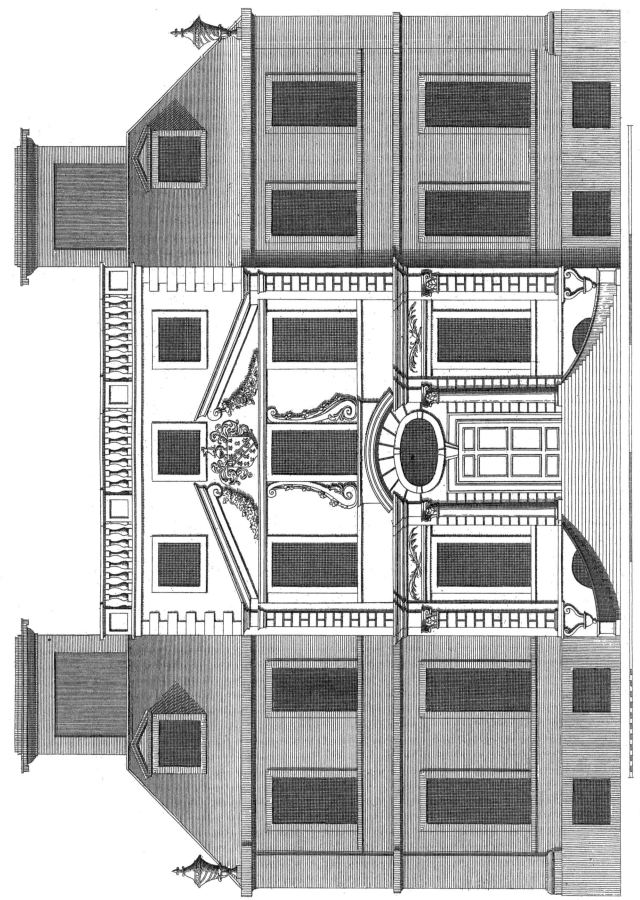

The Elevation of Sr Walter Yonge Bart his house in Devonshire To whom ye plate is most humbly inscrib'd
Elevation de La Maison du Mr Yonge Chevalier Bart dans La Conté de Devon.

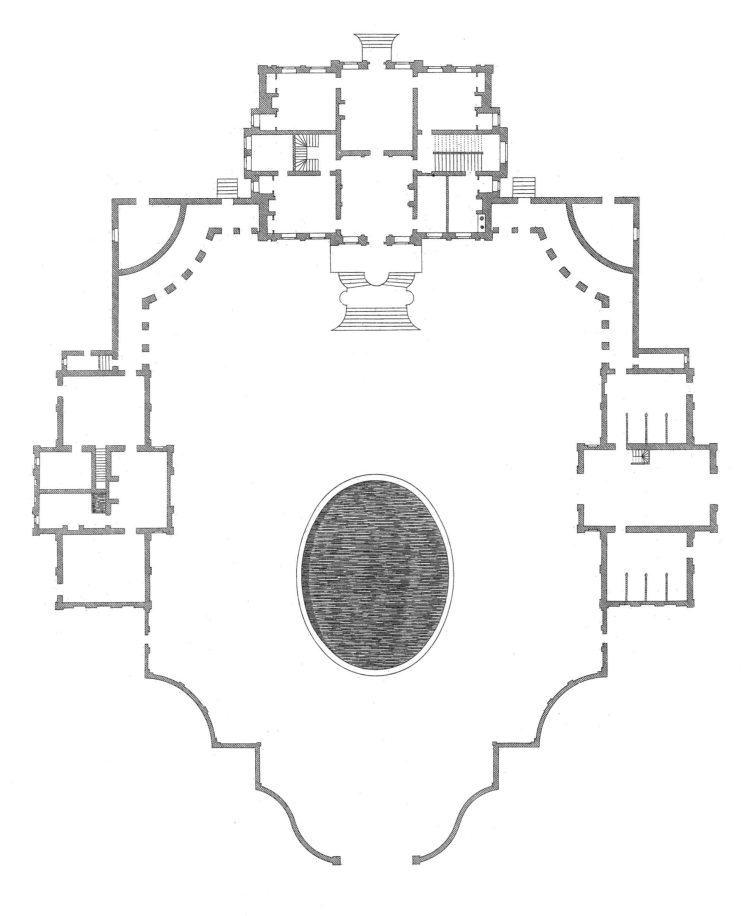

40 Feet ⊏⊔⊔⊔⊔⊔⊔⊐━━━━━━━━⊐ Extends 188

Plan of Ronhampton houfe

Plan de la Maifon de Ronhampton

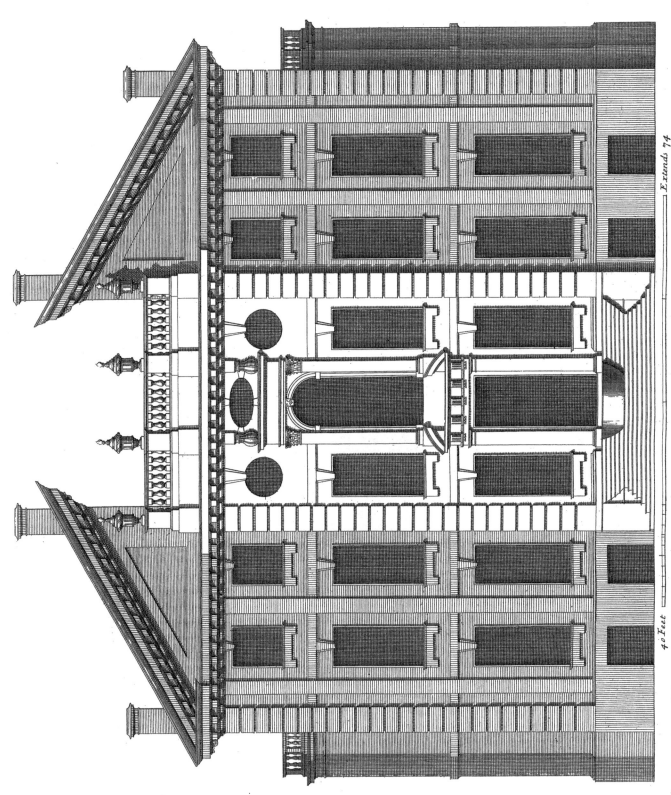

40 Feet ————— Extends 74

The Elevation of Ronhampton house in Surrey the Seat of Thomas Cary Esqʳ: To whom this Plate is most humbly Inscribed . Invented by Thomas Archer Esqʳ: 1712

Ca: Campbell Delin:

Elevation de la Maison de Ronhampton dans la Comté de Surrey.

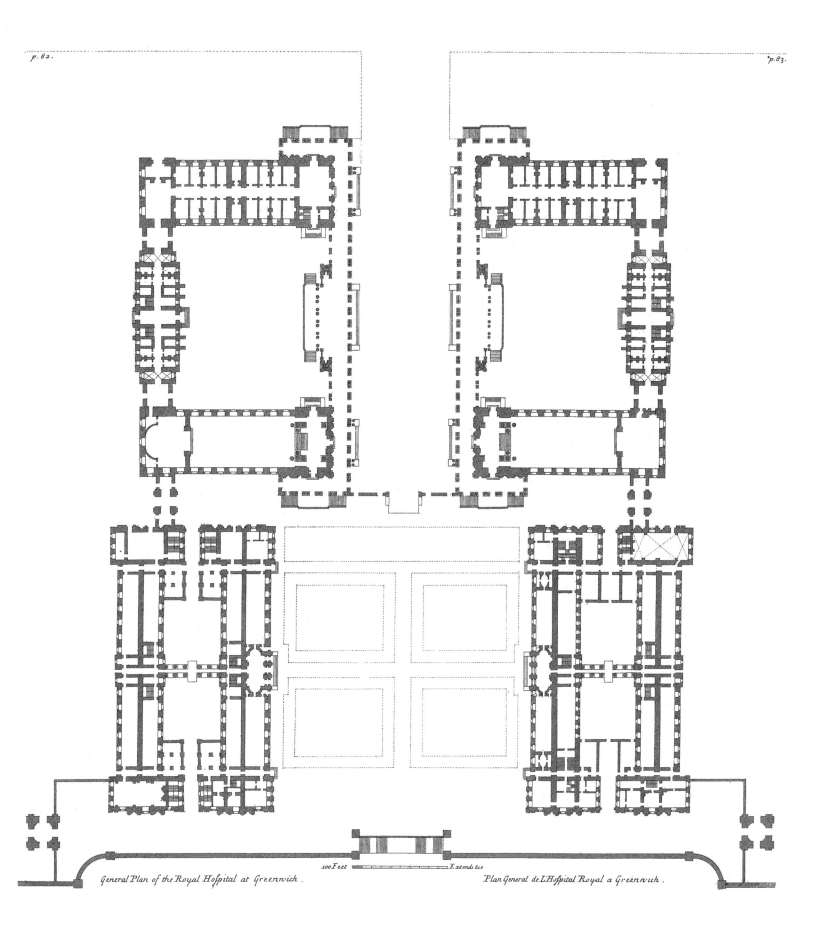

General Plan of the Royal Hospital at Greenwich.   100 Feet   Extends 610   Plan General de L'Hospital Royal a Greenwich.

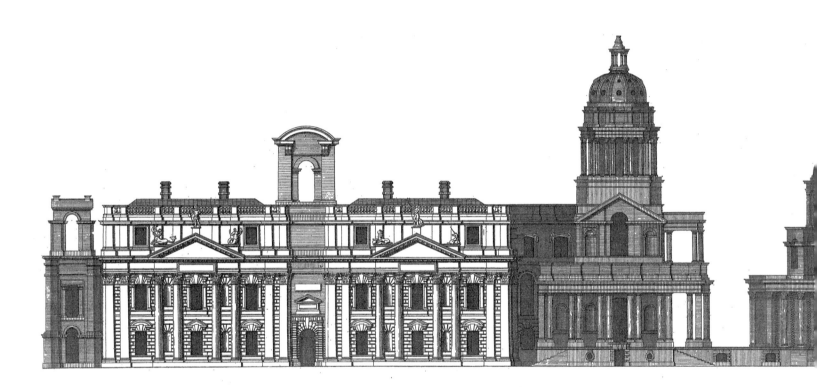

a Scale of 100 Feet

The General Front of the Royal Hofpital at Greenwich, is moft humbly Infcrib'd to the Hon.ble Ma.

Elevation General de L'Hofp.

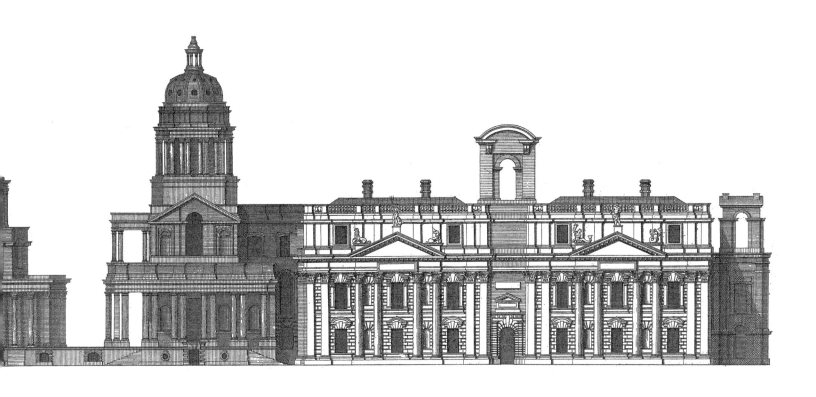

Extends 670

r Eſq. Governour of the Hoſpital. and Admiral of his Majeſty's Fleet &c:

a Greenwich.

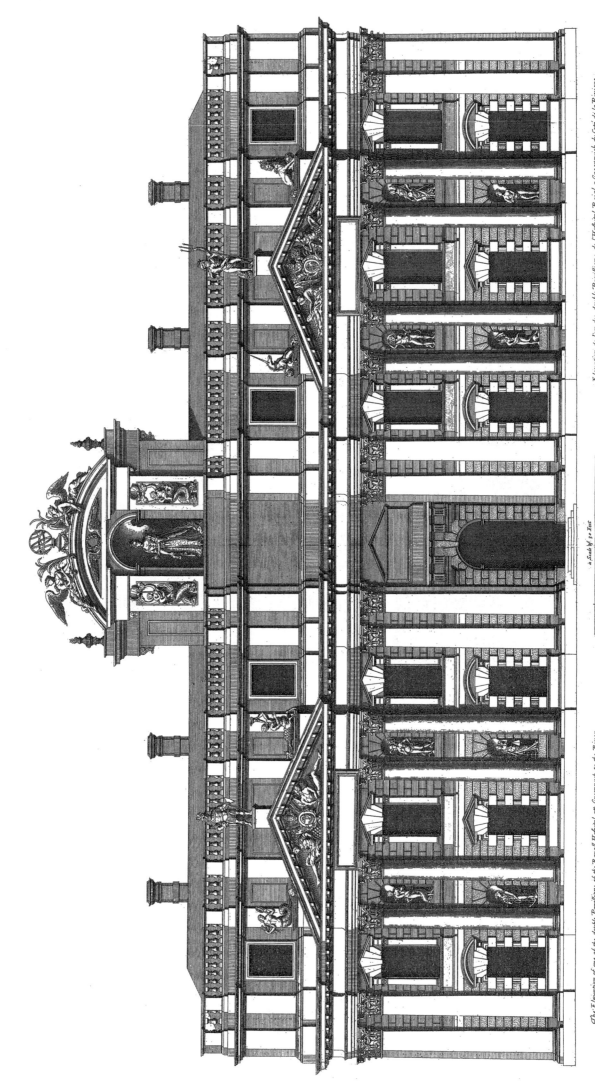

The Elevation of one of the double Pavillions of the Royall Hospital att Greenwich to the River.
I most humbly Inscribed to his Royall Highness the Prince of Wales &c.

Co. Campbell delin.

à Scale of 30 Feet

Extibit 972

I. Fonas Inuen:

Elevation de l'un des double Pavillions de l'Hospital Roial a Greenwich du Coté de la Riviere,
tres humblement dedieé a son Altesse Roiale le Prince de Galles &c.

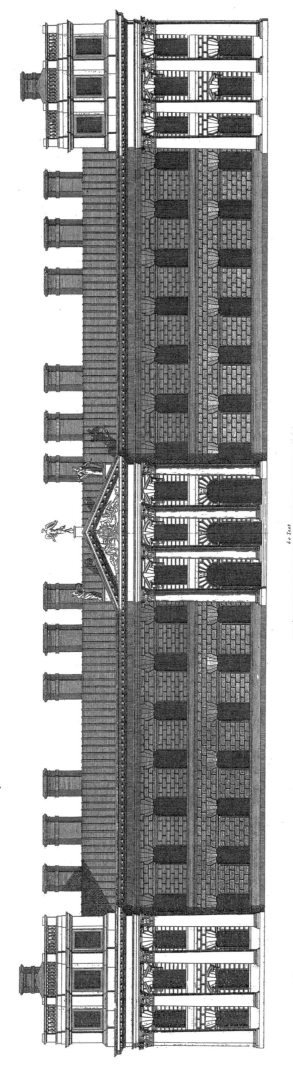

The Elevation of one Wing of the Great Court of Greenwich Hospital.
is most Humbly Inscribed to the Rt. Honourable the Lord Somers &c.

Elevation d'une Aile du côté du Grand Court de l'Hospital Roial a Greenwich.

Co: Campbell Delin:

60 Feet

Extends 289

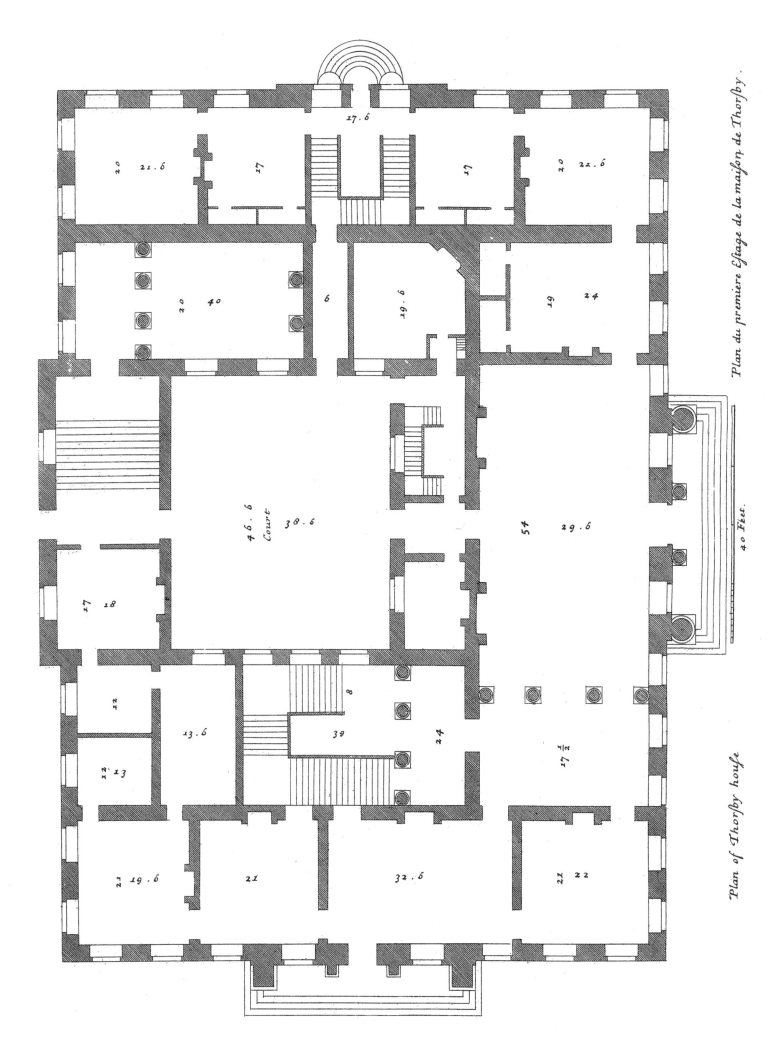

17.6

20 · 21.6 · · · 17 · · · 17 · · · 20 · 21.6

20 · 40 · · · 6 · · · 19.6 · · · 19 · 24

46.6 · Court · 38.6 · · · 54 · · 29.6

17 · 18

12 · · 8

13.6 · · 39 · · 24

12 · 13 · · · 17 ½

21 · 19.6 · · 21 · · 32.6 · · · 21 · 22

40 Feet.

Plan du premiere Estage de la maison de Thorsby.

Plan of Thorsby house

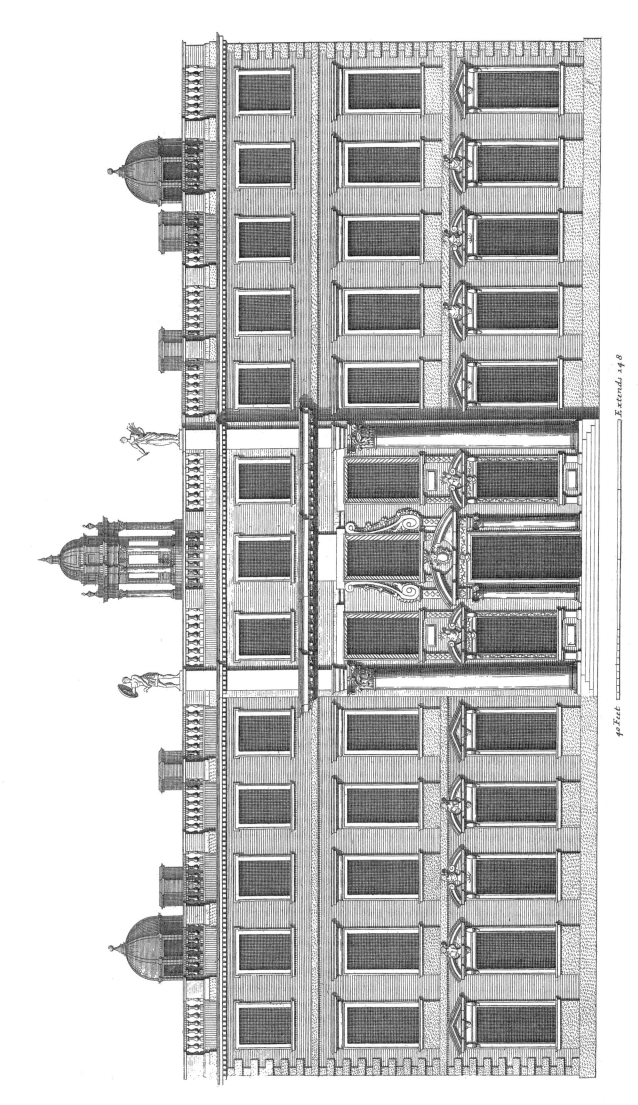

The Elevation of Thorsby house in the County of Nottingham the Seat of the Rt Honble the Marquiß of Dorchester to whom this plate is most humbly Inscribed

Elevation de la Maison de Thorsby dans la Comté de Nottingham.

Ca: Campbell Delin.

Extends 148

40 Feet

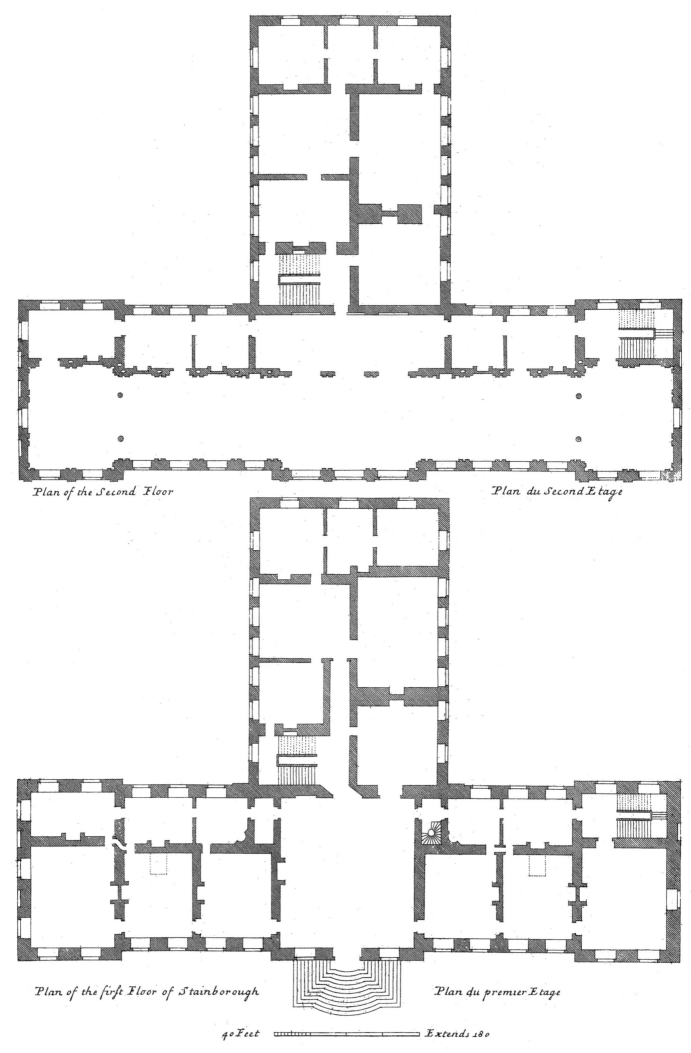

Plan of the Second Floor   Plan du Second Etage

Plan of the first Floor of Stainborough   Plan du premier Etage

40 Feet   Extends 180

40 Feet

Extends 180

The Elevation of Stainborough in Yorkshire the Seat of the R.t Hon.ble The Earl of Strafford &c: Knight of the most Noble Order of the Garter: to whom this Plate is most humbly Inscribed.

Elevation du Chateau de Stainborough dans la Comté de York.

Ca: Campbell Delin:

C. 1, PL. 93-94

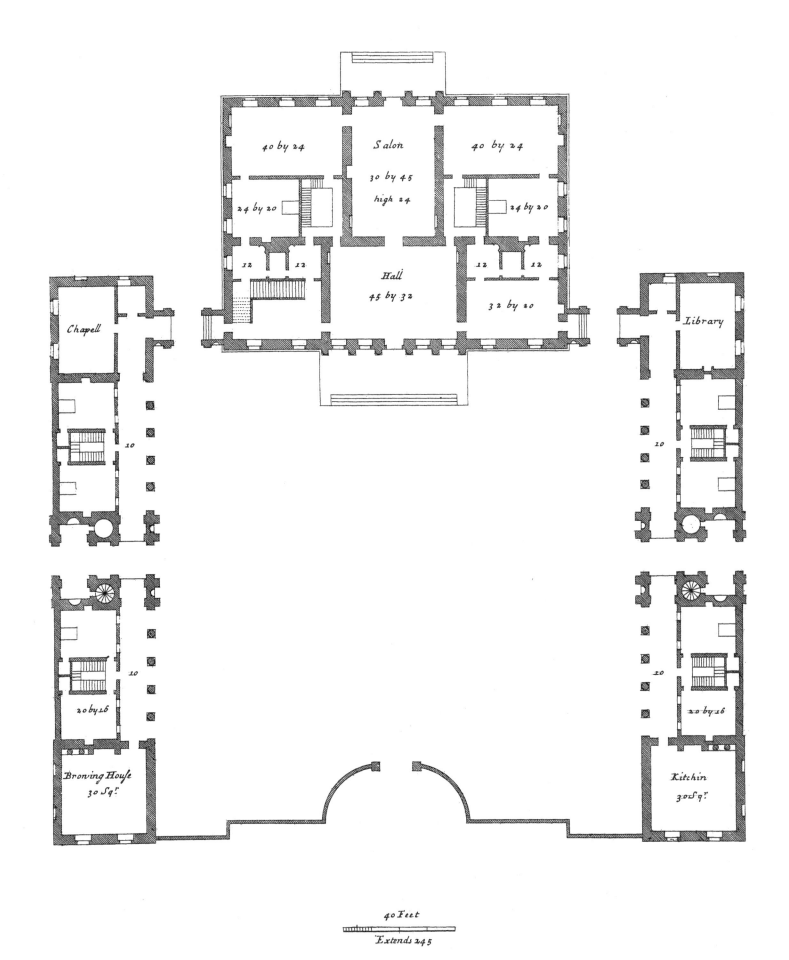

40 by 24 Salon 40 by 24

30 by 45

high 24

24 by 20 24 by 20

12 12 Hall 12 12

45 by 32

32 by 20

Chapell Library

10 10

20 by 16 20 by 16

10 10

Broning House Kitchin
30 Sq.r 30 Sq.r

40 Feet

Extends 245

General Plan of a new Design for the Lord Percival.

Plan d'un Nouveau Dessein pour My Lord Percival.

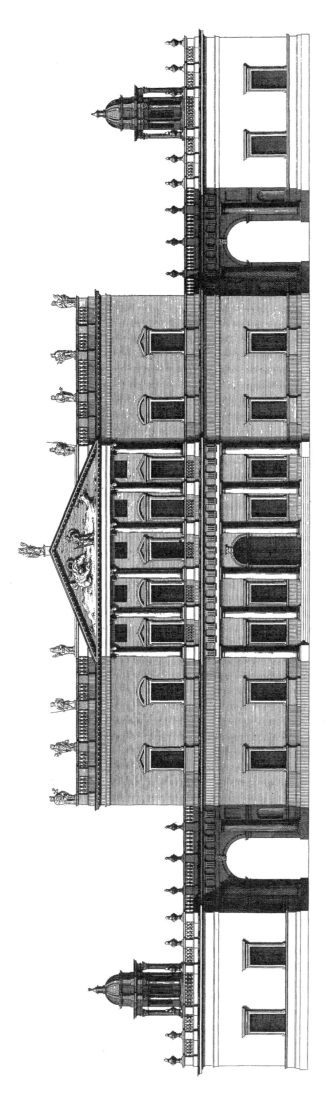

This New Design of my Invention is most humbly Inscrib'd to the R.t Hon.ble the Lord Percival &c:

Elevation d'un Nouveau Dessein de mon Invention Dedié a My Lord Percival &c:

a Scale of 40 Feet

Extends 245

Ca: Campbell Inv: et Delin:

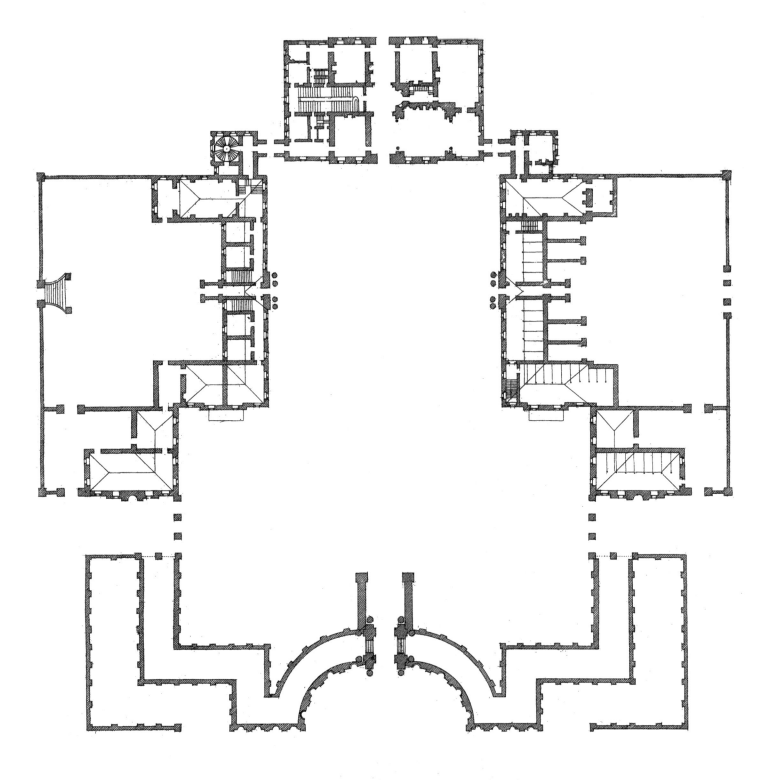

100 Feet |⊞⊞⊞⊞⊞⊞——————————————————| Extends 370

Plan of the Lord Leimpster's house.

Plan de la Maison du my Lord Leimpster.

The Elevation of the Rt. Honourable the Lord Leimpster's houfe in Northamptonfhire to whom this Plate is moft humbly Infcribed.

Elevation de la Mayfon du my Lord Leimpfter dans la Comté de Northampton.

60 Feet   Extends 320

Mr. Hawkfmoor Inv:

Ca: Campbell Delin:

VITRUVIUS BRITANNICUS,

or

The British Architect,

Containing

The Plans, ELEVATIONS, and Sections

of the Regular Buildings, *both*

PUBLICK and PRIVATE,

IN

GREAT BRITAIN,

With Variety of New Defigns; *in* 200 *large* Folio Plates, *Engraven by the* beſt Hands; *and Drawn either from the* Buildings *themſelves, or the* Original Defigns *of the* Architects;

In II VOLUMES

VOL. II   *by* Colen Campbell Efq.ʳ

VITRUVIUS BRITANNICUS,

ou

L'Architecte Britannique;

Contenant

Les Plans, *ELEVATIONS*, & Sections

des Bâtimens Reguliers, *tant*

PARTICULIERS que PUBLICS

de la Grande Bretagne,

Compris en 200 *grandes* Planches *gravez en taille douce par les* Meilleurs Maitres, *et tous ou deſſinez des* Bâtimens *memes, ou copiez des* Deſſeins Originaux *des* Architectes:

EN DEUX TOMES.

TOME II   *Par le Sieur* Campbell.

CUM PRIVILEGIO REGIS.

Sold by the Author over againſt Douglas Coffee-houſe *in* St. Martins-lane, *John Nicholſon in* Little Britain, *Andrew Bell at the* Croſs-Keys *in* Cornhil, *W. Taylor in* Pater-Noſter-Row, *Henry Clements in* St. Pauls Church-yard, *And Jof. Smith in* Exeter-Change. LONDON MDCCXVII.
J. Sturt ſculp.

A N
EXPLANATION

Of all the

PLATES in the Second Volume.

White-hall, *as defign'd by* Inigo Jones, *from p. 2, to p. 19. inclufive.*

FTER much Labour and Expence I have at laft procured thefe excellent Defigns of *Inigo Jones*, for *White-hall*, from that ingenious Gentleman *William Emmet* of *Bromley*, in the County of *Kent*, Efq; from whofe Original Drawings the following 5 Plates are publifh'd, whereby he has made a moft valuable Prefent to the Sons of Art. In the Firft is the General Plan of the *Piano Nobile*, which contains 6 Courts; that next the Park is an exact Square of 245 Foot of each Side are two Squares of 250 by 125, being 2 Squares. The Middle Court next the River is 125 by 85, being a Diagonal; and the two Side-Courts this Way are fo proportioned, that the Length and Breadth are as 5 to 3. So that here is a variety of excellent Proportions, and all the Apartments are difpofed either for State or Conveniency, thofe to the River being moft proper for the Summer Seafon, and thofe to the Park for Winter, having the *South-Weft* Sun. I have omitted the Ground Plan, which may be eafily collected from this and the general Section. The fecond Plate is the Front to the Park, which is the *Banquetting-Houfe*, with a Chapel correfponding to it: In the Middle is a noble Entry after the manner of a double Triumphal Arch; the Angles are terminated with two lofty Towers of an elegant Compofition, and two *Cupolas* crown the Building. Our Architect has drefs'd the Front with the *Ionick* and *Corinthian* Orders: In the third is the Front to the *Thames*, the Orders are *Dorick* and *Ionick*, as moft proper for this Situation, with great Variety of the *Venetian* Windows; the Towers are the fame as in the firft and in the other Fronts: In the fourth is the Front to *Charing-Crofs*, with a noble *Dorick* Arcade; the Superior Order is *Ionick*, and all the Ornaments are beautiful, graceful and fignificant; the Front to *Weftminfter* being the fame is here omitted. In the fifth Plate is the general Section which difcovers the three principal Courts, the great Piazzas, and height of the different Stories.

Covent-Garden, *p. 20, 21, and 22.*

I Have made one fingle and one double Plate of this noble Square, which for the Grandure of Defign, is certainly the firft in *Europe*. In the firft Plate is the general Plan of the Piazza, the Plan, Section and *Weft* Front of that elegant Church, the only Piece the Moderns have yet produced, that can admit of a juft Comparifon with the Works of Antiquity, where a Majeftick Simplicity commands the Approbation of the Judicious. In the double Plate are two Elevations of the great Piazza *Weftwards*, and of the Church to the *Eaft*; the Afpect is *Antes*, the Or-

der is *Tufcan, Tetraftile Areoftile:* The *Ruftick* Arcade round the Square is of an excellent Compofition, the Arches are 10 Foot wide and 20 high, the Piers are 4 Foot in Front, which is two Fifths of the Arch, and 8 at the Angles; above the Arcade is one grand Story and an Attick, the Windows are drefs'd with a regular Entablature, in Width are equal to the Piers and two Diameters in height, the Attick Windows are under the Square. It were to be wifhed our Artificers wou'd obferve this juft Proportion in Piers and Widows, which wou'd prevent the Lanthorn way of Building fo much in Practice of late Years.

The Royal-Exchange, *p. 23, 24, and 25.*

THIS Structure was raifed foon after the Fire of *London*, in the Year 1666, and however inferior to thofe Pieces of *Inigo Jones*, yet may very juftly claim a Place in this Collection, being the moft Confiderable of this Kind in *Europe*; I have made one fingle and one double Plate: In the firft is the Plan containing 205 Foot by 180; the fecond is the principal Front to *Cornhill*; in the Middle is a Piece of the *Corinthian* Order, with a very bold Arch, and two fmall ones of each Side; from this rifeth a lofty Tower compofed of 3 Orders: The *Ruftick* Arcade in this Building is generally condemned by the Criticks, for having Piers but one fourth of the Arch, which renders it weak.

Bow *Steeple. p. 26.*

I Have brought the Plans, Section and Elevation of this Tower into one Plate, and of this Kind 'tis efteemed one of the beft in the Kingdom.

A *Defign for a Church of my Invention, p. 27.*

THE Afpect of this Church is *Proftile, Hexaftile, Euftile*, which by *Vitruvius, Palladio*, and the general Confent of the moft judicious Architects, both Ancient and Modern, is efteem'd the moft beautiful and ufeful Difpofition, being a Medium between the *Picnoftile* and *Areoftile*, the firft being too clofe and the laft too open. The Order is *Ionick*, and in one Plate I have given 4 Defigns: In the firft is the Plan, where the Cella is 54 by 74, which is a Diagonal Proportion; the Side Walls are 6 Foot thick, and with 3 more for the ¼ Columns amounts to 9 Foot, which is one Sixth of 54, and the whole Width being 72, the two Walls make one Fourth of the fame. The fecond Defign is the Side of the Church, where I have abftained from any Ornaments between the Columns, which would only ferve to enflame the Expence and clog the Building. In thofe admirable Pieces of Antiquity, we find none of the trifling, licentious, and infignificant Ornaments, fo much affected by fome of our Moderns. The Ancients placed their chief Beauties in the juftnefs of the Intercolumnations, the precife Proporti-

A   on

ons of the Orders and the greatnefs of Parts; nor have we one Precedent either from the *Greeks* or *Romans*, that they practifed two Orders, one over another in the fame Temple in the Outfide, even in the moft confiderable, much lefs to divide it into little Parts; and whereas the Ancients were contented with one continued Pediment from the Portico to the Paftico, we have now no lefs than three in one Side where the Ancients never admitted any. This Practice muft be imputed either to an entire Ignorance of Antiquity, or a Vanity to expofe their abfurd Novelties, fo contrary to thofe excellent Precepts in *Vitruvius*, and fo repugnant to thofe admirable Remains the Ancients have left us. The third Defign is the Front, where I have alfo abftained from any unneceffary Ornaments, the Door is drefs'd after the beft Models of Antiquity. The fourth is the Section, which fhews the Elevation of the Infide and manner of the Vaulting; the whole Height is 54, equal to the Width, and that being divided into 4 Parts, one of them determines the height of the Vault, and the 3 other Parts are given to the perpendicular Wall. In the *Eaft* End I have made a *Venetian* Window, which will fufficiently illuminate the whole Church; here I have practiced an *Ionick* Pilaftrade with Niches, and over them enriched Compartments.

York *Stairs*, *p.* 28.

THIS Gate was erected by the firft Duke of *Buckingham*, when Lord High Admiral of *England*, *Anno* 1626, by *Inigo Jones*.

Cobham *Hall in* Kent, *p.* 29, 30.

WAS the Seat of the Dukes of *Lenox* and *Richmond*, now of the Lady *Theodofia Blyth* and *John Blyth* Efq; 'Tis a large ancient Fabrick, and has one Front by *Inigo Jones*, with a *Corinthian* Pilaftrade, and an Attick of the higheft Proportion and Baluftrade; the great Hall is two Stories high.

Cholmondeley *Hall in* Chefhire, *p.* 31, 32, 33 *and* 34.

IS the Seat of the Earl of *Cholmondeley*, of which I have made 4 Plates; the firft is the general Plan of the firft Story, being a large Quadrangle open to the *North*: The fecond is the *North* Front drefs'd with a *Corinthian* Pilaftrade, and a proper Baluftrade: The third is the *South* Front with the fame Ornaments; and the laft is the *Weft* Front with fix ½ Columns. The whole Fabrick was rebuilt and finifhed in a fumptuous manner in the Year 1715: Here are fine Gardens, and all is agreeable to the Magnificence of the noble Patron.

Eaton *Hall in* Chefhire, *p.* 35 *and* 36.

THE Seat of Sir *Richard Grofvenor* Bart. in two Plates; the firft contains the general Plan of the Offices and principal Story, which is very Handfom and Commodious; in the Plan one may obferve a great Regard to State and Conveniency, the Size of the Rooms being judicioufly varied, and generally the Rules of Proportion are maintained in all the Apartments: In the fecond Plate is the Front of the Houfe and Offices, the Corners are drefs'd with Rufticks of a good Taft, and the Fabrick is crown'd with a *Cupola*.

Belton *in* Licolnfhire, *p.* 37, 38.

THIS is the Seat of Sir *John Brownlow* Bart. in 2 Plates; the firft contains the Plans of the two principal Stories, where are many very good Apartments, noble and convenient: The fecond is the Front in which the Windows are handfomly drefs'd with Architrave, Frife and Cornice, and the whole Compofition is regular; here are curious Gardens, a large Park, and many other Improvements.

But above all the polite Literature, the great Civility, and uncommon Generofity of the Patron deferves to be tranfmitted to Pofterity.

High-Meadow *in* Gloucefterfhire, *p.* 39, 40.

THE Seat of *Thomas Gage*, Efq; in two Plates; the firft contains the Plans of the two principal Floors: The fecond is the Front which has a noble Entry, the Windows are well drefs'd, but the Piers are too narrow, and in the Wings the large Space from the Window to the Corner has a good Effect.

A New Defign for Tobias Jenkyns, Efq; *p.* 41, 42.

I Have infcribed this fmall Effay of my Invention to this ingenious Gentleman, whofe Knowledge in the moft polite Learning is equal to his extream Modefty, in endeavouring to conceal what fo many do falfly affume, and his particular Atachment to Architecture muft draw a deep Refpect from all that profefs any Love or Efteem for that ufeful and noble Art. In the firft Plate is the Plan of the firft Story, extending 120 Foot, here is the double and fingle Cube, the Hall being 27 by 54; here is 18 by 27, which is the *Sefqui altera*, and 21 by 27, the *Sefqui tertia*, and you pafs gradually from the larger to the leffer. Right againft the Entry I have placed the great Pair of Stairs, which is free and fpacious, and leads up to the principal Story which is the fame with the firft, excepting that the Salon which is over the Hall, is 27 Foot high and has two Degrees of Windows; the two pair of Back Stairs go from the Foundation to the Top, and will ferve all the Apartments: In the fecond Plate is the Front with a Ruftick Bafement and two Orders of Pilafters in the Theatrical, which admits of more Gayety than is proper either for the Temple or Palatial Stile.

Boddington *Place in* Surrey, *p.* 43, 44, 45.

IS the ancient Seat of Sir *Nicholas Carew* Bart. of which I have made 3 Plates; the firft contains the Plans of the two principal Floors, where is a very noble Hall, in Height two Stories, and many large and fpacious Apartments: In the fecond is the *Weft* Front drefs'd with a Compofite Pilaftrade and other Ornaments: The third Plate is the Garden Front, and tho' more plain yet has a good Effect by reafon of the large Solids between the Windows. The Houfe ftands in a large Park, the Gardens are very curious and artful, the Orangery is efteemed the beft in the Kingdom; here is great Plenty of excellent Water, with Canals and Cafcades; and indeed every thing is truly worthy of fo generous a Patron, who has fpared no Coft to rebuild and imbellifh his Seat.

Mr. Hudfon's *Houfe at* Sunbury *in* Middlefex, *p.* 46.

I Have given the general Plan of the firft Floor and Offices with the general Front in one Plate, the Apartments are handfom, the Furniture fumptuous, and the Offices commodious; and tho' there is but little Ornament in the Outfide, the Materials being good and the Work well executed, it makes a fine Appearance: Here are fine Gardens with a charming Profpect to the *Thames*; it was defigned and conducted by Mr. *Fort*, *Anno* 1712.

Mr. Waller's *Houfe in* Beaconsfield, *p.* 47.

I Have alfo given the general Plan of the Offices and firft Floor, with the general Front in one Plate; the Offices are joined to the Houfe, with a handfom Corridore of the *Corinthian* Order, defigned by *Thomas Milner* Efq; *Anno* 1712.

Mr. Rooth's *Houfe at* Epfom, *p.* 48, 49.

IN the firft Plate you have the Plans of the firft and fecond Story, and in the fecond is the Front, and
tho'

tho' but of fmall Extent, yet is moft conveniently laid out and well finifhed.

Melvin *Houfe in* Scotland, *p.* 50.

THE Seat of the Earl of *Lewin*; in this Plate I have given the Plan of the principal Story and Front; here is a very good Salon with two noble Apartments, with two convenient Back Stairs; it was defigned by the moft experienc'd Architeft of that Kingdom, Mr. *James Smith, Anno* 1692.

Mr. Campbell's *Houfe at* Glafgow, *p.* 51.

DAniel Campbell of Shawfield Efq; has built this Houfe after my Defign, in *Glafgow*, the beft fituated and moft regular City in *Scotland:* The principal Apartment is in the firft Story, the Stair-cafe is fo placed in the Middle as to ferve 4 good Apartments in the fecond Story; the Front is drefs'd with Rufticks of a large Proportion, and a *Dorick* Cornice and Baluftrade; the Garrets receive Light from the Roof inwardly; the whole Building is of good Stone and well finifhed, *Anno* 1712.

A New Defign for a Perfon of Quality in Somerfetfhire, *p.* 52, 53, 54, 55.

THE firft Plate prefents you with the general Plan of the Offices and principal Floor raifed 10 Foot above the Court, which lands in a Portico, from thence to a noble Sale and Salon, and of each Side a grand Apartment: The fecond Plate is the principal Front adorned with a *Corinthian* Tetraftile and Pediment: The third is the Garden Front, and the laft is one End with a fine *Venetian* Window, with feveral other Embellifhments, all defigned by the learned and ingenious Sir *John Vanbrugh*, 1716.

Maiden Bradley *in* Wiltfhire, *p.* 56.

IS the Seat of Sir *Edward Seymour* Bart. In this Plate I have given the general Plans of the two principal Stories both of the Offices and beft Apartments, with the Elevation of the Fronts; the Windows of the firft are well drefs'd with Pediments, and the fecond have Windows with Architrave, Frieze and Cornice only: It was begun by the late Sir *Edward*, and finifhed by the prefent in a handfom manner.

Hampton Court *in* Herefordfhire, *p.* 57, 58.

IS the ancient Seat of the Lord *Coningesby*, built by *Henry* IV. King of *England* when he was Duke of *Hereford*, above 300 Years paft, which is the oldeft Building in this Colleftion: His Lordfhip has lately repaired it with great Expence and Magnificence; here are 7 very noble Apartments richly furnifhed, with many convenient fmall ones; here are alfo fine Gardens, a large Park, a well ftock'd Decoy, and all other Advantages both for Pleafure and Conveniency, and truly worthy of fo noble and polite a Patron.

Shobden Court *in* Hereforfhire, *p.* 59, 60.

THE Seat of Sir *James Bateman*, Bar. Lord Mayor of *London*, of which I have made two Plates; the firft contains the Plan of the principal Floor, where is a lofty Hall, in height 2 Stories, and 4 good Apartments: The fecond is the Front with Ruftick Corners and a Pediment: Sir *James* is now improving his Gardens and Plantations, with many other Embellifhments, as lafting Monuments of his Magnificence.

Wilton, *from p.* 61 *to p.* 67, *inclufive.*

THIS is the ancient Seat of the Earls of *Pembroke* and *Montgomery*, begun in the Reign of *Henry* VIII. The great Quadrangle was finifhed in the Time of *Edward* VI. and the Porch was defign'd by *Hans Holbin*. The Hall Side being burnt about 12 Years ago, was rebuilt by the prefent *Thomas* Earl of *Pembroke*, then Lord High Admiral of *England*, in a very noble and fumptuous Manner. The other Parts rebuilt by the firft *Philip* Earl of *Pembroke*, who was Lord Chamberlain, being all defigned by *Inigo Jones*, and finifhed by him in the Year 1640, are what I have here publifhed, 1 double and 5 fingle Plates. In the firft are the Plans of the two principal Floors, with the Garden Front 194 Foot long, which is juftly efteemed one of the beft Pieces of that great Architeft: 'Tis univerfally acknowledged that the grand Apartment is one of the nobleft Architefture has yet produced, particularly the Sale and Salon, whofe Seftions I give in the following Plates. In the firft you have the Seftion of the Sale, long 60 Foot, high 30, and in Breadth the fame; in one end of the Room is the celebrated Family Pifture by *Vandyke*, 20 Foot long and 12 high, containing 13 Figures as big as the Life, which rather appear as fo many real Perfons than the Produftion of Art, and all the other Piftures in the Seftion are of the fame incomparable Hand; in the fecond Plate is firft the Seftion of the fame Room towards the great geometrical Stair-Cafe, the firft of this kind in the Kingdom, with a rich and magnificent Door-Cafe; in this Plate is alfo the Seftion of the Salon, which is a Cube of 30 Foot: In both thefe Rooms, and in moft of the other Apartments, are Marble Chimney Pieces of the moft exquifite Work and moft elegant Compofition I have feen in the Kingdom, all carved in *Italy* and brought over by the firft *Philip* Earl of *Pembroke*, with many curious Statues, *Baffo Relievo's*, and other things of Marble, and Piftures of the moft famous Mafters. The third is the Loggio in the Bowling-Green, with an *Ionick* Arcade; the Pilafters are moft beautifully rufticated, and the Defign is enriched with Niches and Statues: In this Plate alfo is the Grotto, the Front being curioufly carved without, and all Marble within, having black Pilars of the *Ionick* Order, with Capitels of white Marble and 4 fine *Baffo Relievo's* from *Florence*. In the fame Plate is 1 Side of a Ruftick *Ionick* Door, in the Garden whereof there are 2 fronting each other two ways. The fourth is the Stables difpofed in a very handfome Manner. The fifth is a Ruftick Gate, which may ferve for a Model to direft our Workmen on the like Ocafion; the Columns frofted on each fide this Gate are on the Stable-Bridge. There remains fo much to be faid of this charming Place, that to give a true Account of it would require an entire Volume of a much more artful Pen; but I hope this will be accepted of by the candid Reader as fufficient from me till I publifh my Third Volume in Perfpeftive, where I intend a more ample Defcription.

Longleate, *in* Wiltfhire, *p.* 68, 69.

THE Seat of the Right Honourable the Lord Vifcount *Weymouth*, founded by Sir *John Thynne*, the great Reftorer of that ancient and honourable Family, in the Reign of *Edward* the Sixth, and of this Date, is efteemed to be the moft regular Building in the Kingdom, being above 160 Years ago. In one double Plate I have given firft the Plans of the two principal Floors, where is a noble Hall in Height two Stories, the Apartments are numerous, large and fumptuous; in the third Story, not here defigned, is a fpacious Gallery, and in the fame Line a very curious Library, in all 220 Foot long, befides 4 handfome Apartments in the Gallery. In the Library is an excellent Colleftion of the beft Authors of the moft correft Editions, with many rare and valuable Manufcripts. The Front is of a large Extent, being 220 Foot long, and adorned with three Orders of Pilafters, the *Dorick, Ionick,* and *Corinthian*, with their proper Pedeftals; the Proportions of each Order, their Intercolumnation and gradual Diminution is duely obferved, and the Fabrick is

crowned

crowned with a handfome Baluftrade, feveral Cupola's and Statues, erected by the late Lord; who alfo greatly adorned this Seat by the noble Gardens, Fountains, Canals, perpetual Cafcades, curious Plantations, and many other magnificent Monuments of his Grandeur.

Cliefden Houfe, *in* Buckinghamfhire, *p.* 70, 71, 72, 73, *and* 74.

THE Seat of the Right Honourable the Earl of *Orkney*, founded by the late Duke of *Buckingham*, but greatly improved and adorned by the prefent noble Patron, who after the dangerous Fatigues of thirty Campaigns, (*forfan & hæc olim meminiffe juvabit*,) with immortal Honour to himfelf and Country, has now the Pleafure of this delightful Retreat, when the Bufinefs of his King and Country does not call for his Service. I have made one fingle and two double Plates; in the firft is the general Plan of the Offices and firft Story, the Apartments are noble, richly furnifhed, and commodious. Here is one of the moft confiderable Terraffes in the Kingdom, being 24 Foot above the Parterre, and is as high as the Level of *Windfor* Caftle, and is 433 Foot long, adorned with a curious Baluftrade of *Portland* Stone; under the great Court in Front are arched Corridores that communicate from one fide of the Offices to the other; a thing of great Ufe and Conveniency: Here is alfo a curious Grotto, with a great Number of large and fpacious Vaults, and many other fubterraneous Conveniencies. The fecond and third Stories contain many fine Apartments magnificently furnifhed. The fecond Plate is the chief Front to the North, having the Offices joined to the Houfe by Corridores of the *Ionick* Order, defigned by Mr. *Archer*. The third Plate is the South Front with the fore-named Terrafs, which affords one of the moft beautiful Profpects in the Kingdom.

Hopeton-houfe, *in* Scotland, *p.* 75, 76, *and* 77,

IS the Seat of the Right Honourable the Earl of *Hopeton*. The Defigns were given by Sir *William Bruce*, who was juftly efteem'd the beft Architect of his time in that Kingdom; it was begun about the Year 1698, and finifhed four Years after. I have made one fingle and one double Plate; the firft contains a general Plan of the Offices and firft Story, where is a Portico, Hall, and 4 very handfome Apartments; in the middle is a Geometrical Octagon Stair-Cafe, which leads up to the fecond Story, and over the Hall is a noble Salon and the fame Number of Apartments as below, and all well finifhed and fumptuoufly furnifhed. The fecond Plate gives the general Front of the Houfe and Offices, the whole being executed in very good Stone; the Windows are well-proportion'd and handfomely dreft, the Fafcade is rufticated in the *French* Manner, and finifhed with Rail and Baluftrade, Statues, Vafes, and a Stone Cupola over the great Stair-Cafe.

Lowther Houfe, *in* Weftmorland, *p.* 78, 79, *and* 80.

THE Seat of the Right Honourable the Lord Vifcount *Lonfdale*, in 1 fingle and 1 double Plate. The firft is the general Plan of the Offices and principal Story extending 337 Foot; here are ftately Apartments, Coridores, large Galleries, a noble Library and Chapel. In the fecond Plate you have the general Front, in Height three Stories; the Windows of the middle Story are dreft with Pediments in a very handfome manner; the Fabrick is finifhed with a Baluftrade, Figures and Vafes, and a large Pediment at each End, which has a good Effect: Here are fine Gardens, a noble Park, and many other ufeful and magnificent Improvements, anfwerable to the Grandeur of fo noble and generous a Patron.

Braman Park, *in* Yorkfhire, *p.* 81 *and* 82.

THE Seat of the Right Honourable the Lord *Bingley*. In one double Plate is firft the general Plan of the Principal Story extending 240 Foot, including the Pavilions. The flooping Terrafs leads up to the grand Floor, where is a noble Hall an exact Cube of 30 Foot, moft artfully decorated, and all the Apartments are fpacious and convenient; above is an Attuk Story for the Family, and two Stair-Cafes that are very well illuminated by raifing the inward Walls above the Leads. The Front is of an elegant tho' plain Manner, with a regular Cornice and Baluftrade; the Pavilions are joined to the Houfe with two *Tufcan* Colonades. Here are curious Gardens laid out with great Judgment, and all the other additional Improvements were happily finifhed by the noble Patron, *Anno* 1710.

A new Defign infcribed to Mr. Walpole. *p.* 83 *and* 84.

IN this Defign of my Invention, I have endeavoured to introduce the *Temple* Beauties in a private Building. The Plan of the principal Houfe is a Square of 100 Foot. In the Ground Story, which is 20 Foot high, the Hall under the Salon is divided with 4 Columns both to fupport the Floor and Proportion the Room: The Plan defcribed here is that above, to which you afcend by a double Stair-cafe without, which leads into a noble Salon, being a Cube of 40 Foot; here are four Apartments, and over them is the Bed-Chamber Floor: The Offices are joined to the Houfe by 2 Galleries; the Towers are 40 Foot each, and the Galleries 60 Foot, fo that the whole Extent is 300, the Houfe making one third. In the Front you have a large Ruftick Bafement, which fupports an Octaftyle of the Compofite Order, where a lofty Pediment covers the entire Fabrick: The Towers are fet at a convenient Diftance, and are dreft with a *Tufcan* Arch and Attick; in one you have the Chapel, *&c.* and in the other a Library, *&c.* What is moft remarkable in this Defign is, that it has the Appearance of a large and magnificent Structure, when in Effect it is of a moderate Bignefs, being no more than a Square of 100 Foot.

Chevening Houfe *in* Kent, *p.* 85.

THIS was the Seat of the Right Honourable the late Earl of *Suffex*, now of the Right Honourable *James Stanhope*, Efq; principal Secretary of State. In this Plate I have given the Plans of the 2 Principal Stories, where the Apartments are very good and the Rooms large and well-proportion'd: the Windows in the Front are regular and dreft with a proper Architrave Frife and Cornice; over the fecond Story are Attick Windows, and a regular Entablature crowns the whole Building, and is faid to be defigned by *Inigo Jones*.

A new Defign infcribed to Mr. Secretary Stanhope. *p.* 86.

IN this Effay of my Invention I have given the two principal Plans; in the firft is a Cube of 30 Foot, with a large Apartment on each fide, in which is a Variety both of Size and Proportions; in the middle is a handfome Stair-Cafe, with Light from above, and behind it a Garden-Room; in the fecond Plan are 4 Apartments and a convenient Library; on each fide is a circular Pair of back Stairs, and above this is an Attick Story for the Family. The Front is richly dreft with a large *Corinthian* Colonade of ¼ Columns, and a leffer Pilaftrade of the fame Order to diftinguifh the two Stories; at the two Angles are 2 fmall ¾ Columns which fupport a *Mars* and *Pallas*, as *Palladio* has done in the Palace of *Vilmaran a* at *Vicenfa*, whofe Example I think a fufficient Authority.

Sir

Sir Charles Hotham, *Bart. his Houſe at* Beverly *in* Yorkſhire, *p.* 87.

AT the Deſire of this worthy Gentleman I gave the following Deſign, who in Harveſt laſt laid the Foundation of it and finiſh'd the Vaults, and intends this Summer to cover in the Houſe with Lead. It being a Cube of 56 Foot, here are the Plans of the two Principal Stories. The firſt is 14, the ſecond is 13, and the third is 11 Foot high; the Proportions of each Room are all exactly figured in the Plate. In the Front the Windows of the firſt Story have Pediments, the next have Architrave Friſe and Cornice, and the third has Attick Windows, all regularly dreſt, and at proper Diſtance, an Obſervation never to be neglected: Here is alſo a handſome *Ionick* Porch; All the Ornaments are of *Roch Abby Stone,* being eſteemed the beſt in the Kingdom; the Fabrick is crowned with a regular Cornice and Baluſtrade: The Offices are joined to the Houſe by a Ruſtick Arch of each ſide, which, in my weak Opinion, has no ill Effect; and upon the whole I have endeavoured to render it worthy of ſo generous and honourable a Patron.

Cheſter-Lee-ſtreet *in the Biſhoprick of* Durham,*p.*88.

THE Seat of *John Hedworth,* Eſq; for whom I made this Deſign. In this Plate you have the general Plan of the Principal Floor, extending 128 Foot, of which the main Houſe has 64 and 48 Foot deep; the other half is equally divided between the Offices of each Side: The Front is South, and the North Proſpect not being very favourable, is the Reaſon why I have made no Windows in that Side but to the two Stair-Caſes; the Windows in the firſt Story are without Pediments, the better to ſet off that of the Door-Caſe, but I have uſed them in the ſecond Story: There being ſufficient Space from the Windows to the Coines, I have dreſt them with large Ruſticks of different Lengths, as moſt proper to expreſs the true Office of thoſe Stones, which is to croſs-bind the Angles, and not as the *French* and ſome others have introduced them, of the ſame Extent in Place of Pilaſters. The Roof is flat with Cornice and Baluſtrade.

A new Deſign inſcribed to Mr. Secretary Methuen, *p.* 89 *and* 90.

I Have made two Plates of this Deſign: In the firſt are the Plans of the two Principal Stories; the firſt is raiſed 6 Foot above the Court, where is a ſpacious Hall of 60 by 30 Foot, and in Height 21; but to preſerve a due Proportion, as I have often obſerved, 'tis ſubdivided by 4 Columns into three Parts, ſo as the middle becomes a Square: In this Story are 4 very good Apartments all exactly figured, and two Pair of winding Stairs. The great Pair of Stairs lead up to the *Piano Nobile,* where is a lofty and ſpacious Salon of the ſame Extent as the Hall below, but has 30 Foot in height, which makes two Cubes, here are 4 very handſome Apartments both for State and Conveniency, and the whole Extent of this Plan is 100 by 70 Foot. In the ſecond Plate you have the Front in the Theatrical Stile, with a Ruſtick Baſement ſupporting two and in the middle three Orders to give a ſufficient height to the Salon, over all the ſmall Rooms next the Back Stairs are Interſoles.

High Wittham *in* Somerſetſhire, *p.* 91, 92.

THE ancient Seat of Sir *William Windham,* Bart. in two Plates: Firſt the general Plan of the principal Floor where is a noble and ſpacious Hall, with many large and handſome Apartments, and when the whole Deſign is finiſhed, there will be abundance of State and Accommodation. In the ſecond Plate is the Front to the Gardens, with a Compoſite

Hexaſtile, which makes a beautiful Portico, to the Court; the reſt of the Front is adorned with a Pilaſtrade of the ſame Order, over which is an Attick and Cupola, and many other Decorations that ſufficiently expreſs the Magnificence of the generous Patron. *Anno* 1717.

Dyrham Houſe *in* Gloceſterſhire. *p.* 91, 93.

THE Seat of *William Blathwayt,* Eſq;. Firſt I have given the general Plan of the principal Story, which is very large and convenient, with a Variety of very good Apartments. In the ſecond Plate is the Garden Front extending 130 Foot; the firſt Story is entirely ruſticated, and the Coines to the Cornice. In the ſecond Story the Windows are dreſt with alternate Pediments, over which are Attick Windows, which is finiſhed with a handſome Cornice and Baluſtrade, adorned with Trophies and Vaſes of an excellent Choice; and the learned Patron has ſpared no Expences in leaving ſuch laſting Monuments of his Liberality. The Deſign was given by the ingenious Mr. *Talmen, Anno* 1698.

Newbold-Hall *in* Warwickſhire, *p.* 94.

IS the Seat of Sir *Fullwar Skipwith,* Bart. In this Plate I have deſigned the Plans of the two principal Stories; in the firſt is a ſpacious Hall in Height two Stories, with many large and convenient Apartments; in the Front the Coines are ruſticated after the *French* manner, and finiſhed with a regular Cornice, Baluſtrade, and other proper Ornaments. *Anno* 1716.

Althrop *in* Northamptonſhire, *p.* 95, 96, 97.

THE Seat of the Right Honourable the Earl of *Sunderland,* of which I have made 1 ſingle and 1 double Plate. In the firſt are deſigned the Plans of the two principal Stories, where are great Variety of noble and ſpacious Apartments, extending 140 Foot in Front, and deep 180. Here is a very large Stair-Caſe, and in the ſecond Story a moſt magnificent Gallery 120 Foot long, richly adorned with many excellent original Pieces of the moſt celebrated Painters, particularly of *Vandyke.* Here is alſo a moſt curious and valuable Library, and the whole is finiſhed and adorned in a very ſumptuous Manner, anſwerable to the Magnificence of the noble Patron. In the ſecond Plate I have deſigned the principal Front, which is dreſt with two Orders of Pilaſters, the *Corinthian* and *Compoſite,* and which are continued round the whole Building; the ſecond Order is remarkable in having no Architrive or Friſe, but only a Cornice, over which is a Baluſtrade. It was built by the late Earl, in the Year 1688.

A new Deſign inſcribed to the Lord Cadogan, *p.*98, 99, *and* 100.

OF this Eſſay of my Invention I have made 1 ſingle and 1 double Plate. In the firſt I have given the Plans of the two principal Stories, being 180 Foot in Front and 150 deep; the firſt Floor is raiſed above the Court by 4 Steps, which leads into a Hall 44 Foot ſquare and 24 Foot high, but divided as in my other Deſigns, with 4 Columns; here are 4 large Apartments, and over the ſmall Rooms are Interſoles. In the middle is the great Stair-Caſe 44 Foot Square, with a Corridore round of 10 Foot, which is of ſingular Uſe to the whole Houſe in paſſing from one Apartment to another. In the ſecond Story, which is the *Piano Nobile,* is firſt a Salon an exact Cube of 44 Foot, with a very noble Apartment of each Side; to the Garden Front is a large Gallery 110 Foot long, 30 broad, and in the Height the ſame, with a great Apartment at each End; here are convenient Back Stairs and an Attick Story for the Family. The Front is in the *Pallatial* Stile,

C whereſe

where a large Ruftick Bafement fupports an *Ionick* Colonade of ¼ Columns 4 Foot Diameter, and in Height 36. I have returned the Angles with Pila- fters to ftrengthen the Coines, the Fabrick is crown- ed with a regular Entablature and Baluftrade, and with it I finifh this Second Volume.

A LIST *of what is contain'd in the Second Volume.*

A LIST of the SUBSCRIBERS.

A

Setts.

DUKE of St. *Albans*, Captain of the Band of Penfioners. — 1
Duke of *Ancafter*, Lord Great Chamberlain — 2
Duke of *Argyle* — 2
The Marquis of *Annandale* — 2
Earl of *Albermarle* — 2
Earl of *Arran* — 1
The Lord *Afhburnham* — 1
Sir *John Anftruthers*, Bar. — 1
Sir *Jacob Aftley*, Bar. — 1
Sir *Robert Adair*, Knt. — 1
Jofeph Addifon, Efq; — 1
John Arthbuthnott, M. D. — 2
David Anderfon, S. T. D. — 1
James Anderfon, D. V. M. — 1
Mr. *Gabriel Appleby* — 1
James Anderfon, Gent. Waiter to the Signet in *Edinborough* — 1
Sir *H. Aucher*, Bart. — 1
The Honourable *John Aiflabie*, Efq; Treafurer to the Navy — 1
Jacob Aickworth, Efq; Surveyor of his Majefty's Navy — 1
John Allen, Efq; — 1
Thomas Archer, Efq; — 1
Francis Annefley, Efq; — 1
Alexander Abercrombie, Efq; — 1
Col. *John Armftrong* — 1
Mr. *James Ayres* — 1
Mr. *Francis Anderton* — 1

B.

HIS Highnefs Prince *Auguftus Wilhelm*, Duke of *Brunfwick Lunenberg* — 1
Duke of *Bedford* — 1
Duke of *Beaufort* — 2
Duke of *Buckingham* — 2
Duke of *Bolton* — 2
Dutchefs of *Buccleugh* — 2
Earl of *Bridgewater* — 2
Earl of *Burlington* — 2
Earl of *Brodalbin* — 1
Earl of *Buchan* — 1
Earl of *Bute* — 1
Lord Vifcount *Bolingbroke* — 1
Lord *Balmerinoch* — 1
Lord *Bruce* — 1
Lord *Bathurft* — 1
His Excellence Baron *Bothmar* — 1
Lord *Berkely* of *Stratton* — 1
Lord *Bingly* — 1
Sir *William Bennet*, one of the Commiffioners of Excife for *North-Britain* — 1
Sir *Juftus Beck*, Bar. — 1
Sir *John Brownlow*, Bar. — 1
Sir *Roger Bradfhaw*, Bar. — 1
Sir *Jacob Banks*, Knt. — 1
Sir *James Bateman*, Bar. Lord-Mayor of *London* — 1
The Honourable *George Baily*, Efq; Commiffioner of the Admiralty — 1
The Right Hon. *William Bromley*, Efq; — 1
The Rt. Hon. *William Blathwayt*, Efq; — 1
William Benfon, Efq; — 1
J. Barington Shute, Efq; — 1
John Boulter, Efq; — 1
Nathaniel Blackerby, Efq; — 1
William Burnet, Efq; — 1
Harry Benfon, Efq; — 1
Stephen Biffe, Efq; Commiffioner of the Equivalent — 1
John Basket, Efq; Printer to the King's moft Excellent Majefty — 1
Tho. Baker, Efq; — 1
John Bligh, Efq; — 1
———*Baird*, Efq; — 1
The Honourable *John Bylos*, Efq; — 1
Mr. *Charles Bridgman*, Gardener — 1
Mr. *Robert Barker*, Joyner — 1
Mr. *Thomas Bowls* — 1
John Blake, Sen. of the Office of Ordnance in the *Tower* of *London* — 1
The Reverend Mr. *Bethem* — 1
Mr. *Bofwell* — 1
Dr. *Brooks*, M. D. — 1
Mr. *Daniel Brown*, Bookfeller — 1
Mr. *Jonas Brown*, Bookfeller — 1

Setts.

Mr. *William Brown* of *Shaftsbury* — 1
Mr. *Nicholas Blake*, Carpenter — 1
Mr. *Richard Brown* — 1
Mr. *James Bateman* — 1
Mr. *James Blacket*, Joyner — 1
Mr. *Francis Bird*, Statuary — 1

C.

WIlliam Lord *Cowper*, Lord High-Chancellor of *Great Britain* — 2
Earl of *Carlifle* — 2
Earl of *Carnarvan* — 2
Earl of *Cholmondeley*, Treafurer of the Houfhold — 2
His Excellence the Lord *Cadogan* — 1
Lord *Cobham* — 1
Lord *Caftle-Comer* — 1
Lord *Craven* — 1
Lord *Colerane* — 1
Lord *Coningsby* — 1
Lord *Conway* — 1
Lady *Cairnes* — 1
The Lady *Cary* — 1
Sir *Thomas Clargis*, Bar. — 1
Sir *Nicholas Carew*, Bar. — 1
The Right Hon. *Thomas Coke*, Efq; Vice Chamberlain — 1
Sir *Archibald Campbell*, Knt. — 1
Sir *Duncan Campbell*, Bar. — 1
Sir *Hugh Campbell* of *Calder*, Bar. — 1
Sir *James Campbell* of *Ardkinglafs*, Bar. — 1
Sir *James Campbell* of *Achinbrake*, Bar. — 1
Sir *James Campbell* of *Abruchill*, Bar. — 1
The Honourable *John Campbell*, Efq; — 1
The Hon. Coll *James Campbell*, Efq; — 1
The Hon. Coll. *John Campbell*, Efq; Gentleman of the Bed-Chamber to his Royal Highnefs — 1
Archibald Campbell, Efq; — 1
Daniel Campbell, Efq; — 1
Duncan Campbell, Efq; — 1
Capt. *Matthew Campbell*, Efq; — 1
John Campbell, Efq; Lord Provoft of *Edinburgh* — 1
John Campbell of *Caldes*, Efq; — 1
Colen Campbell, Efq; — 1
Sir *Richard Child*, Bar. — 3
Sir *James Carmichel*, Bar. — 1
Sir *James Cuningham*, Bar. — 1
Sir *Thomas Crofs*, Bar. — 1
Sir *Robert Child*, Knt. — 1
Sir *Alexander Cummins*, Knt. — 1
The Honourable *George Clark*, Efq; — 1
George Lockhart of *Carnwath*, Efq; — 1
R. *Crefwell*, Efq; — 1
George Culworth, Efq; — 1
Thomas Cary, Efq; — 2
Henry Cuningham, Efq; — 1
Charles Cæfar, Efq; — 1
Courtney Crooker, Efq; — 1
The Honourable *Charles Cecil*, Efq; — 1
William Chetwynd, Efq; — 1
Rt. Hon. *Spencer Compton*, Speaker of the Houfe of Commons — 1
William Clayton, Efq; — 1
Edmund Clarke, Efq; of the *Inner Temple* — 1
———*Cholmley*, Efq; of *Vale Royal*, *Chefhire* — 1
Arthur Croft of *Croft Caftle*, in *Herefordfhire*, Efq; — 1
Mr. *Cranenburgh*, late Refident for his Majefty — 1
Mr. *Chetwynd* — 1
Mr. *John Churchill*, Mafter Carpenter to his Majefty — 1
John Corbett, LL. D. — 1
Mr. *Clements*, Bookfeller in *Oxford* — 1
Knightley Chetwood, D. D. Dean of *Gloucefter* — 1
Mr. *Edward Cowper* — 1
Mr. *Jofeph Carter* of St. *Albans* — 1

D.

DUKE of *Devonfhire*, Lord Prefident of the Council — 2
Duke of *Douglafs* — 1
Earl of *Derby* — 1
Earl of *Dartmouth* — 1
Earl of *Dorfet* — 2
Earl of *Denbigh* — 1
Earl of *Dundonald* — 2
Lord *Digby* — 1

Setts.

Sir *David Dalrymple*, Bar. — 1
Sir *Matthew Decker*, Bar. — 1
The Hon. *George Doddington*, Efq; one of the Lords of the Admiralty — 1
Montague Gerrard Drake, Efq; — 1
William Dafhwood, Efq; — 1
William Dun of *Liveyeard*, Efq; — 1
Archibald Douglafs of *Cavers*, Efq; — 1
Thomas Dawfon, D. D. — 1
Mr. *Decaux*, Merchant — 1
Capt. *N. Duboife* — 6
Mr. *Dodd* of *Lincolns-Inn* — 1
Mr. *William Dickinfon* — 1
Mrs. *Dolben* — 1
Mr. *Peter Dunoyer*, Bookfeller — 1
Mr. *John Darby*, Printer — 1

E

RIght Hon. Lieut. General *Earl* — 1
Sir *John Evelyn* — 1
Sir *Gilbert Elliot* of *Munto*, Bar. one of the Senators of the College of Juftice — 1
R. *Edgecomb*, Efq; one of the Commiffioners of the Treafury — 1
His Excellence Baron *D'Erfe* — 1
William Emmett, Efq; — 1
Mr. *William Elliot* — 1

F.

EARL of *Findlator* and *Seafield* — 1
Lord *Foley* — 1
Lord *Forrefter* — 1
Sir *Compart Fytch*, Bar. — 1
Sir *Robert Furnefe*, Bar. — 1
Sir *Thomas Frankland*, Bar. — 1
Richard Fuller, LL. D. — 1
Mr. Auditor *Foley* — 1
Thomas Frankland, Efq; — 1
James Fury, Efq; — 1
John Forbes of *Colloden*, Efq; — 1
William Freeman, Efq; — 1
The Reverend Mr. *Forfter* — 1
Mr. *Alexander Fort*, Under Store-Keeper at *Hampton-Court* — 1
Mr. Baron *Fortefque* — 1
Mr. *Benjamin Fairfax* — 1

G.

DUKE of *Grafton* — 2
The Earl of *Godolphin* — 2
Lord *Guilford* — 1
His Excellency the Lord Baron *Goerts*, &c. — 1
Sir *Richard Grofvenar*, Bar. — 1
Sir *Robert Gordon*, Bar. — 1
Sir *William Gordon*, Bar. — 1
Alexander Gordon of *Pitburg*, Efq; — 1
Alexander Grant, Efq; Brigadier General — 1
Francis Gwynn, Efq; — 1
William Le Grand, Efq; — 1
Richard Golph, Efq; — 1
Sir *Samuel Garth*, M. D. — 1
Orlando Gee, Efq; — 1
Thomas Gage Efq; — 1
Mr. *Nathaniel Guftuies* — 1
Mr. *Grahame* — 1
Robert Gray, M. D. — 1
Mr. *Tho. Granger* of the *Eaft India Houfe* — 1
Mr. *Andrews Gelph* — 1

H.

DUtchefs of *Hamilton* and *Brandon* — 2
Earl of *Hallifax* — 2
Earl of *Hopeton* — 2
Earl of *Haddington* — 1
Lord *Harley* — 1
Lord *Haverfham* — 1
Sir *Thomas Hanmer*, Bar. — 1
Sir *Roger Hill*, Bar. — 1
Sir *Jof. Hodges*, Bar. — 1
Sir *Charles Hotham*, Bar. — 1
Sir *John Harper*, Bar. of *Calk* in *Derbyfhire* — 1
Sir *David Hamilton*, Knt. — 1
John Henly of *Briftol*, Efq; — 1
Richard Hill of *Richmond*, Efq; — 1
William Herbert, E q; — 1
William Hedworth, Efq; — 1
John Huggins, Efq; — 1
Nicholas Hawkfmoor, Efq; Clerk of his Majefty's Works — 1
Roger Hudfon, Efq; — 1
Francis Haws, Efq; — 1
John Hallingins, Efq; — 1

Mr.

Setts.

Mr. *John Hare* ... 1
Mr. *Thomas Hinton* ... 1
Mr. *Robert Hynd* ... 1
Mr. *Hattorf* ... 1
Mr. *Robert Halton* ... 1
Mr. *Henemines* ... 1
Mr. *John Harris* ... 1
Mr. *John Hulton* ... 1
Michael Hutchinson, D. D. ... 1
Mr. *John Hodges of Derbyshire* ... 1
Mr. *Henry Hare of Docking* ... 1

I.

EARL of *Islay*, Lord Register and Justice General of *North-Britain* ... 2
Sir *Theodore Jansen*, Knt. and Bar. ... 1
Sir *Henry Innes*, Bar. ... 1
Sir *William Johnston*, Bar. ... 1
The Right Hon. *James Johnston*, Esq; ... 1
Tobias Jenkyns, Esq; ... 1
Thomas Jett, Esq; ... 1
Benjamin Jackson, Esq; his Majesty's Master Mason ... 1
Mr. *Andrew Johnson* ... 1
Mr. *William Jelks of Burton upon Trent* ... 1
Mr. *Andrews Jelf* ... 1
Mr. *John James of Greenwich* ... 1
Mr. *William Jones* ... 1
Mr. *Henry Joines of Woodstook* ... 1
Mr. *Edward James* ... 1
Mr. *William Jones*, F. R. S. ... 1

K.

DUKE of *Kingston*, Lord Privy Seal ... 1
Duke of *Kent*, Lord Chamberlain ... 2
Earl of *Kinnoul* ... 1
Lord Viscount *Kilsyth*. ... 1
Lord Chief Justice *King* ... 1
Robert Keck, Esq; ... 1
Mr. *Thomas Kynaston* ... 1
John King, D. D. Master of the *Charter-House* ... 1

L.

DUKE of *Leeds* ... 2
Earl of *Lowdon* ... 2
Lord *Longueville* ... 1
Lord *Lansdown* ... 1
Lord *Leimster* ... 1
Lord *Langsdale* ... 1
Lord Bishop of *London* ... 1
Nicholas Lechmere, Esq; ... 1
Samuel Lynn, Esq; ... 1
Christopher Lister, Esq; ... 1
Benjamin Lacy, Esq; ... 1
Collonel *Leley* ... 1
Mr. *John Law of High-Wickham* ... 1
Mr. *Daniel Lock* ... 1
Mr. *Lockman, St. James's* ... 1
Mr *John Leggat* ... 1
Mr. *William Law* ... 1

M.

DUKE of *Marlborough*, Captain General of all His Majesty's Forces ... 2
Dutchess of *Marlborough* ... 2
Duke of *Montague* ... 2
Dutchess of *Montague* ... 2
Duke of *Montrosse* ... 2
Earl of *Mareshall* ... 2
Earl of *Marr* ... 2
Lord *Mansell* ... 1
Lord *Middleton* ... 1
Sir *William Mansell*, Bar. ... 2
Sir *Christopher Musgrave*, Bar. ... 1
Sir *Nicholas Morice*, Bar. ... 1
Sir *Robert Masham*, Bar. ... 1
The Right Hon. *Paul Methuen*, Esq; principal Secretary of State ... 1
John Montgomery, Esq; ... 1
Humphry Milway, Esq; ... 1
Edward Minshowl, Esq; ... 1
Thomas Milner, Esq; ... 1
William Maynard, Esq; of *Curryglass in Ireland* ... 1
William Monck, Esq; of *Ireland* ... 1
George Maddison, Esq; ... 1
Abraham Meure, Esq; ... 1
Capt. *Mandell* ... 1
Doctor *Mede*, M. D. ... 1
Doctor *John Milbourne*, M. D. ... 1
Mr. *John Mum Moor*. ... 1
Mr. *Arthur Manley* ... 1
Mr. *George Montgomery* ... 1
Mr. *Isaac Mars* ... 1
The Reverend *John Maxwell* ... 1

Setts.

Mr. *Mahomet of St. James's* ... 1
Mr. *Mustapha* ... 1
Mr. *John Meards* ... 1
Mr. *John Manley* ... 1

N.

DUKE of *Newcastle* ... 2
Earl of *Nottingham* ... 2
Earl of *Northampton* ... 1
Grey Neville, Esq; ... 1
Edward Nicolas, Esq; ... 1

O.

LATE Duke of *Ormond* ... 2
Earl of *Orford*, first Lord of the Admiralty ... 2
Earl of *Orrery* ... 1
Earl of *Orkney* ... 2
Earl of *Oxford* ... 1
The Honourable *Thomas Onslow*, Esq; ... 2
Mr. *Isaac Olley*, Clerk of the City Works ... 1

P.

DUKE of *Powis* ... 2
Duke of *Portland* ... 2
Earl *Paulet* ... 1
Earl of *Pembroke* ... 2
Lord *Polworth* ... 1
Lord *Percival* ... 1
Lord Chief Justice *Parker* ... 1
Sir *Robert Pollock*, Bar. ... 1
Sir *Joseph Pringle* ... 1
Sir *Walter Pringle* ... 1
Sir *John Packington*, Bar. ... 1
His Excellence Major General *Pepper* ... 1
His Excellence Governour *Pitts* ... 1
William Pulteny, Esq; Secretary of War ... 1
Robert Pringle, Esq; Under-Secretary ... 1
Blackwell Perkins, Esq; ... 1
John Pringle of Haining, Esq; ... 1
Uvedale Price, Esq; of *Foxley* in *Herefordshire* ... 1
Silvester Pettyt of *Bernard's-Inn*, Gent. ... 1
Mr. *John Price*, Jun. ... 8
Mr. *Francis Price* ... 1
Mr. *Alexander Prichard*, Mason ... 1
Mr. *Plummtree* ... 1
Dr. *Prat*, Provost of *Dublin* ... 1
Mr. *John Pris of Richmond*, Jun. ... 1
Mr. *James Paget*, Mason ... 1
Captain *Charles Pearce* ... 1
Mr. *Andrew Peters*, Painter ... 1
Mr. *Bart. Peisley of Oxon*, Mason ... 1

Q.

DUKE of *Queensbury* ... 2

R.

DUKE of *Richmond* ... 2
Duke of *Roxburgh*, principal Secretary of State ... 2
Duke of *Rutland* ... 2
Earl of *Rochester* ... 1
Earl of *Rothes* ... 1
Earl of *Roseberry* ... 1
Right Honourable the Lord *Romney* ... 1
Sir *William Robinson*, Bar. ... 1
Thomas Rawlinson, Esq; ... 1
Richard Rooth, Esq; ... 1
Hugh Rose of Kilravock, Esq; ... 1
Benjamin Robinson, Esq; ... 1
Samuel Ravenel, Esq; ... 1
John Rudg, Esq; ... 1
Mr. *John Richards* ... 1
Mr. *Henry Ribboteau*, Bookseller ... 1
Mr. *John Roper* ... 1

S.

DUke of *Somerset* ... 2
Duke of *Shrewsbury* ... 2
Marquess of *Seaforth* ... 2
Earl of *Sunderland* ... 2
Earl of *Scarborough* ... 2
Earl of *Strafford* ... 2
Earl of *Sutherland* ... 1
Earl of *Stairs* ... 2
Lord *Somers* ... 1
Lord *Shelburne* ... 1
Sir *Fullwar Skipwith*, Bar. ... 1
Sir *William Stewart*, Bar. ... 1
Sir *John Smith*, Bar. ... 1
Sir *Edward Seymore*, Bar. ... 1
Sir *Edward Simeon*, Bar. ... 1
Sir *Edmund Smith* of Hill Hall in *Essex*, Bar. ... 1
Sir *Thomas Seabright*, Bar. ... 1

Setts.

The Right Honourable *Edward Southwell*, Esq; ... 1
The Right Hon. *James Stanhope*, Esq; principal Secretary of State ... 1
Sir *James Stuart*, his Majesty's Solicitor for *North-Britain* ... 1
Sir *Edward Smith* of Hill Hall, *Essex* ... 1
Brigadier General *Stearne* ... 1
Doctor *Steygersdale*, Physician to his Majesty ... 1
His Excellence, Baron *Shack*, Resident from his *Czarian* Majesty. ... 1
William Strickland, Esq; ... 1
Mrs. *Elizabeth Southwell* ... 1
Thomas Strangeways, Esq; ... 1
James Sadler, Esq; ... 1
Hans Sloane, M. D. ... 1
Joseph Smith, D. D. ... 1
Mr. *Edward Strong*, Jun. ... 4
Mr. *John Sturges* ... 1
Mr. *Andrew Smith* ... 1
Mr. *Thomas Sadler* ... 1
Mr. *George Sampson* ... 1
Mr. *Richard Sanders*, Joyner ... 1
Mr. *John Sturt*, Engraver ... 1

T.

MArquess of *Tweeddale* ... 1
Earl of *Thanet* ... 1
Lord Viscount *Townshend*, Lord Lieutenant of *Ireland* ... 1
Lord *Thomond* ... 1
Col. *Tyrell*, Groom of the Bed-Chamber to his Majesty ... 1
James Taylor, Esq; ... 1
Cholmondeley Turner, Esq; ... 1
John Talbot, Esq; ... 1
William Tomlins, Esq; ... 1
John Talman, Esq; ... 1
Samuel Thompson, Esq; ... 1
Capt. *Tufnel of Westminster* ... 1
Mr. *James Thornhill*, Painter ... 1
Mr. *Thomas Taylor* ... 1
Mr. *Turvin* ... 1
Mr. *Joseph Towtnum* ... 1
Mr. *Taylor of Stafford* ... 1

V.

HIS Excellence Baron *Doiver Voirde*, Ambassador Extraordinary from the States General ... 1
Count *Volkra*, Envoy from his Imperial Majesty ... 1
Sir *John Vanbrugh*, Knt. Comptroller of His Majesty's Works ... 1
Henry Vernon, Esq; of *Sudbury* ... 1
James Vernon, Esq; ... 1
Mr. *Vanhuls* ... 1

W.

MArquess of *Wharton* ... 1
Earl of *Weymise* ... 1
Earl of *Warwick* ... 1
The Lord Viscount *Weymouth* ... 1
Lord Bishop of *Winchester* ... 1
Lord Bishop of *Waterford* ... 1
The Rt. Hon. *Robert Walpole*, Esq; first Lord Commissioner of the Treasury ... 1
Sir *William Wyndham*, Bar. ... 1
Sir *John Walter*, Bar. ... 1
Sir *Thomas Webster*, Bar. ... 1
Sir *Robert Worsley*, Bar. ... 1
Sir *Nicholas Wolstenholme*, Bar. ... 1
Sir *Christopher Wrenn*, Knt. Surveyor-General of his Majesty's Works ... 1
Christopher Wrenn, Esq; ... 1
Thomas Woodcock, Esq; ... 1
John Wallop, Esq; ... 1
William Wickham, Jun. Esq; ... 1
Thomas Walker of the Temple, Esq; ... 1
Humphry Wild, Esq; ... 1
Richard Wynne, Esq; ... 1
Leonard Wooddison, Clerk of his Majesty's Works and Store-keeper of *Winchester* ... 1
Doctor *Welwood*, M. D. ... 1
Mr. Serjeant *Wynne* ... 1
Mr. *Samuel Waters* of the *East-India House* ... 1
Mr. *Robert Wood* ... 1
Mr. *James Williams*, Mason ... 1
Mr. *Isaac Whood*, Painter. ... 1

Y.

SIR *Walter Yonge*, Bar. ... 1

N. B. The Author has made a great Progress in a Third Volume, containing the Geometrical Plans of the most considerable Gardens and Plantations, with large Perspectives of the most Regular Buildings, in a Method intirely new, and both instructing and pleasant.

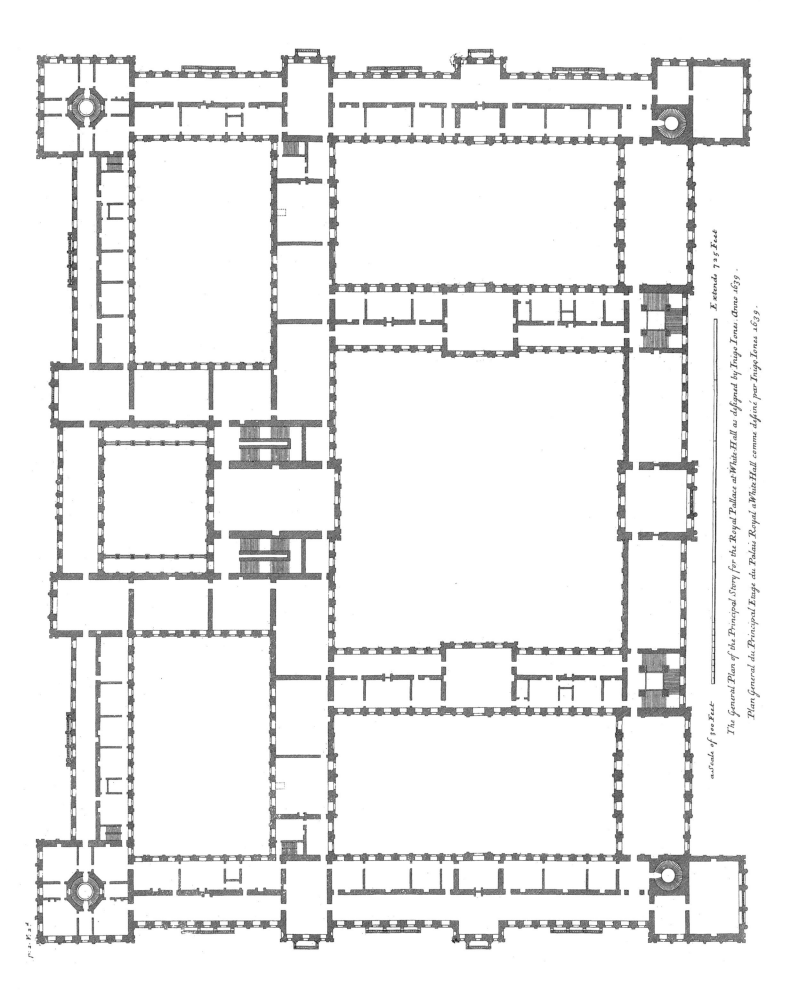

a Scale of 300 Feet

Extends 725 Feet

The General Plan of the Principal Story for the Royal Pallace at White-Hall as designed by Inigo Iones. Anno 1639.

Plan General du Principal Etage du Palais Royal a White-Hall comme dessiné par Inigo Iones 1639.

C. 2, PL. 2-3

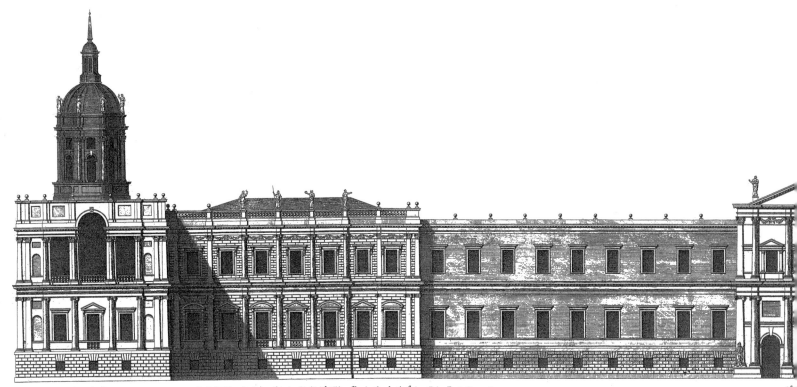

The Elevation of a Design for the Pallace at White-Hall, towards the Park, as it was presented to his Majesty King Charles the . by the famous Inigo Iones Anno 1639.
Is most humbly Inscrib'd to his most Sacred Majesty King George .

Ca: Campbell Delin:

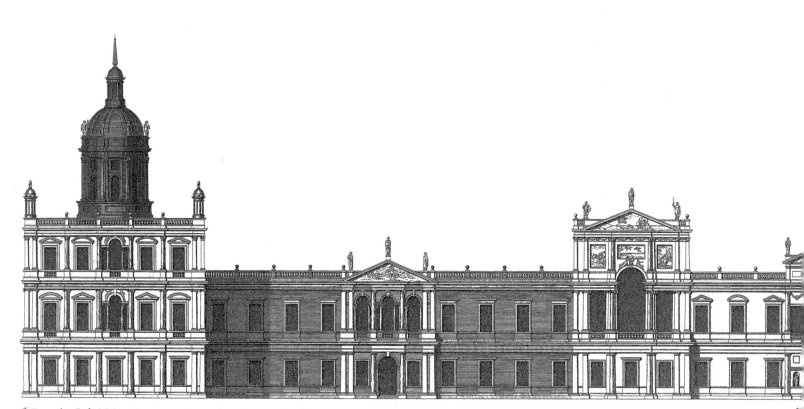

The Elevation of a Design for the Pallace at White-Hall, towards the River. as it was presented to his Majesty King Charles I. by the celebrated Inigo Iones Anno 1639. but interrupted by the Civil Warrs .
Is most humbly Inscrib'd to his Royal Highness the Prince of Wales &c .

Ca: Campbell Delin:

Elevation d'un Nouveau Dessein pour le Palais Royal a White-Hall du coté du Parc, Inventé par le fameux Inigo Iones. premier Architec du Roy Charles I. Anno 1639
Est tres humblement Dedié au Roy.

H. Hulsbergh Sculp:

C. 2, PL. 4-7

Elevation d'un Nouveau Dessein pour le Pallais Royal a White-Hall du coté de la Riviere, comme il a été presenté au Roy Charles I. par le celebre Inigo Iones. Anno 1639.
Est tres humblement Dedié a Son Altesse Royale le Prince de Galles &c.

H. Hulsbergh Sculp:

C. 2, PL. 8-11

The Elevation of a Design for the Pallace at White-Hall, towards Charing-Cross, as it was presented to his Majesty King C:I. by Inigo Iones Anno 1639. is most humbly Inscrib'd to her Royal Highness the Princess of Wales &c.

Ca: Campbell Delin:

The Section of the Royal Pallace at White-Hall as designed by the renowned Inigo Iones 1639.

Is most humbly Inscrib'd to his Royal Highness Prince Frederick &c:

Ca: Campbell Delin

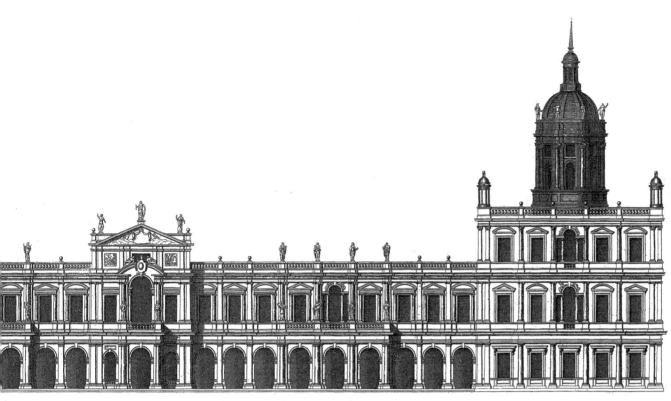

Elevation d'un nouveau Dessein pour le Palais Royal a White Hall, du coté Oriental, comme il a été presenté au Roy Charles I. par le celebre Inigo Iones Anno 1639 . est tres humblement Dedié a Son Altesse Royale la Princess de Galles &c.

H. Hulsbergh Sculp:

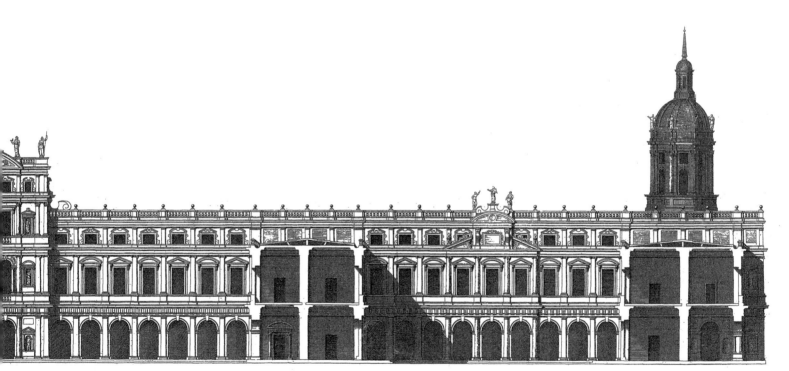

La Section du Palais Royal a White-Hall comme dessiné par le renommé Inigo Iones, premier Architec du Roy Charles I. Anno 1639 .

Dedié a son Altesse Royale le Prince Frederick &c.

H. Hulsbergh Sculp:

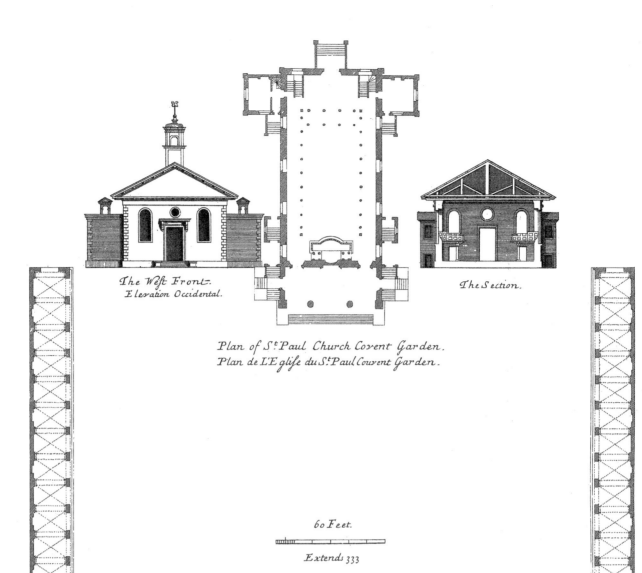

The West Front.
Elevation Occidental.

The Section.

Plan of S.t Paul Church Covent Garden.
Plan de L'Eglise du S.t Paul Couvent Garden.

60 Feet.

Extends 333

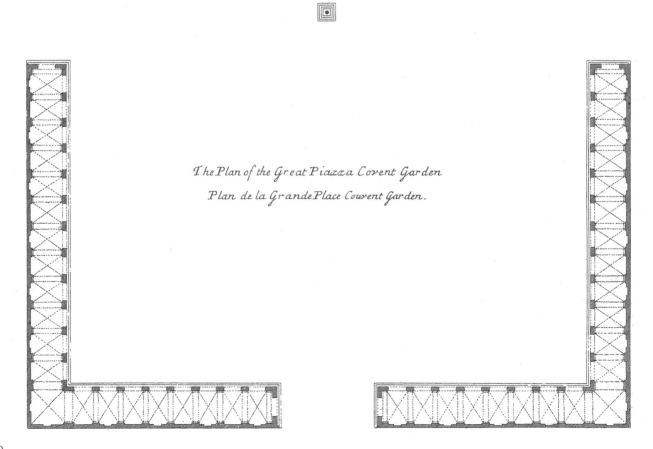

The Plan of the Great Piazza Covent Garden
Plan de la Grande Place Couvent Garden.

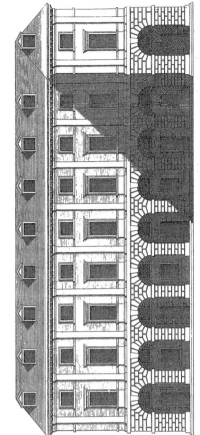

The East prospect of St Paul Church Covent Garden to the Great Square.
Elevation Oriental de L'Eglise du St Paul Covent Garden du coté de la grande Place.

a Scale of 100 Feet.

The West prospect of Covent Garden Invented by Inigo Iones 1640.
Elevation Occidental de la Grande Place de Covent Garden.

This Plate is most humbly Inscrib'd to her Grace the Duchess of Bedford &c.

H.Hulsbergh Sc:

C. Campbell Delin:

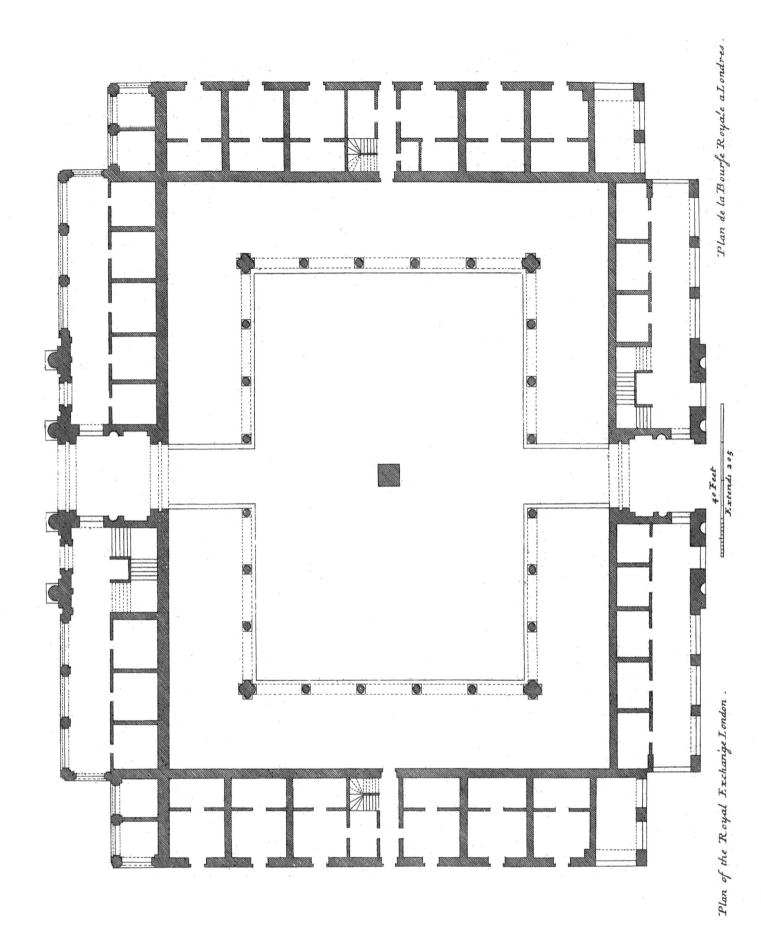

Plan de la Bourſe Royale a Londres.

Plan of the Royal Exchange London.

40 Feet
Extends 205

Gu: Campbell Delin:

The Elevation of the Royal Exchange, Is most humbly Inscrib'd to the Rt Honble Sr James Bateman Bart Lord Major of London &c:

Elevation de la Bourse Royale a Londres.

a Scale of 90 Feet   Extends 207

H.Hulsbergh Sc:

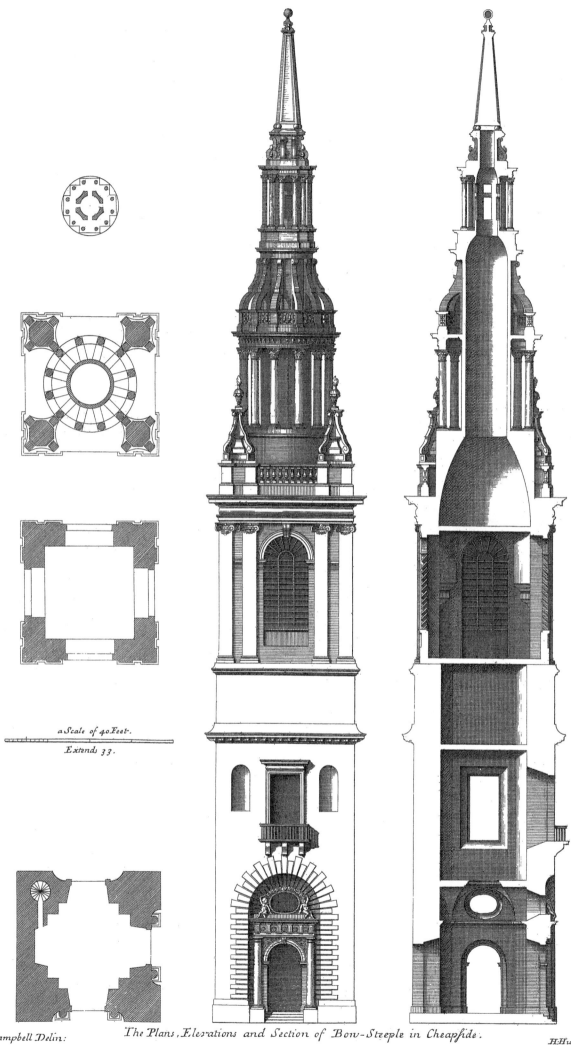

a Scale of 40 Feet.

Extends 33.

Ca: Campbell Delin:

The Plans, Elevations and Section of Bow-Steeple in Cheapside.

H. Hulsbergh Sc:

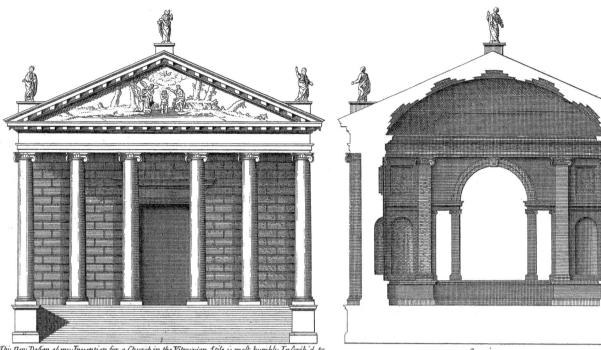

This New Design of my Invention for a Church in the Vitruvian Stile is most humbly Inscrib'd to his Grace William Arch.Bishop of Canterbury &c.
Elevation d'un Nouveau Dessin de mon Invention pour une Eglise a L'Antique.

Section.

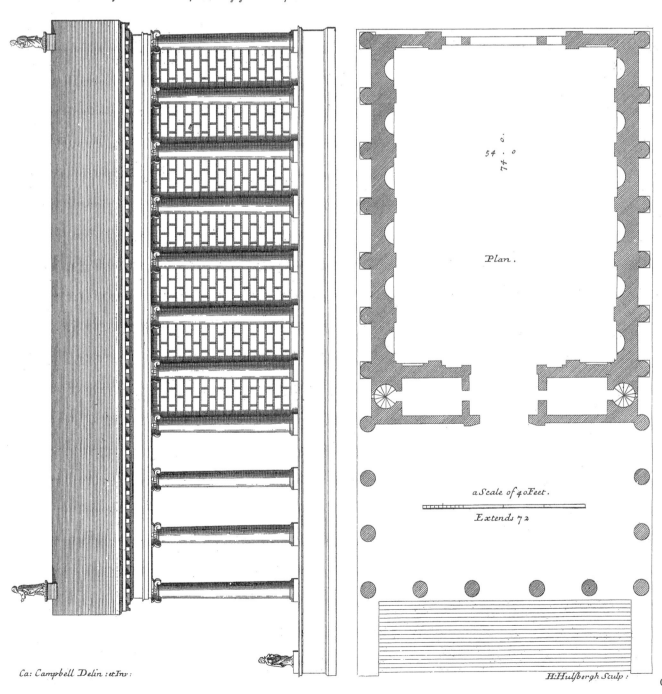

Plan.

54 . 0
74 . 0

a Scale of 40 Feet.

Extends 72

Ca: Campbell Delin : et Inv:

H. Hulsbergh Sculp:

The Elevation of York Stairs to the River, London. Inv: by Inigo Iones 1626. is most humbly Infcrib'd to Sr George Markham Bart.
Elevation d'un grand Efralier du Coté de la Riviere a Londres par Inigo Iones

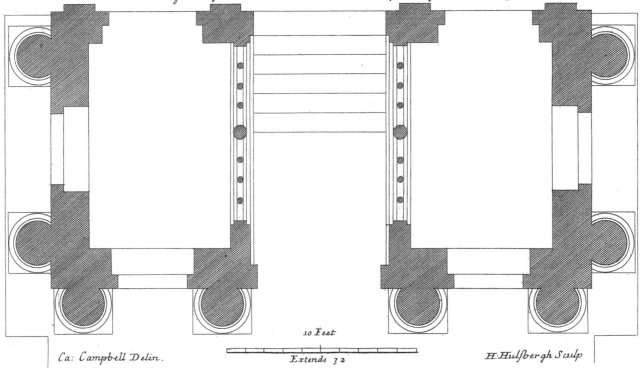

Ca: Campbell Delin.

10 Feet

Extends 32

H. Hulfbergh Sculp

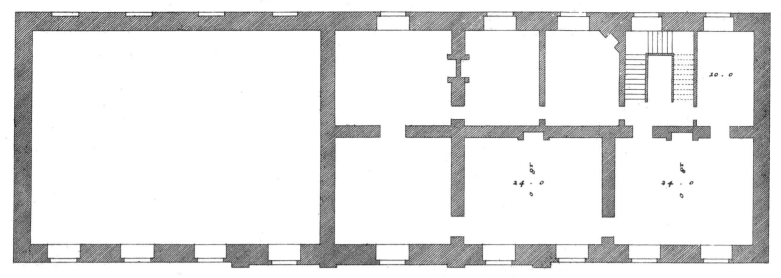

Plan of the Second Floor.
Plan du Second Etage.

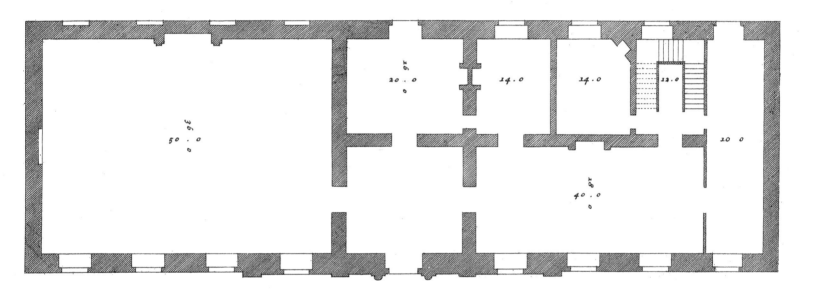

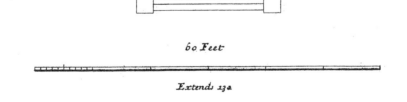

60 Feet

Extend 132

Plan of the first Floor of Cobham Hall.
Plan du Premier Etage de la Maison de Cobham.

The Elevation of Cobham Hall in Kent late the Seat of the Dukes of Lenox and Richmond, now of the R.t Hon.ble Lady Theodofia Blyth, and Iohn Blyth Efq.r her Houfband.
to whom this Plate is moft humbly Infcrib'd .

Elevation de la Maifon de Cobham dans la Comté de Kent .

60 Feet

Extends 132

Inigo Iones Inv:

Ca: Campbell Delin:

H. Hulfbergh Sculp:

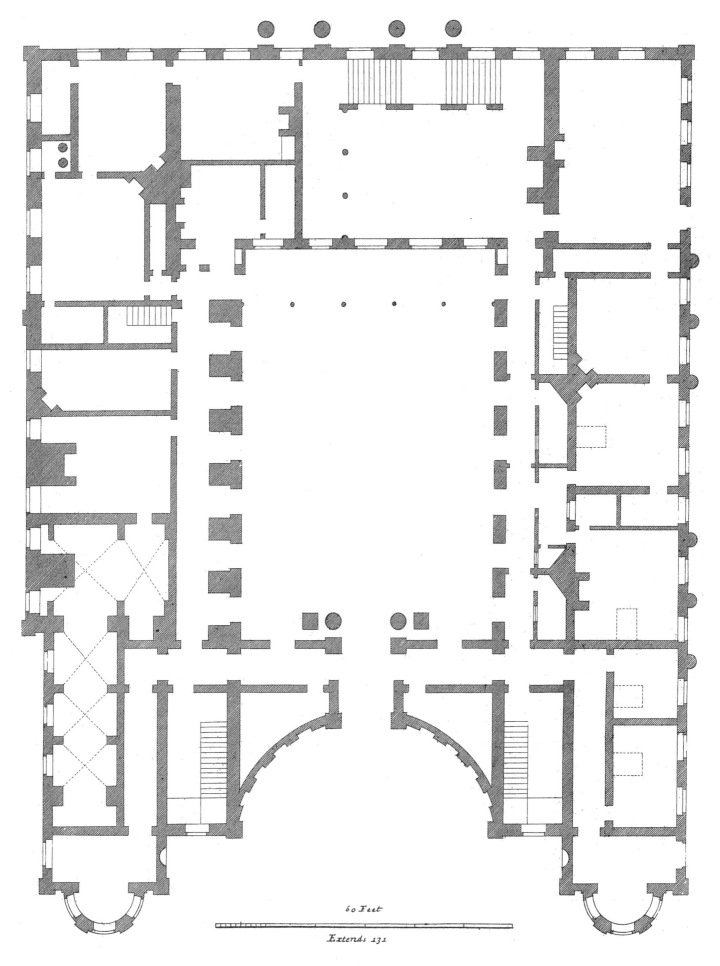

60 Feet

Extends 131

Plan of Cholmondely Hall.

Plan de la Maison de Cholmondeley

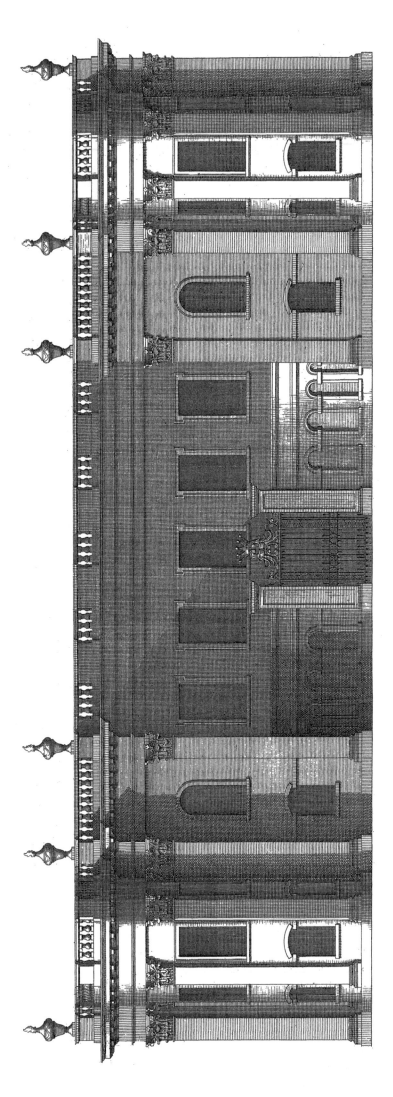

C. 2, PL. 32

Ca: Campbell Delin:

H.Hulsbergh Sculp.

a Scale of 60 Feet

Extends 131

The North Prospect of Cholmondeley Hall in Cheshire. The Seat of the Rt. Honble. The Earl of Cholmondeley, Treasurer of his Majesty's Houshold.
to whom this Plate is most humbly Inscrib'd.

Elevation Septentrionale de la Maison de Cholmondeley dans la Comté de Cheshire.

60 Feet

Extends 135

The South Proſpect of Cholmondeley Hall in Cheſhire. The Seat of the Rt. Honble. The Earl of Cholmondeley, Treaſurer of his Majeſty's Houſhold.

to whom this Plate is moſt humbly Inſcrib'd.

Eʹlevation Midyonale de la Maiſon de Cholmondeley dans la Comté de Cheſhire.

C. 2, PL. 33

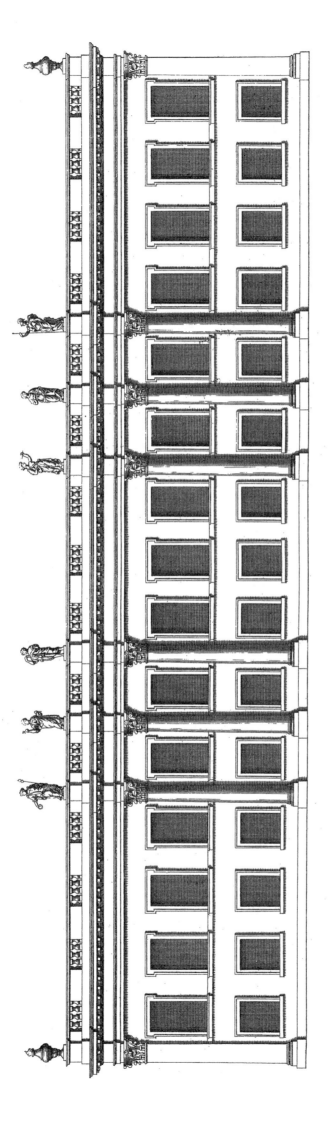

The West Prospect of Cholmondeley Hall in Cheshire. The Seat of the R.t Hon.ble The Earl of Cholmondeley Treasurer of his Majesty's Houshold. to whom this Plate is most humbly Inscrib'd.

a Scale of 60 Feet.

Extends 166.

Elevation Occidentale de la Maison de Cholmondeley, dans la Comté de Cheshire.

Ca:Campbell Delin:

H:Hulsbergh Sculp:

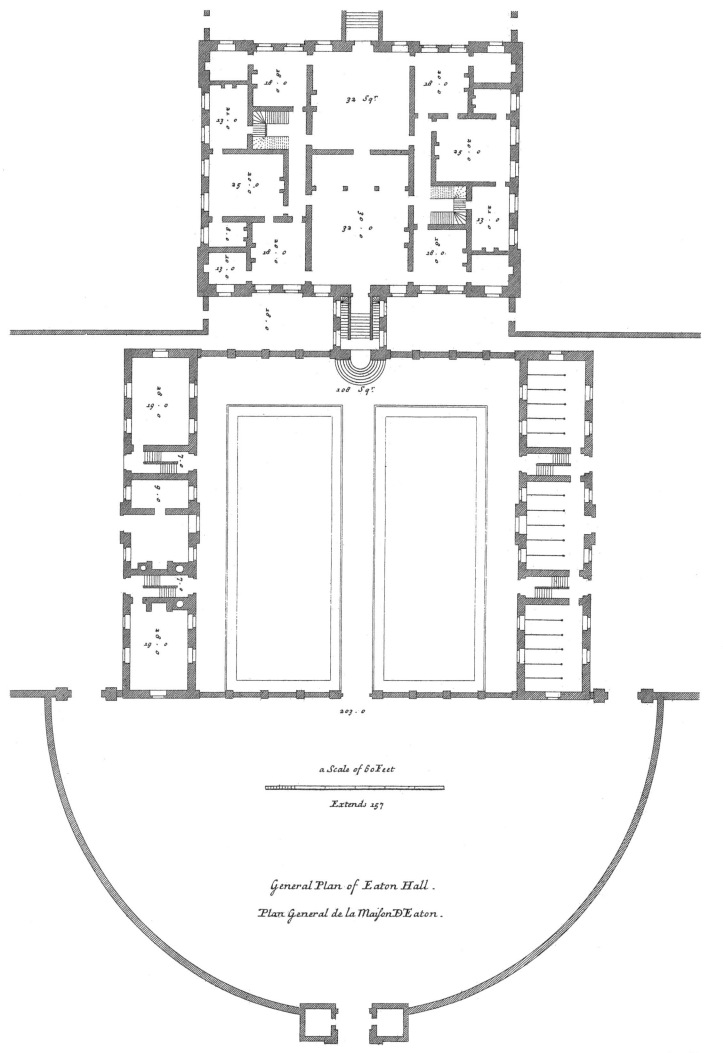

32 Sqr.

108 Sqr.

203.0

a Scale of 60 Feet

Extends 157

General Plan of Eaton Hall.

Plan General de la Maison D'Eaton.

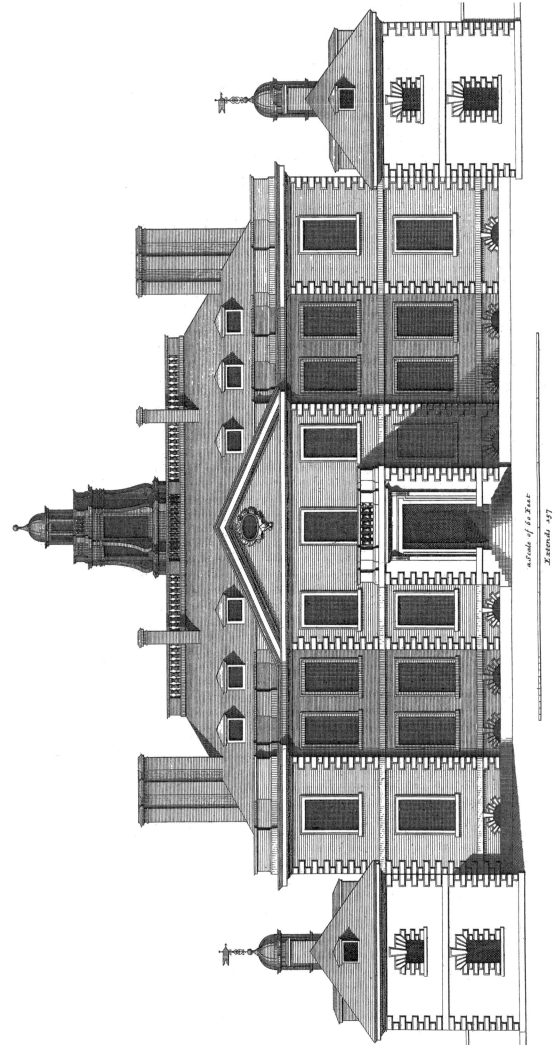

The Elevation of Eaton Hall in Cheshire, The Seat of Sir Richard Grosvenor Bart: to whom this Plate is most humbly Inscrib'd.

Elevation de la Maison D'Eaton.

a Scale of 60 Feet

Extends 157

Ca: Campbell Delin:

H: Hulsbergh Sculp:

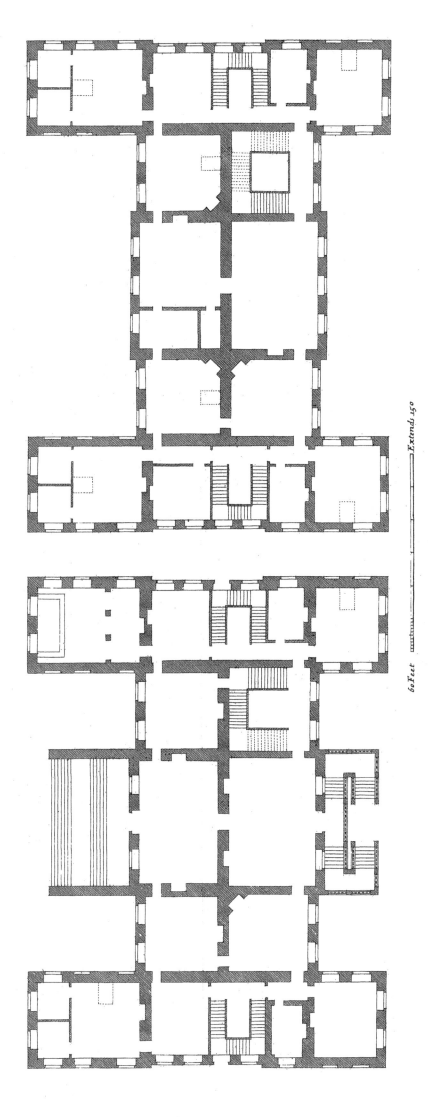

Plan of the 2ᵈ Story.

Plan du Second Etage.

Extends 150

60 Feet

Plan of the First Story of Belton.

Plan du Premier Etage de Belton.

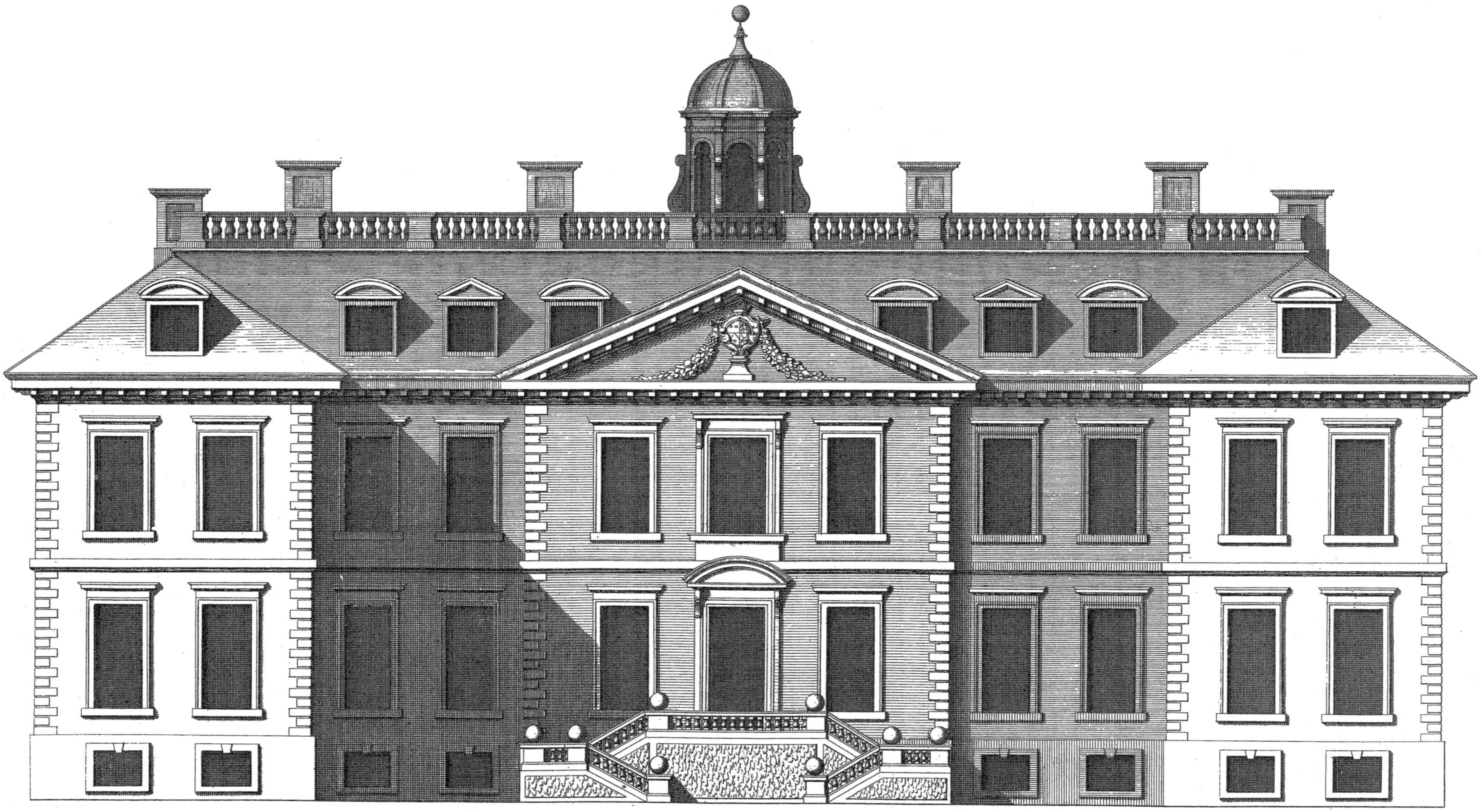

Ca: Campbell Delin:

The Elevation of Belton in Lincolnshire the Seat of S.r Iohn Brownlow Bar.t
to whom this Plate is most humbly Inscrib'd.

Elevation de la Maison de Belton dans la Comté de Lincoln.

60 Feet

Extends 150

H: Hulsbergh Sculp:

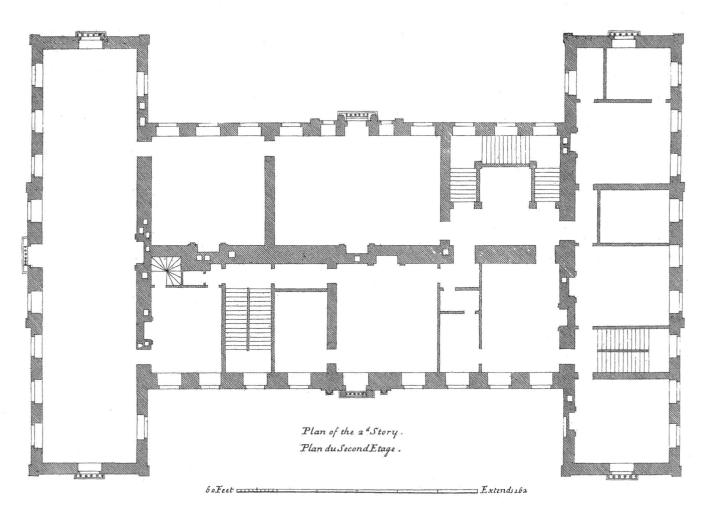

Plan of the 2.ᵈ Story.

Plan du Second Etage.

60 Feet ⊢⊣⊣⊣⊣⊣⊣⊣⊣⊣⊣⊣⊣⊣⊣⊣⊣⊣⊣⊣⊣⊣⊣⊣⊣⊣⊣⊣⊣⊣⊣ Extends 162

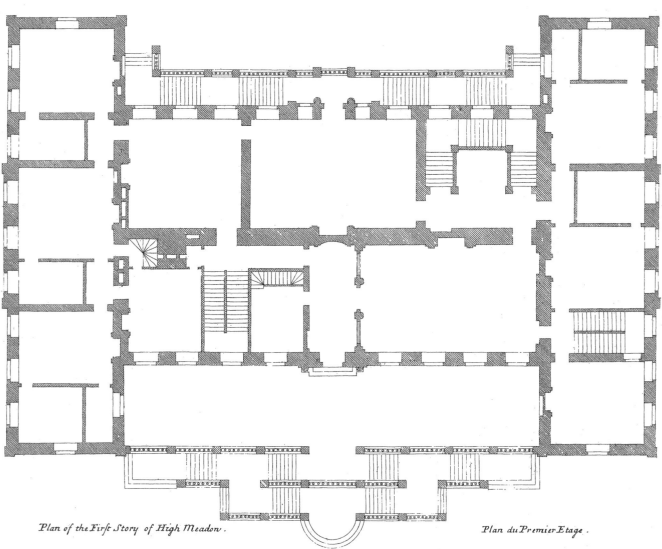

Plan of the First Story of High Meadon.   Plan du Premier Etage.

The Elevation of High Meadow in Glocestershire the Seat of Thomas Gage Esqr.
To whom this Plate is most humbly Inscrib'd.

Elevation de la Maison du Monsieur Gage dans la Comté de Glocester.

60 Feet

Extends 164

Ca: Campbell Delin:

H. Hulsbergh Sculp:

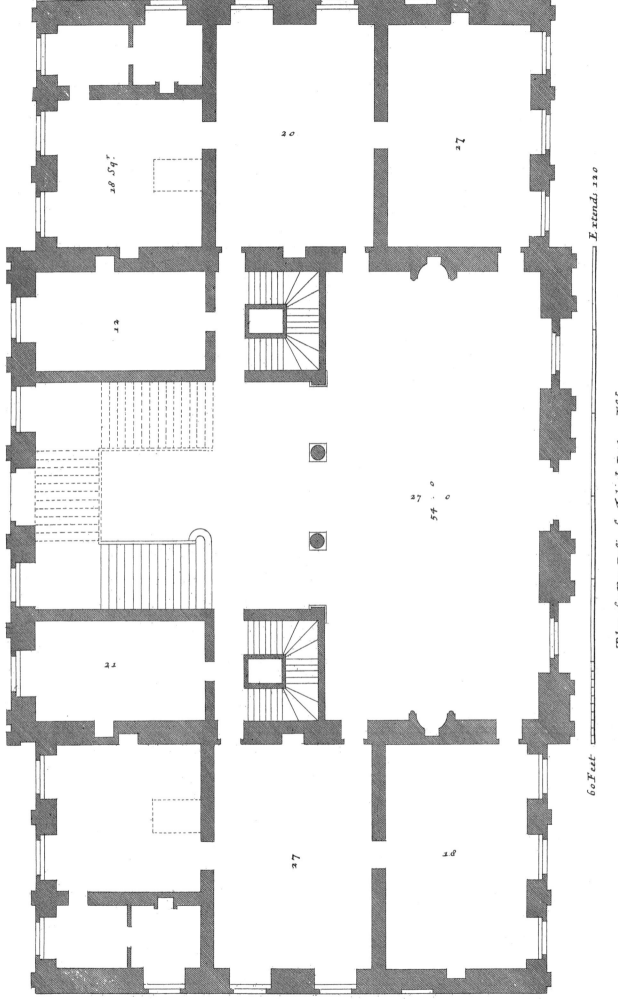

18 Sq.ᵗ

20

27

12

27·0
54·0

21

27

18

Extends 120

60 Feet

Plan of a New Design for Tobiah Ienkyns Esqʳ: —

Plan du Premier Etage.

This New Design of my Invention in the Theatrical Stile

Is most humbly Inscrib'd to Tobiah Jenkyns Esqr:

Elevation d'un Nouveau Dessein de mon Invention a la maniere Theatrale.

60 Feet   Extends 120

Ca: Campbell Inv: Del::   H.Hulsbergh Sc::

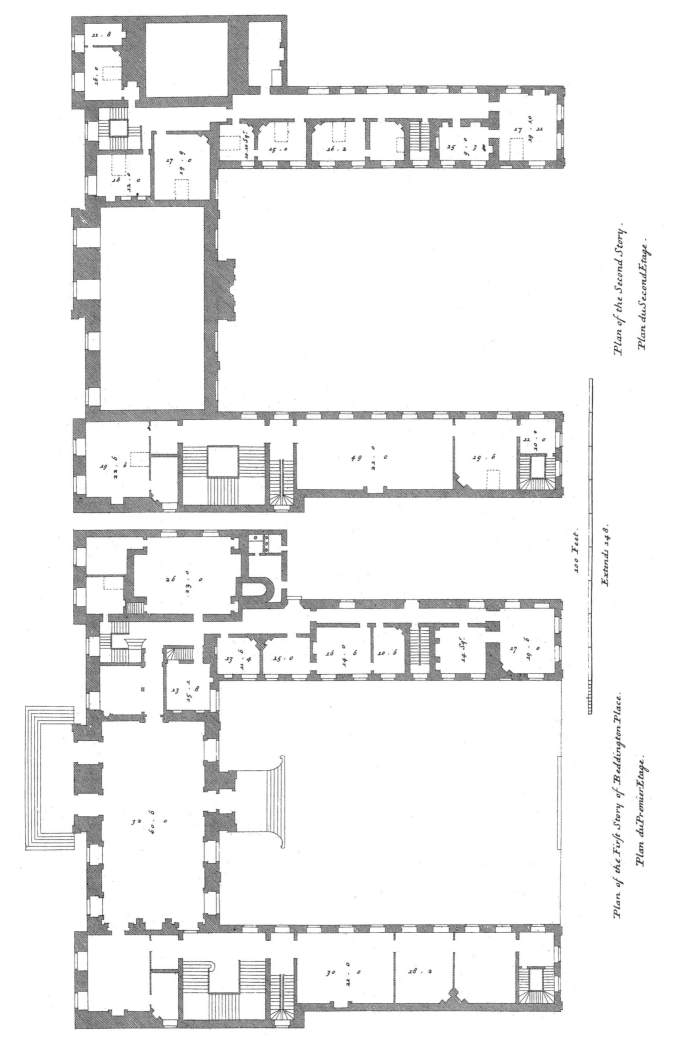

Plan of the Second Story.

Plan du Second Etage.

Plan of the First Story of Beddington Place.

Plan du Premier Etage.

100 Feet.

Extends 148.

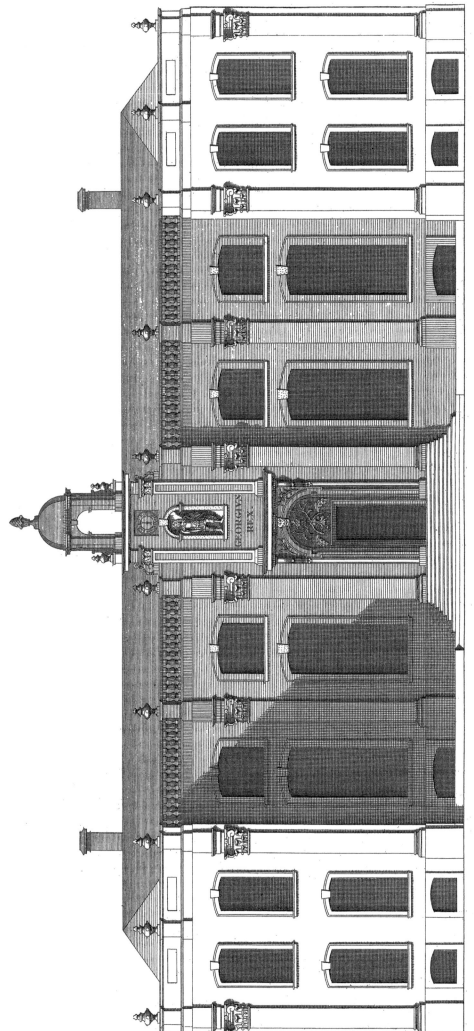

The West prospect of Beddington Place in Surrey, the Seat of Sr. Nicholas Carew Br.
to whom this Plate is most humbly Inscrib'd.

Elevation Occidentale de la Maison de Beddington dans la Comté de Surrey.

60 Feet   Extends 125

Co: Campbell Delin:

H. Hulsbergh Sculp:

C. 2, PL. 44

The East Profpect to the gardens of Beddington Place in Surrey.
is moft humbly Infcrib'd to The Lady Carew.

Elevation Orientale de la Maifon de Beddington dans la Comté de Surrey.

60 Feet

Extends 148

Ca: Campbell Delin:

H: Hulfbergh Sculp:

C. 2, PL. 45

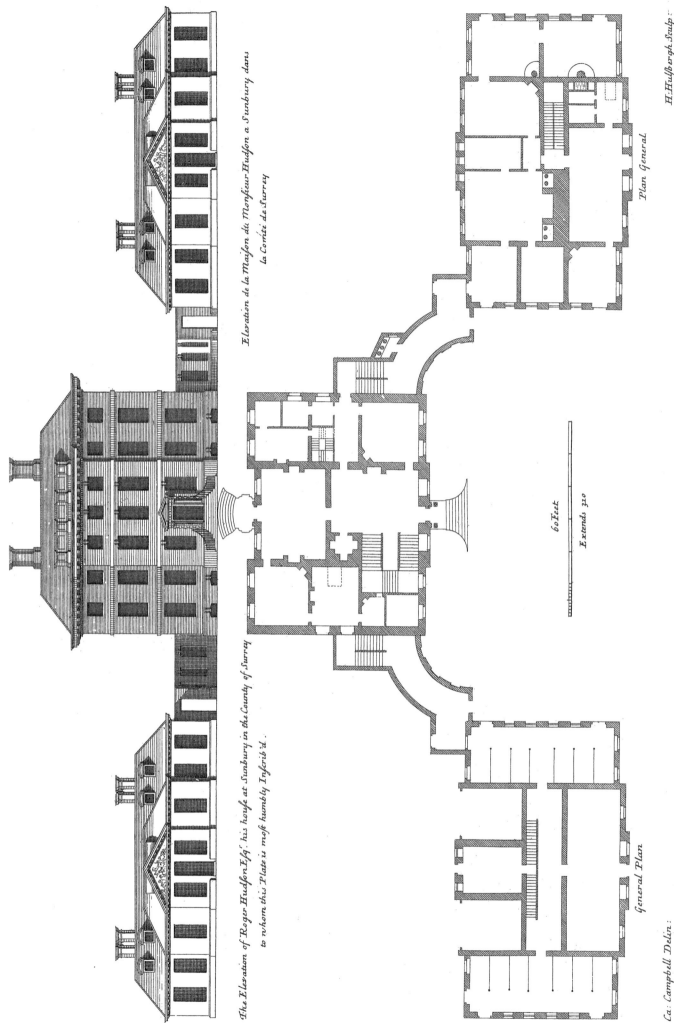

Elevation de la Maison du Monsieur Hudson a Sunbury dans la Comté de Surrey

The Elevation of Roger Hudson Esq: his house at Sunbury in the County of Surrey to whom this Plate is most humbly Inscrib'd.

Plan General

General Plan

60 Feet

Extends 310

C.a: Campbell Delin:

H. Hulsbergh Sculp:

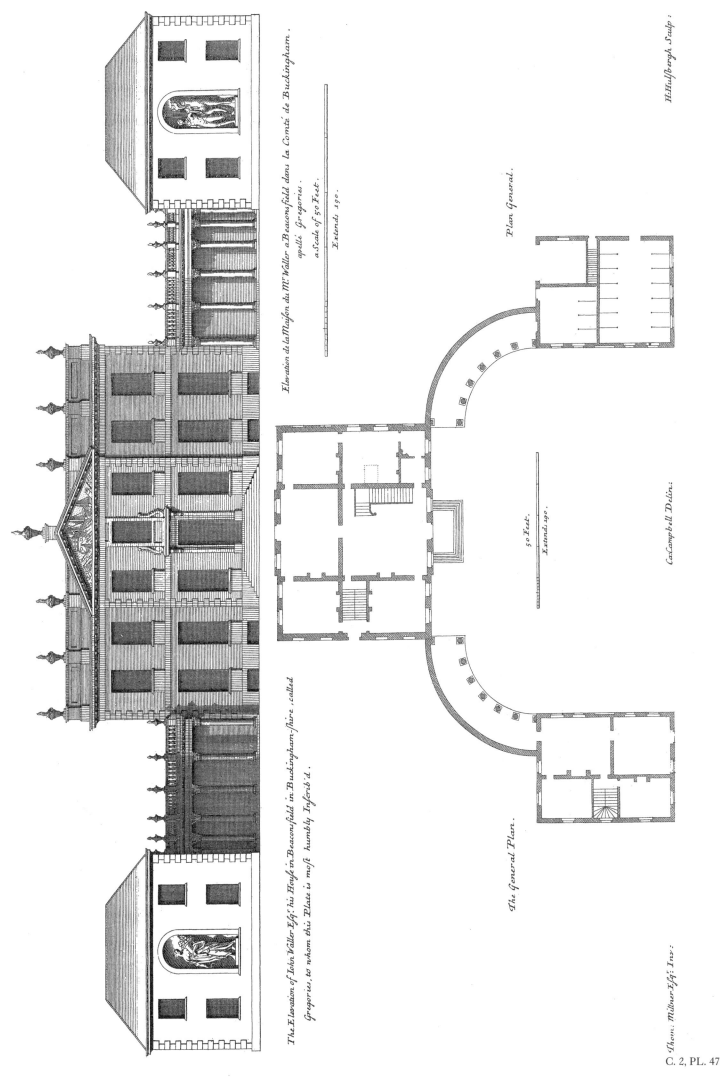

The Elevation of John Waller Esq; his House in Beaconsfield in Buckingham-shire, called Gregories, to whom this Plate is most humbly Inscrib'd.

Elevation de la Maison du Mr. Waller a Beaconsfield dans la Comté de Buckingham. apellé Gregories. a Scale of 50 Feet.

Extends 190.

Plan General.

The General Plan.

50 Feet.

Extends 190.

Thom: Milner Esq; Inv:

Ca.Campbell Delin:

H.Hulsbergh Sculp:

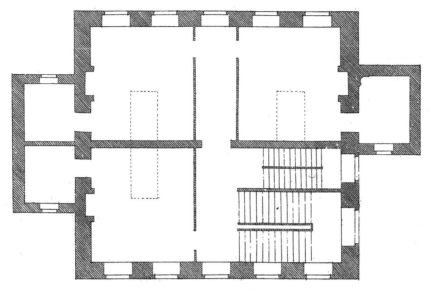

Plan of the Chamber Floor.
Plan du Second Etage.

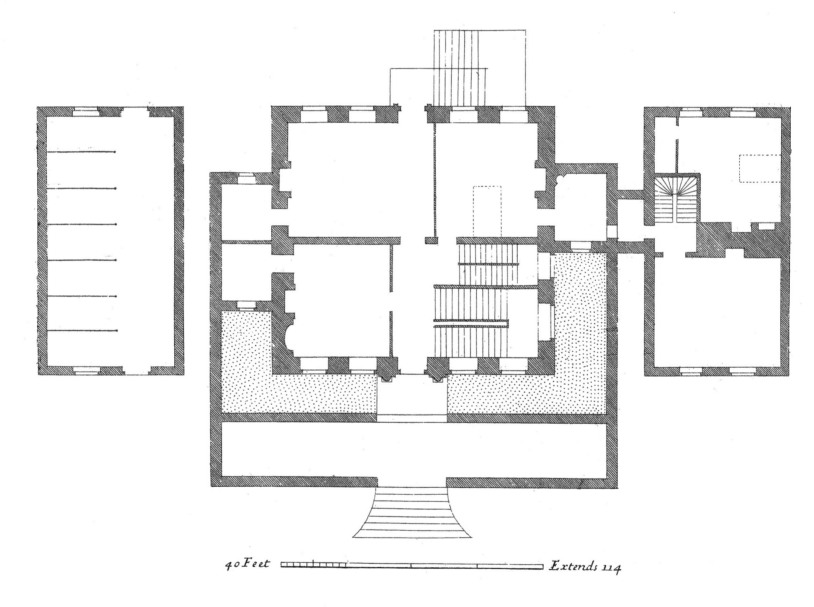

40 Feet   Extends 114

general Plan of Mr. Rooth's house at Epson.
Plan General de la Maison du Monsieur Rooth.

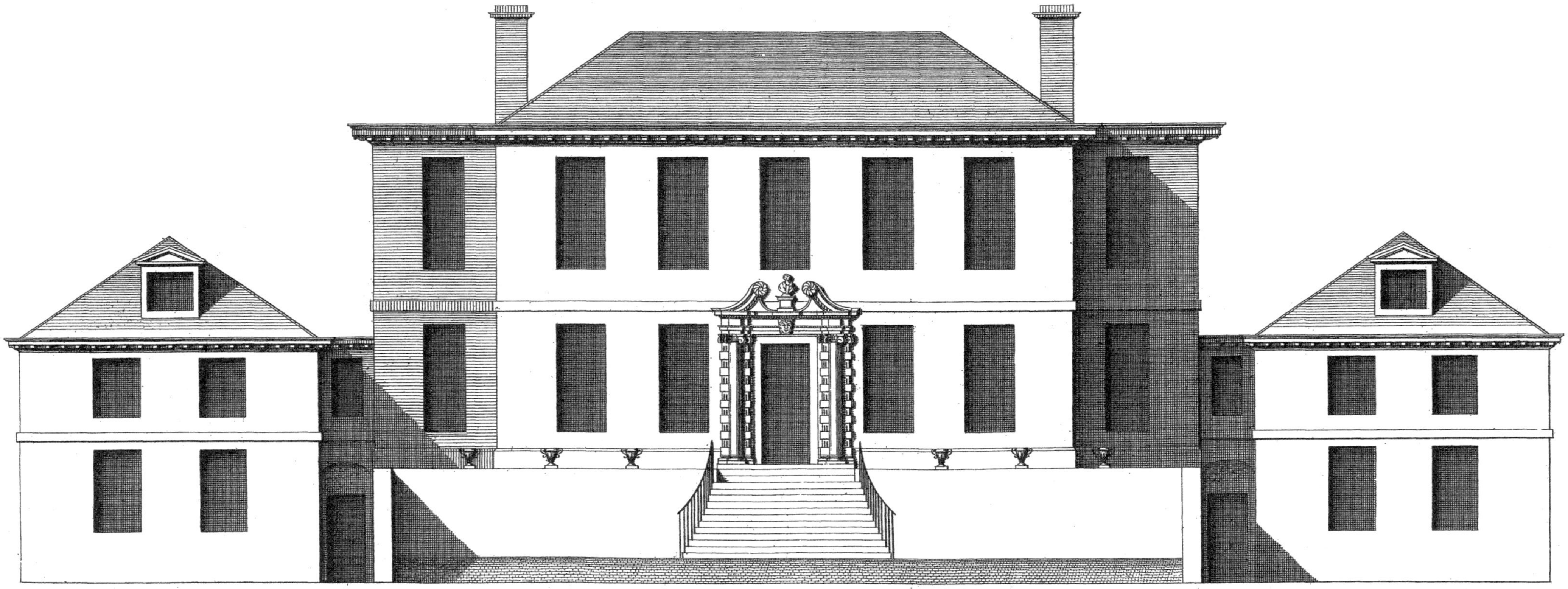

40 Feet

Extendi 114

The Elevation of Richard Rooth Esq.rs Houfe at Epfom in Surrey .

to whom this Plate is moft humbly Infcrib'd .

Elevation de la Maifon du Monfieur Rooth a Epfom dans la Comté de Surrey .

The Elevation of Melvin house in the Shire of Fyfe in Scotland, the Seat of the Rt. Honble. the Earl of Leven —
to whom this Plate is most humbly Inscrib'd.
Elevation de la Maison de Melvin dans la Comté de Fyfe en Ecosse.

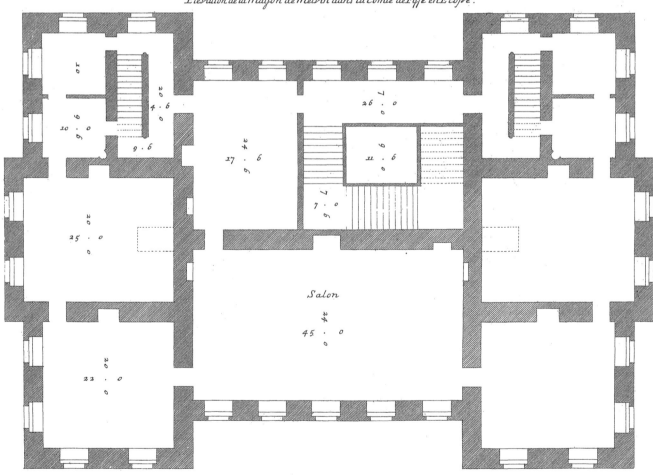

40 Feet ⌐⊏⊏⊏⊏⊏⊏⊏⊏⊏⊏⊐ Extends 100

Plan of the principal Floor.
Plan du principal Etage.

Ca: Campbell Delin

H. Hulsbergh Sc:

40 Feet ⊏▯▯▯▯▯▯▯▯▯▯▯▯▯▯▯▯▯▯▯▯▯▯▯▯▯⊐ Extends 66

The Elevation of Daniel Campbell of Shawfield Esq.r his house in the City of Glaßgow in Scotland.
to whom this Plate is most humbly Inscrib'd.

Elevation de la Maison du M.r Campbell Sieur de Shawfield a Glaßgow en Ecoße.

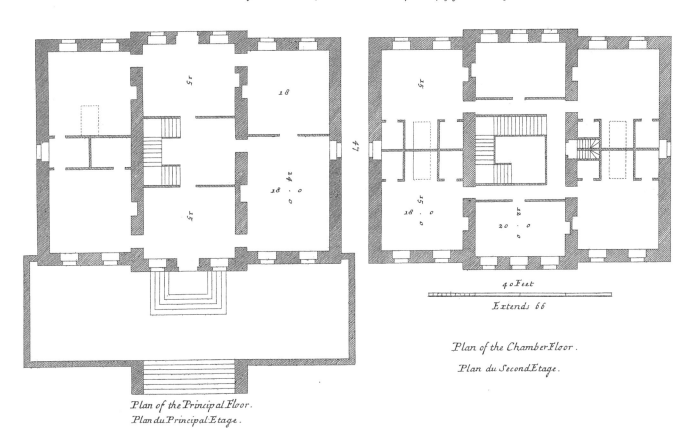

40 Feet ▯▯▯▯▯▯▯▯▯▯▯▯▯▯▯▯▯
Extends 66

Plan of the Chamber Floor.
Plan du Second Etage.

Plan of the Principal Floor.
Plan du Principal Etage.

Ca: Campbell Inv.r et Delin:

H: Hulsbergh Sc:

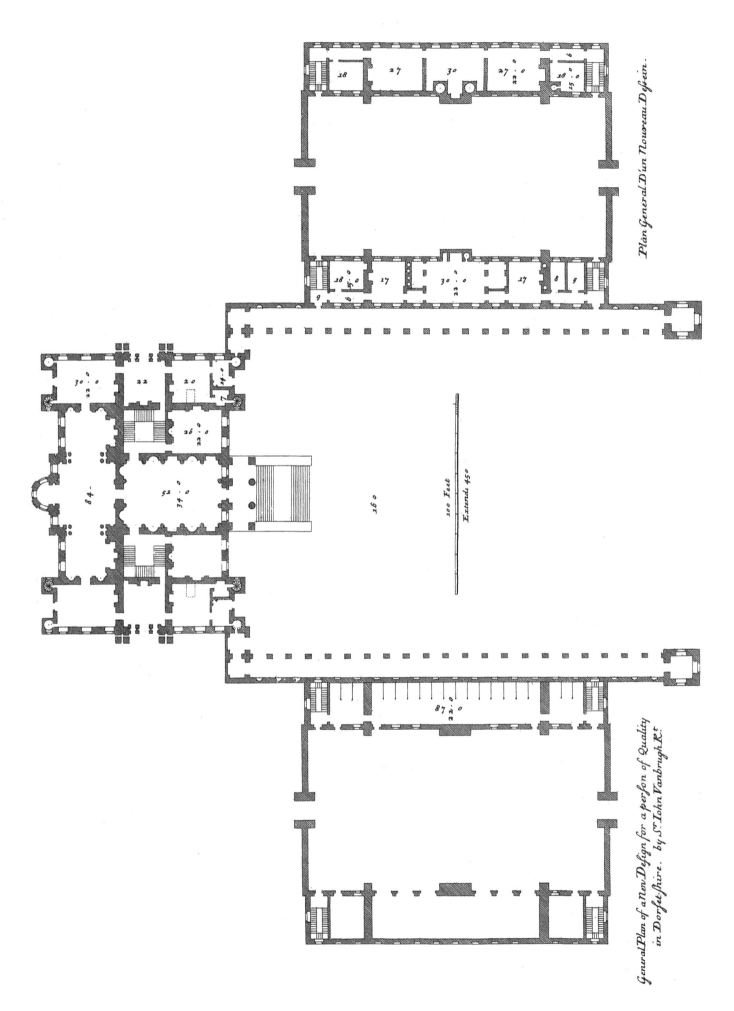

Plan General D'un Nouveau Defsein.

General Plan of a New Defign for a perfon of Quality
in Dorfet-fhire. by Sr John Vanbrugh Kt.

C. 2, PL. 52

Ca: Campbell. Delin:

The Elevation of a New Design for a person of Quality in Dorsetshire as Designed by Sr. John Vanbrugh Kt.
Elevation D'un Nouveau Dessein.

40 Feet ━━━━━━━━━━━━━━━ Extends 140

H: Hulsbergh Sc:

Ca: Campbell Delin:

H: Hulsbergh Sc:

The Garden Front of a New Design for a person of Quality in Dorsetshire, as Designed by Sr. John Vanbrugh Kt.

Elevation D'un Nouveau Dessein du Coté des Jardins.

40 Feet ⊢━━━━━┤   ⊢━━━━━ Extends 140

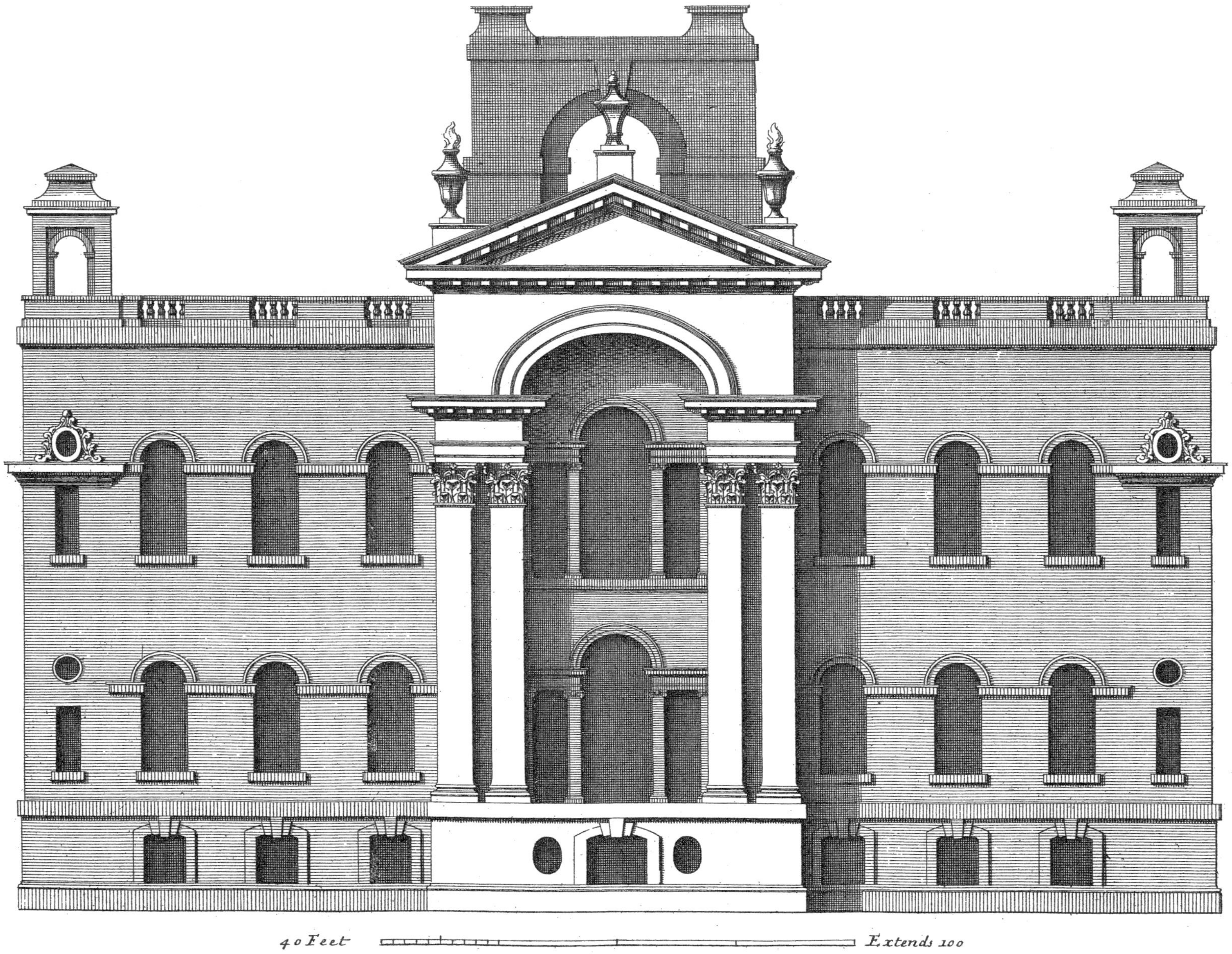
40 Feet
Extends 100

The Elevation of One End of a New Design for a person of Quality in Dorset-shire, as Designed by S^r. John Vanbrugh K^t.

Ca: Campbell Delin:

H: Hulsbergh Sc:

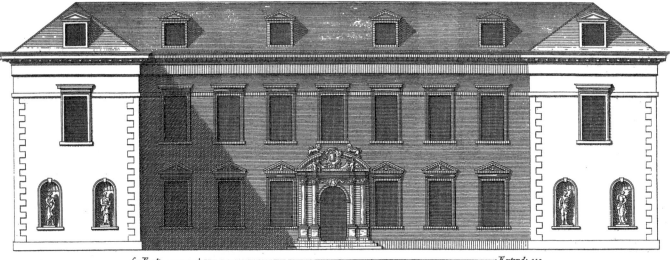

The Elevation of Maiden Bradley in Wiltshire, the Seat of S.ʳ Edward Seymour Bar.ᵗ to whom this Plate is most humbly Inscrib'd.
Elevation de la Maison de Maiden Bradley, dans la Comté de Wilts.

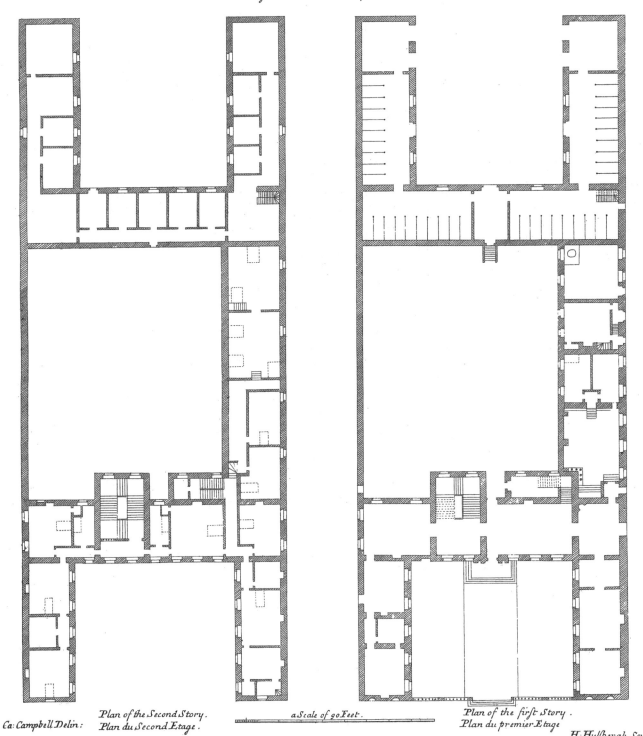

Ca: Campbell Delin:

Plan of the Second Story.
Plan du Second Etage.

a Scale of 90 Feet.

Plan of the first Story.
Plan du premier Etage

H. Hulsbergh Sculp:

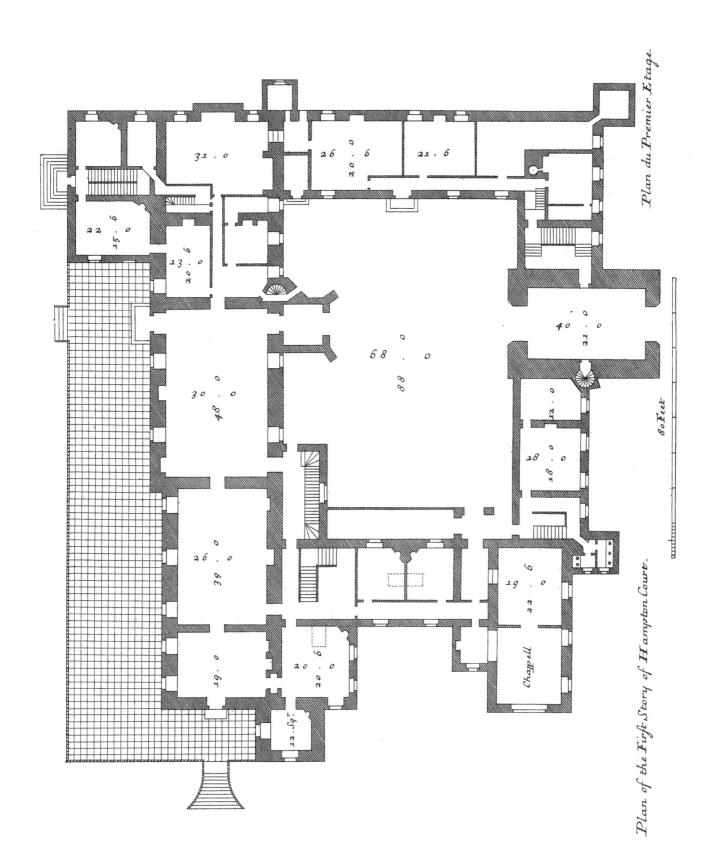

31 . 0

26 . 0

20 . 6

21 . 6

22 . 6

15 . 0

13 . 6

20 . 0

40 . 0

21 . 0

68 . . 0

88 . 0

30 . 0

48 . 0

12 . 0

18 . 0

18 . 0

26 . 0

39 . 0

19 . 0

22 . 6

19 . 0

20 . 6

20 . 0

12. Sq.t

Chapell

8 Feet

Plan of the First Story of Hampton Court.

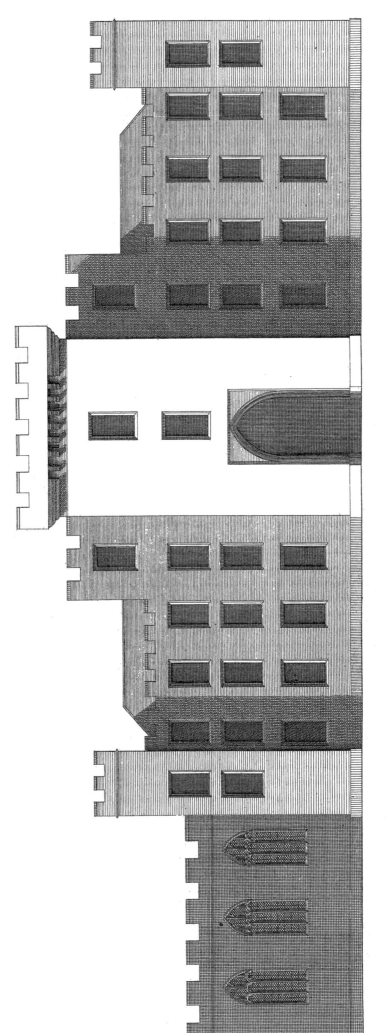

Ca: Campbell Delin:

C. 2, PL. 58

H.Hulfbergh Sculp:

Hampton Court in Herefordshire. built by Henry the 4.th King of England when he was Duke of Herford, the Seat of the Right Hon.ble the Lord Coningesby.

to whom this Plate is most humbly Inscrib'd.

Elevation. D.Hampton Cour dans la Comté 'D.Herford.

Houfe Extends 140

a Scale of 80 Feet

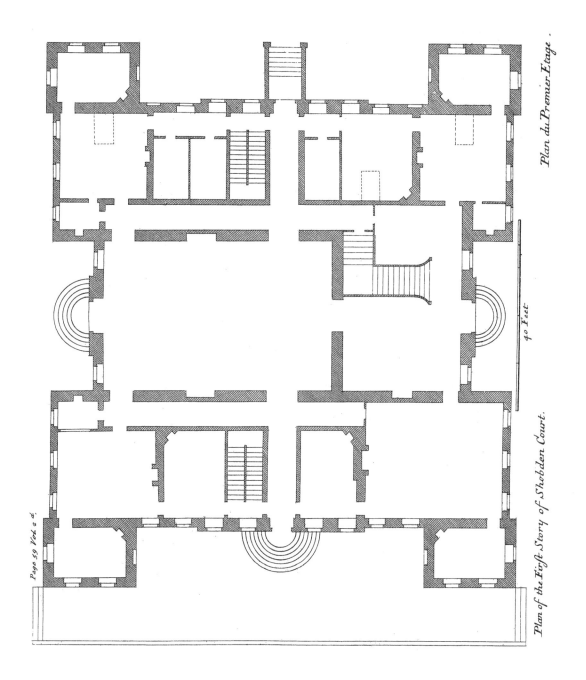

Plan du Premier Etage .

40 Feet

Page 59 Vol 2 d.

Plan of the First Story of Shobden Court.

I:a: Campbell Delin:

Shobden Court in Herefordshire, the Seat of the Rt Honble Sr James Bateman Bart Lord Major of London &c: to whom this Plate is most humbly Inscrib'd.

Elevation de Shobden Cour dans la Comté D'Heriford.

a Scale of 40 Feet

Extend 103

H. Hulsbergh Sculp:

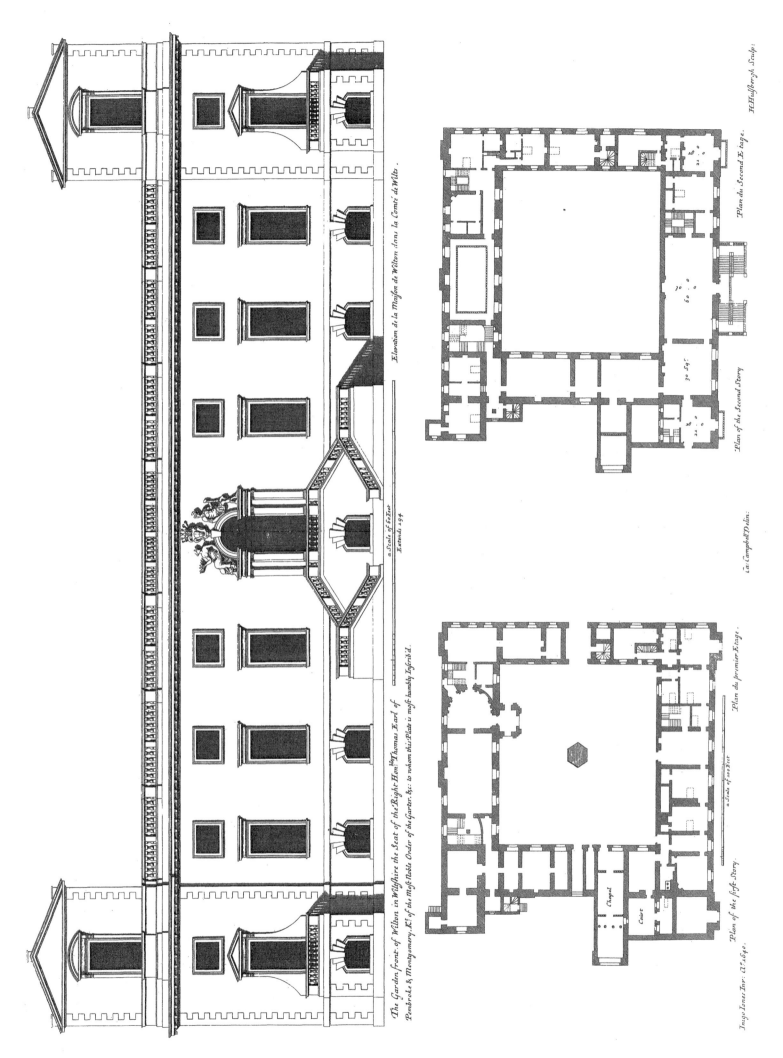

The Garden front of Wilton in Wilshire the Seat of the Right Hon.ble Thomas Earl of
Pembroke & Montgomery, K.t of the Most Noble Order of the Garter, &c:: to whom this Plate is most humbly Inscrib'd.

Elevation de la Maison de Wilton dans la Comté de Wilts.

a Scale of 60 Feet
Extends 194

Plan of the Second Story.

Plan du Second Etage.

Plan of the first Story.

Plan du premier Etage.

a Scale of 120 Feet

Inigo Jones Inv: A°.1640.

Ia: Campbell Delin:

H.Hulsbergh Sculp:

Chapel

Court

C. 2, PL. 61-62

InigoIones Inv:

Section of the Great Dining Room at Wilton.

20 Feet.

Extends 60.

Section de la Grande Sale.

Ca: Campbell Delin:

H: Hulsbergh Sculp:

Section of the Salon.
Section du Salon.

a Scale of 30 Feet

One End of the Great-Dining Room.

Inigo Jones Inv:

Ca: Campbell Delin:

H.Hulsbergh Sc:

a Scale of 30 Feet

Extends 52.

The Loggio in the Bowling Green at Wilton.

La Galerie au Jardins.

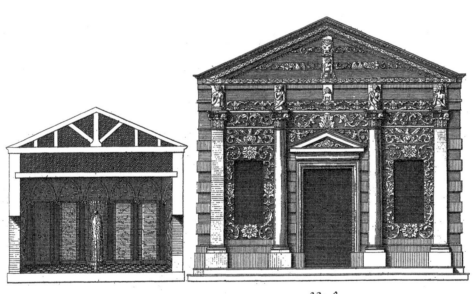

Section of the Grotto.

22. 0

The Garden Door.

Front of the Grotto at Wilton.

Elevation de la Grote.

This Plate is most humbly Inscrib'd to the R.ᵗ Hon.ᵇˡᵉ The Lord Herbert Collonel of his Majesty's Guards,
Lord of the Bed Chamber to his Royal Highneß the Prince of Wales &c: and Son and heir to the R.ᵗ Hon.ᵇˡᵉ the Earl of Pembroke &c:

Inigo Iones Inv: *Ca: Campbell Delin:*   *H:Hulsbergh Sc:*

Plan and Elevation of the out Offices at Wilton.

Plan et Elevation des Equieries de Wilton.

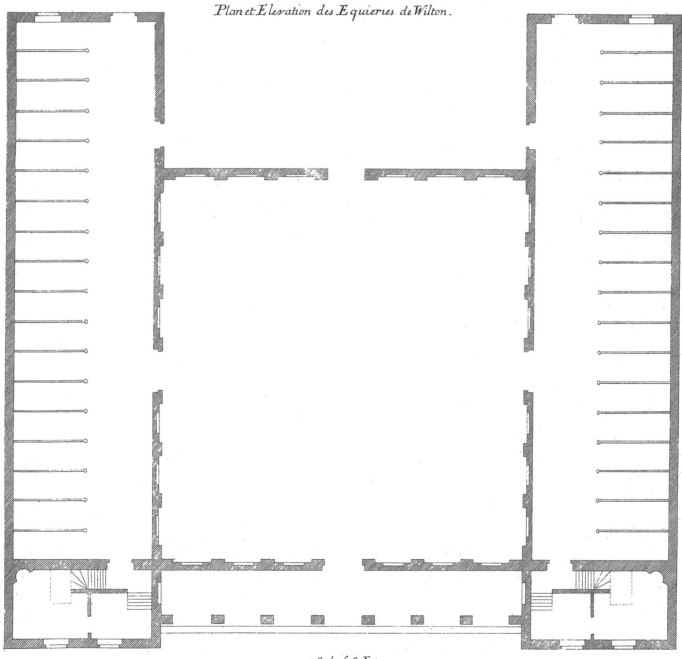

a Scale of 60 Feet

Extends 125

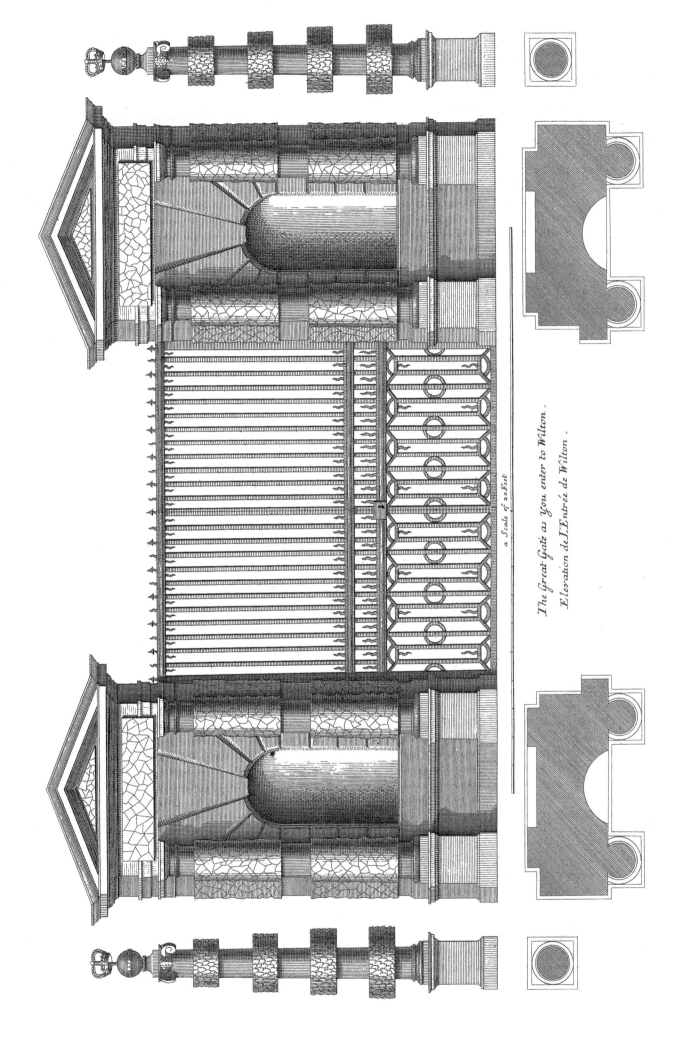

H. Hulsbergh Sc:

The Great Gate as you enter to Wilton.

Elevation de l'Entrée de Wilton.

a Scale of 20 Feet

Inigo Jones Invr:

Ca: Campbell Delin:

C. 2, PL. 67

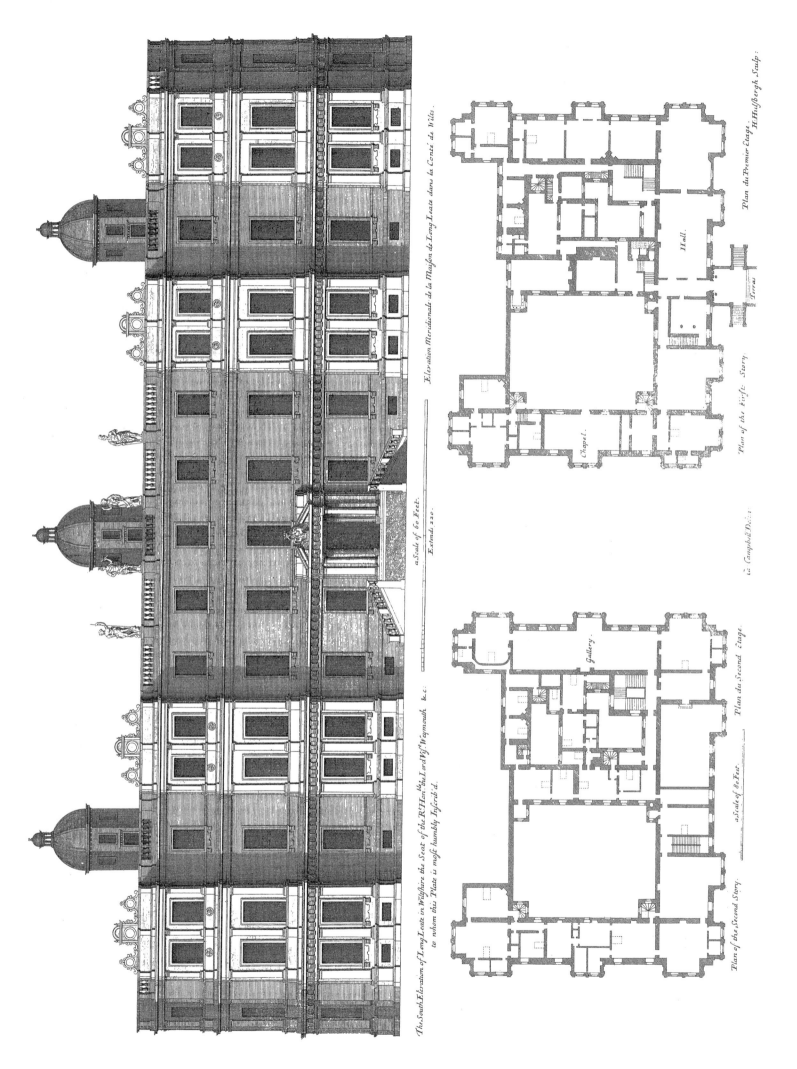

The South Elevation of Long Leate in Wiltshire the Seat of the R.t Hon.ble the Lord V.t Weymouth &c:
to whom this Plate is most humbly Inscrib'd.

Elevation Meridionale de la Maison de Long Leate dans la Conté de Wilts.

a Scale of 60 Feet.

Extends 220.

Plan du Premier Etage.   H.Hulsbergh Sculp:

Plan of the first Story.

Hall.

Terras.

Chapel.

Ca: Campbell Delin:

Gallery.

Plan du Second Etage.

Plan of the Second Story.

a Scale of 80 Feet.

C. 2, PL. 68-69

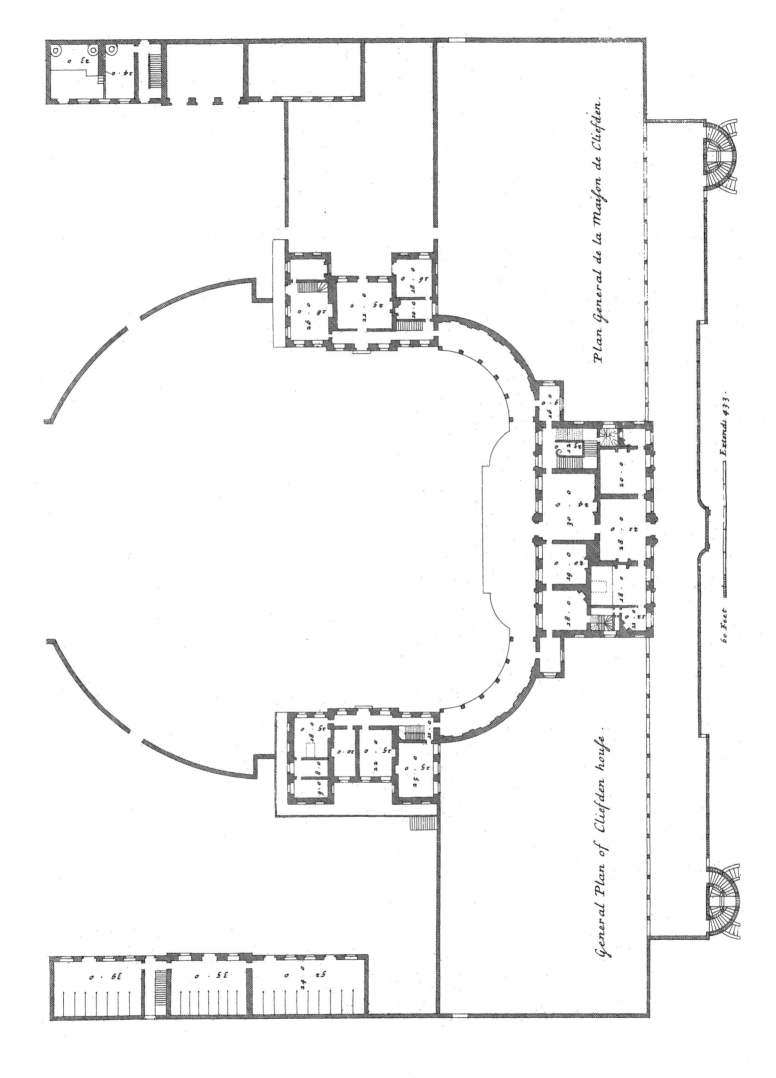

Plan General de la Maison de Cliefden.

General Plan of Cliefden house.

Extend: 433.

60 Feet

The North Prospect of Clifden house in Buckinghamshire the Seat of the Right Hon:ble The Earl of Orkney, Generall of the Infantry, one of the Lords of his Majestyes Bedchamber and Knight of the most ancient Order of the Thistle &c: to whom this Plate is most humbly Inscrib'd.

Elevation Occidentale de la Maison de Clifden dans la Comté de Buckingham.

a Scale of 60 Feet

Extends 245

Ca: Campbell Delin:

H: Hulsbergh Sc:

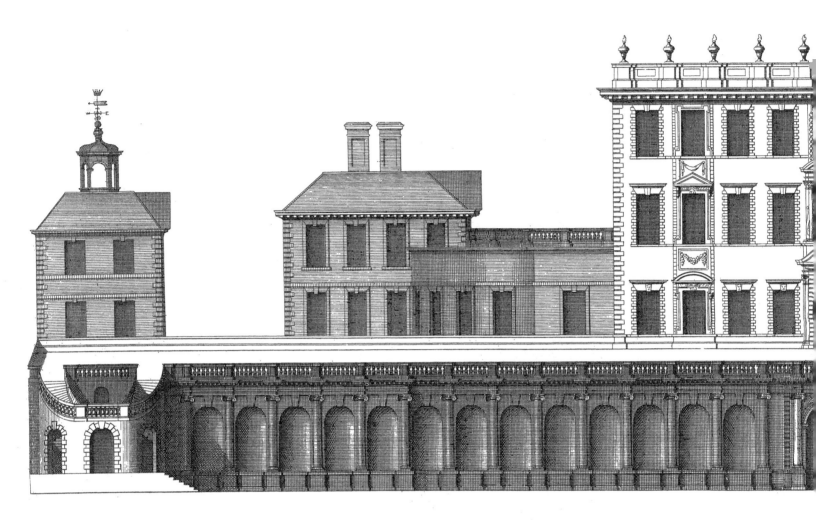

a Scale of 60 Feet

The West-Front of

Is most humbly Inscrib'd to the R.

Elevation Occidentale de la

Ca: Campbell Delin:

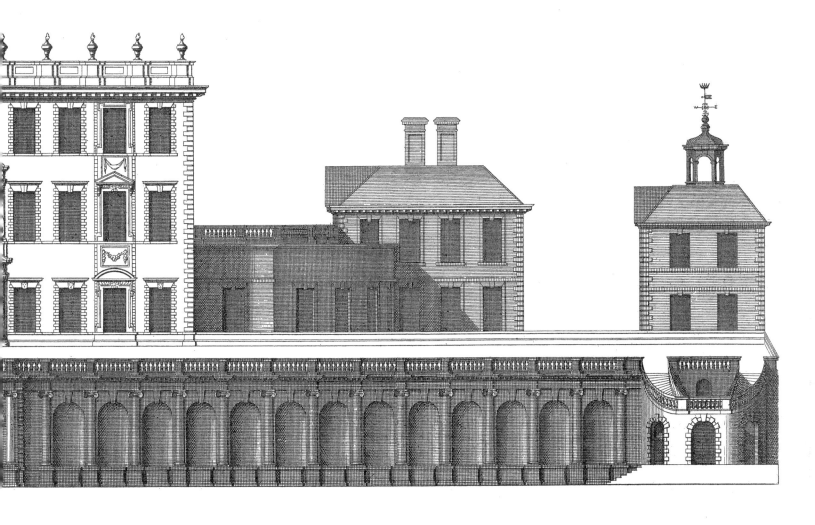

≡══════════════╤═════╤══════════════ *Extends* 360

den House .
^{ble} *the Counteß of Orkney*
on de Cliefden .

H:Hulſbergh Sc:

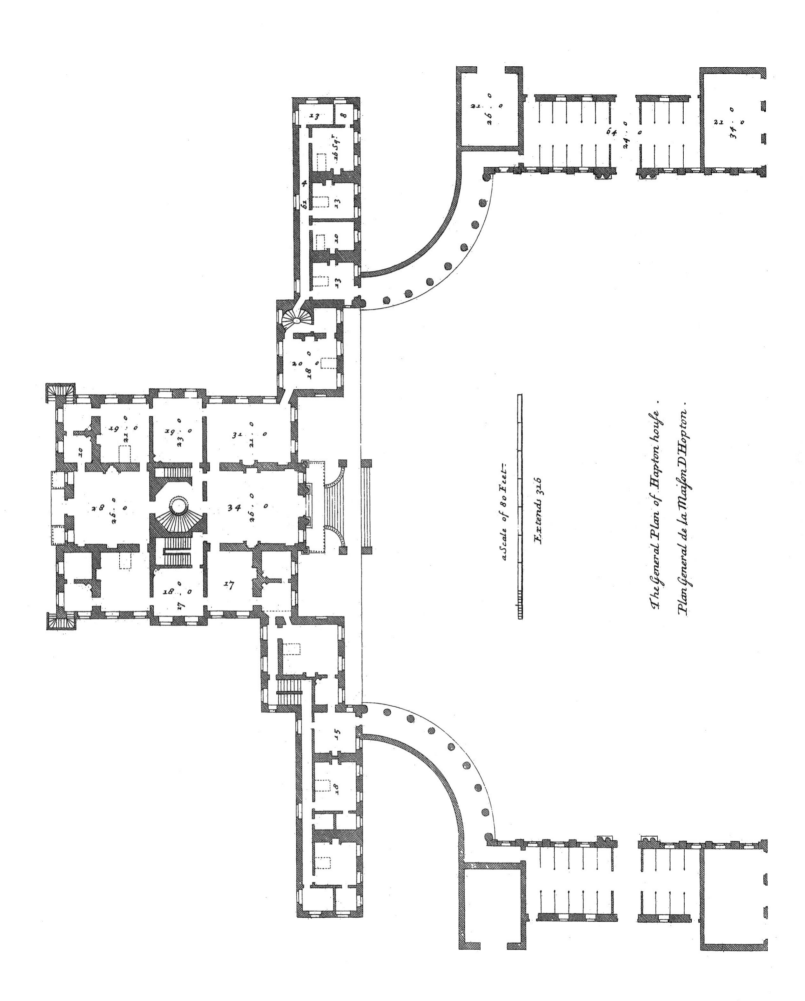

The General Plan of Hopton house.

Plan General de la Maison D'Hopton.

a Scale of 80 Feet.

Extends 316

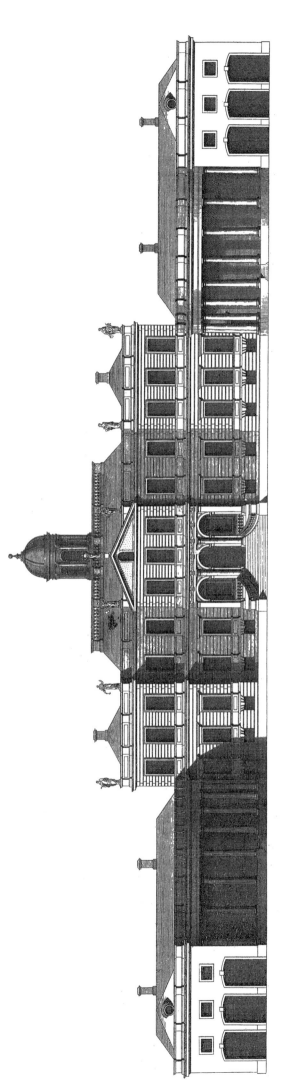

Ca: Campbell Delin:

H.Hulſbergh Sculp.

The Elevation of the East Front of Hoptone houſe in the Shire of Linlithgow in Scotland the Seat of the Rt Honble the Earl of Hoptone.

to whom this Plate is moſt humbly Inſcrib'd. Invented by Sr Wm Bruce. 1700

Elevation Orientale de la Maiſon D' Hoptone dans la Comté de Linlithgow en Eſcoſſe.

80 Feet

Extends 316

C. 2, PL. 76-77

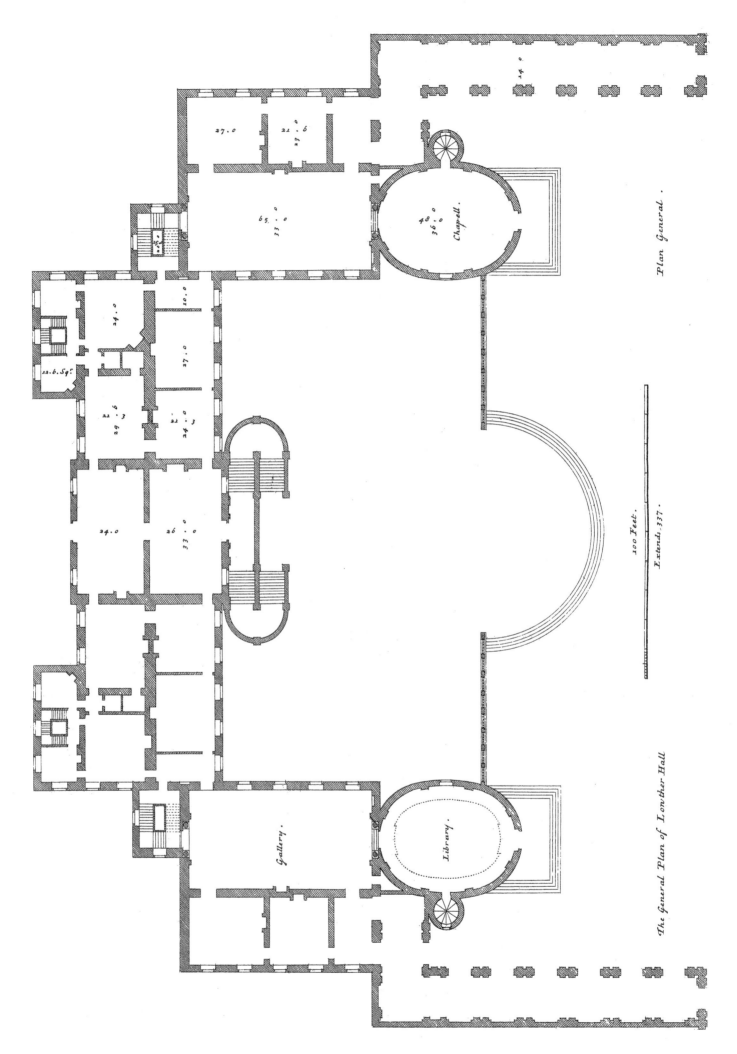

27.0   21.6

27.0

65.0

33.0

48.0

36.0

Chapell.

24.0

10.0

12.6. Sq.

27.0

22.6

29.3

22.0

24.3

24.0

26.0

33.0

14.0

Gallery.

Library.

100 Feet.

Extends. 337.

Plan General.

The General Plan of Lowther Hall

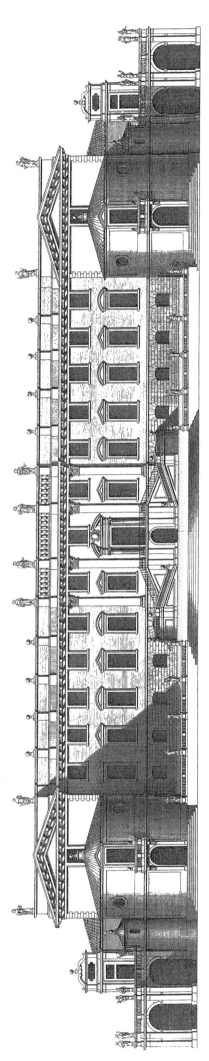

Ca: Campbell Delin:

H: Hulsbergh Sculp:

a Scale of 100 Feet

Extends 337

The Elevation of Lowther Hall in Westmoreland the Seat of the R.t Hon.ble the Lord Viscount Lansdale.
to whom this Plate is most humbly Inscrib'd.

Elevation de la Maison de Lowther dans la Comté de Westmoreland.

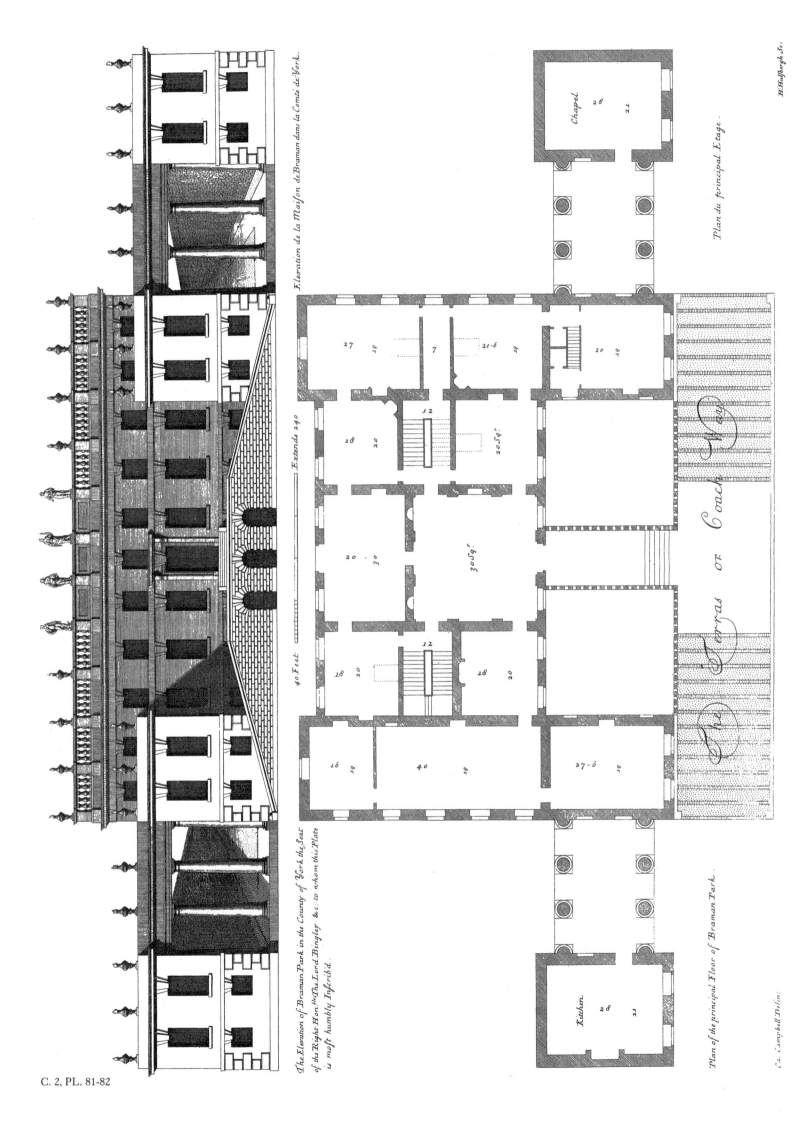

The Elevation of Braman Park in the County of York the Seat
of the Right Hon.ble Th.º Lord Bingley &c: to whom this Plate
is most humbly Inscrib'd.

Elevation de la Maison de Braman dans la Comté de York.

Plan of the principal Floor of Braman Park.

Plan du principal Etage.

Chapel   28   21

Kitchen   28   21

27   19

7   21-6   19

20   19

18   20

20 Sq.r

20   30

30 Sq.r

18   20

18   20

16   19

40   19

27-6   19

The Terras or Coach Way

Extends 240

40 Feet

C. Campbell Delin.

H. Hulsbergh Sc:

C. 2, PL. 81-82

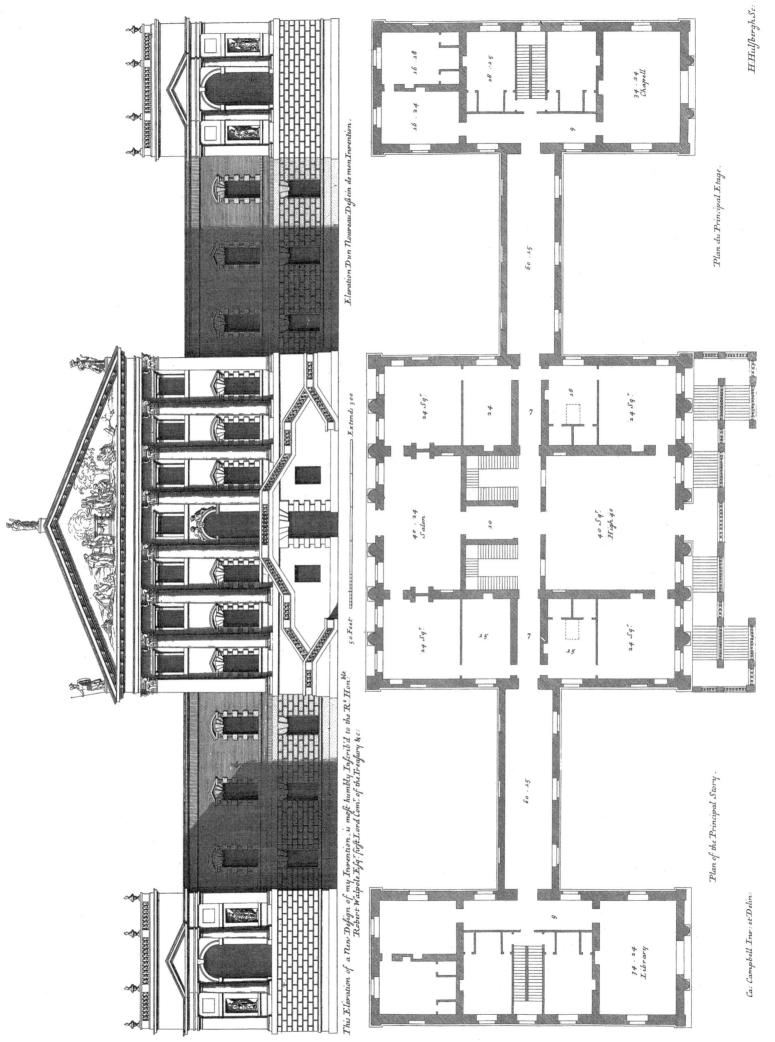

Elevation D'un Nouveau Dessein de mon Invention.

Plan du Principal Etage.

H: Hulsbergh Sc:

Extend 300

50 Feet

Chapell

9

18 . 15

16 . 18

16 . 24

60 . 45

This Elevation of a New Design of my Invention, is most humbly Inscrib'd to the R.t Hon.ble
Robert Walpole Esq.r first Lord Com.r of the Treasury &c:

24 Sq.r

24

7

18

24 Sq.r

40 . 24
Salon

10

40 Sq.r
High 40

24 Sq.r

15

7

15

24 Sq.r

60 . 45

9

34 . 24
Library

Plan of the Principal Story.

Ca: Campbell Inv.t et Delin:

C. 2, PL. 83-84

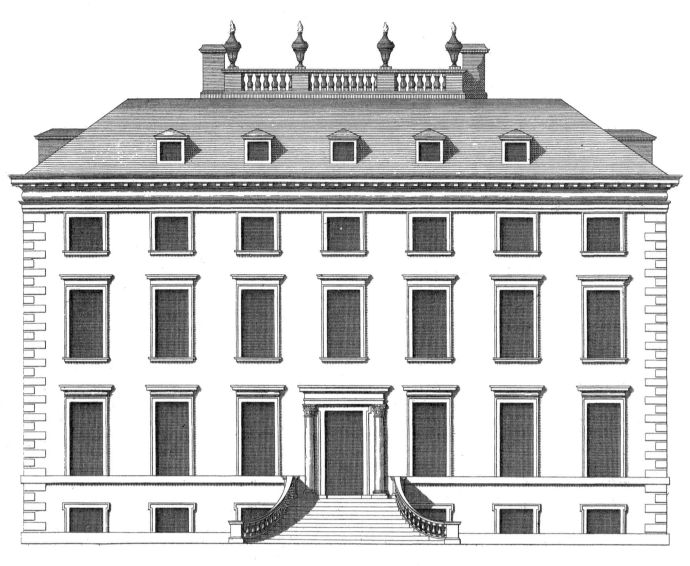

50 Feet   Extends 88

The Elevation of Chevening house in Kent the Seat of the R:t Hon:ble the late Earl of Sußex, is most humbly Inscrib'd
to the R:t Hon:ble the Counteß Dowager of Sußex.

Elevation de la Maison de Chevening dans la Comté de Kent.

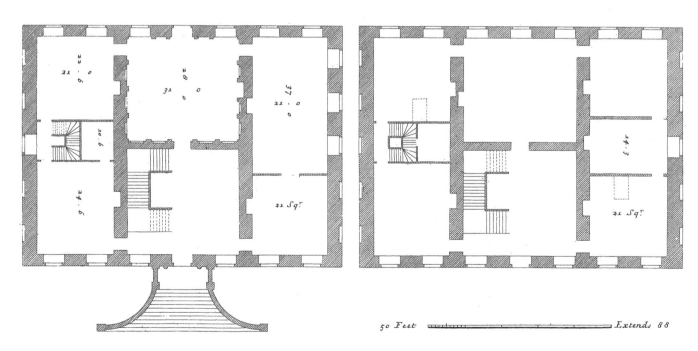

50 Feet   Extends 88

Plan of the First Floor.   *Plan of the Second Floor.*
Plan du Premier Etage.   *Plan du Second Etage.*

Inigo Iones Inv: *Ca: Campbell Delin:*   *H: Hulsbergh Sculp:*

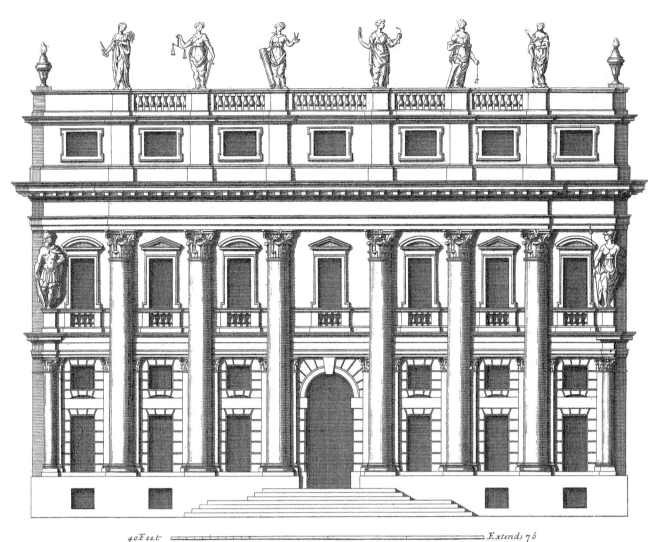

40 Feet   Extends 76

This new Design of my Invention is most humbly Inscrib'd to the Rt. Honble. James Stanhope Esqr. principal Secretary of State &c :
Elevation D'un Nouveau Dessein de mon Invention .

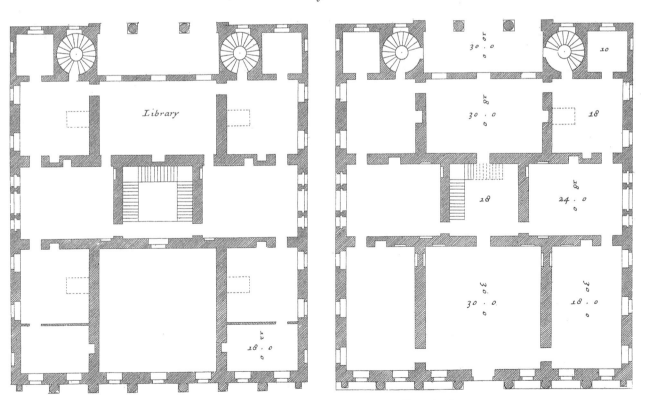

Plan of the Second Story .   40 Feet   Extends 76   Plan of the first Story .
Plan du Second Etage .   Plan du Premier Etage

Ca: Campbell Inv: et Delin: H: Hulsbergh Sc:

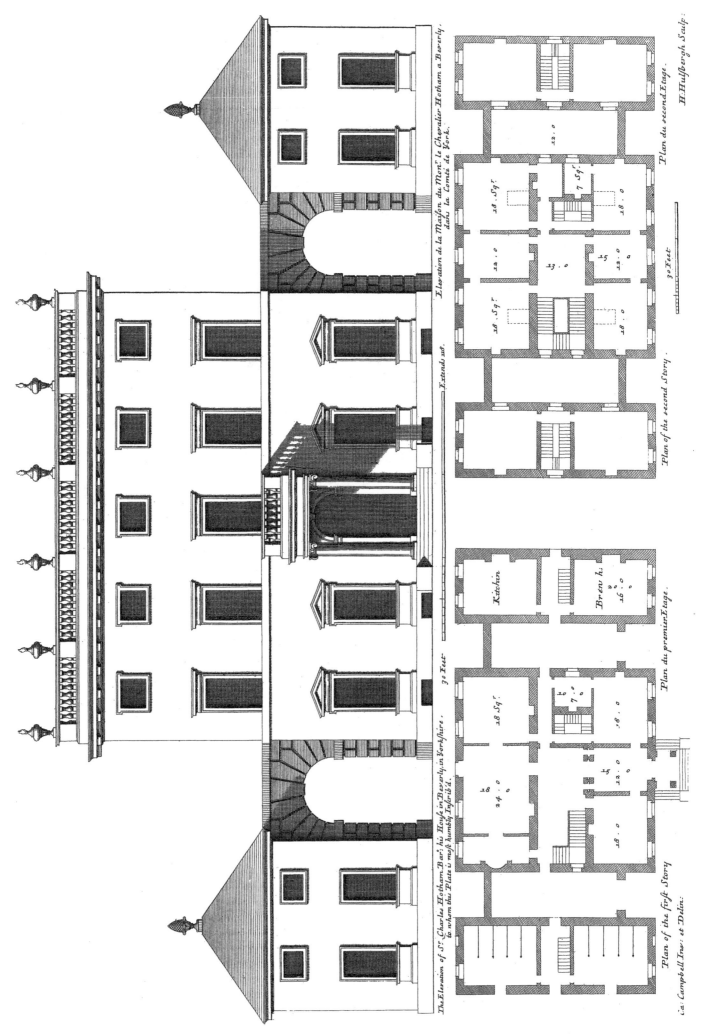

The Elevation of S.r Charles Hotham Bar.t his House in Beverly in Yorkshire.
to whom this Plate is most humbly Inscrib'd.

Elevation de la Maison du Mon.r le Chevalier Hotham a Beverly.
dans la Comté de York.

Extends 118.

30 Feet

Plan of the first Story

Kitchen

Brew h.

Plan of the second Story.

Plan du premier Etage.

Plan du second Etage.

30 Feet

C.a: Campbell Inve.t et Delin::

H. Hulsbergh Sculp:

C. 2, PL. 87

Elevation de la Maison de Chester-Lee-street dans la Comté de Durham.

H. Hulsbergh Sculp:

Extends 128

a Scale of 44 Feet

The Elevation of Chester Lee-street in the County of Durham, the Seat of John Hedworth Esq.r to whom this Plate is most humbly Inscrib'd.

40 Feet

Extends 128

Plan.

C. 2, PL. 88

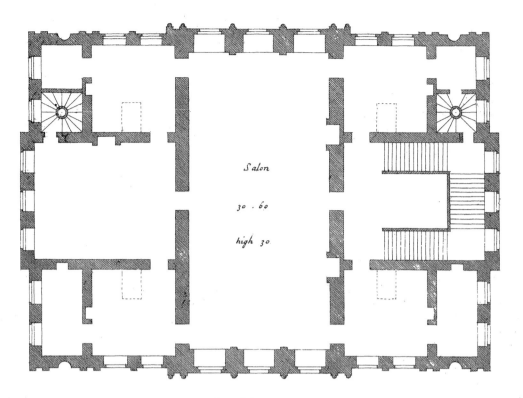

Plan of the Second Story.

Plan du Second Etage.

60 Feet |———————————————| Extends 100

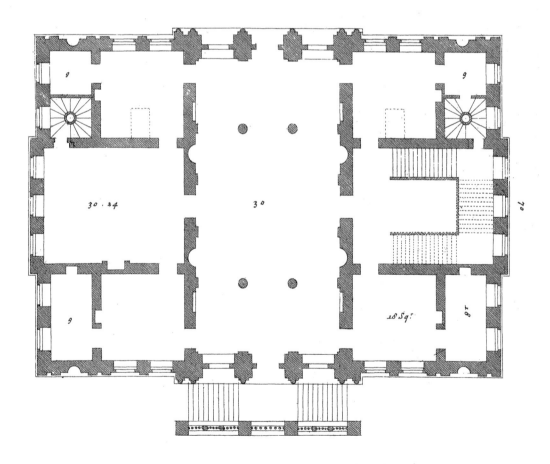

Plan of the first Story of my Design for M.ʳ Secretary Methuen.

Plan du premier Etage.

This New Design of my Invention in the Theatrical Style, is most humbly Inscrib'd to the R.t Hon.ble Paul Methuen Esq.r principal Secretary of State &c:

Elevation d'un Nouveau Dessein de mon Invention.

Co: Campbell Inv: et Delin:

H: Hulsbergh Sc:

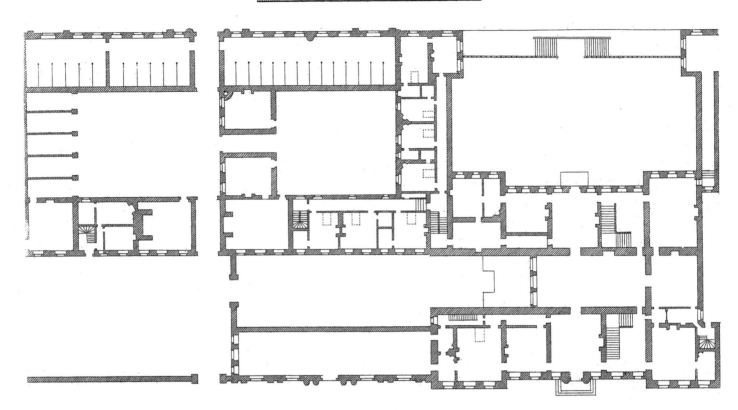

Plan of the principal Story of Dyrham house.

Plan du principal Etage de la Maison de Dyrham.

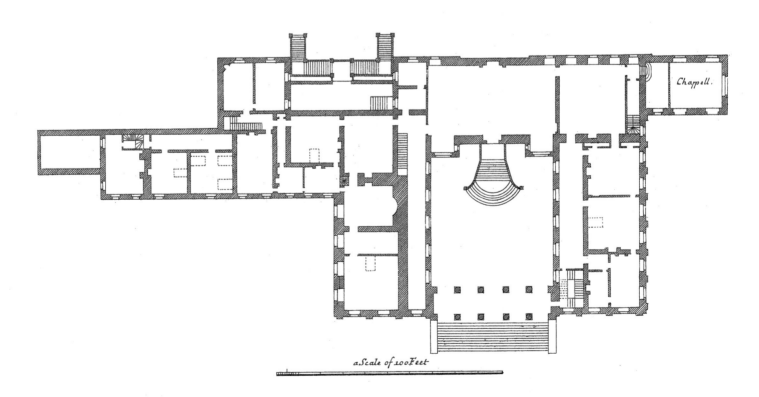

Chappell.

a Scale of 100 Feet

Plan of the principal Story of Wittham.

Plan du principal Etage de Wittham.

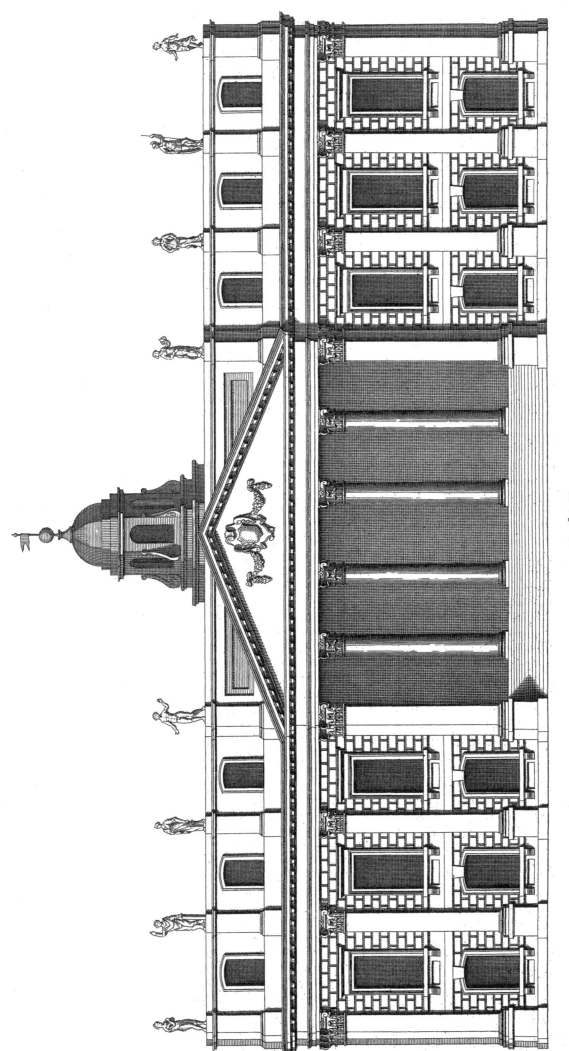

Ca: Campbell Delin:

H:Hulsbergh Sc:

The Elevation of Wittham in Somersetshire, the Seat of the R.t Hon.ble S.r William Wyndham Bar.t: to whom this Plate is most humbly Inscrib'd.

Elevation de la Maison de Wittham, dans la Comté de Somerset.

a Scale of 60 Feet

Extendi 140.

Ca: Campbell Delin:

H.Hulßbergh Sculp:

Extend: 130

40 Feet

The Elevation of Dyrham house in Glocester-shire the Seat of the R.t Hon.ble William Blathwayt Esq.r
to whom this Plate is most humbly Inscrib'd. Invented by M.r Talman.

Elevation de la Maison de Derham dans la Comté de Glocester.

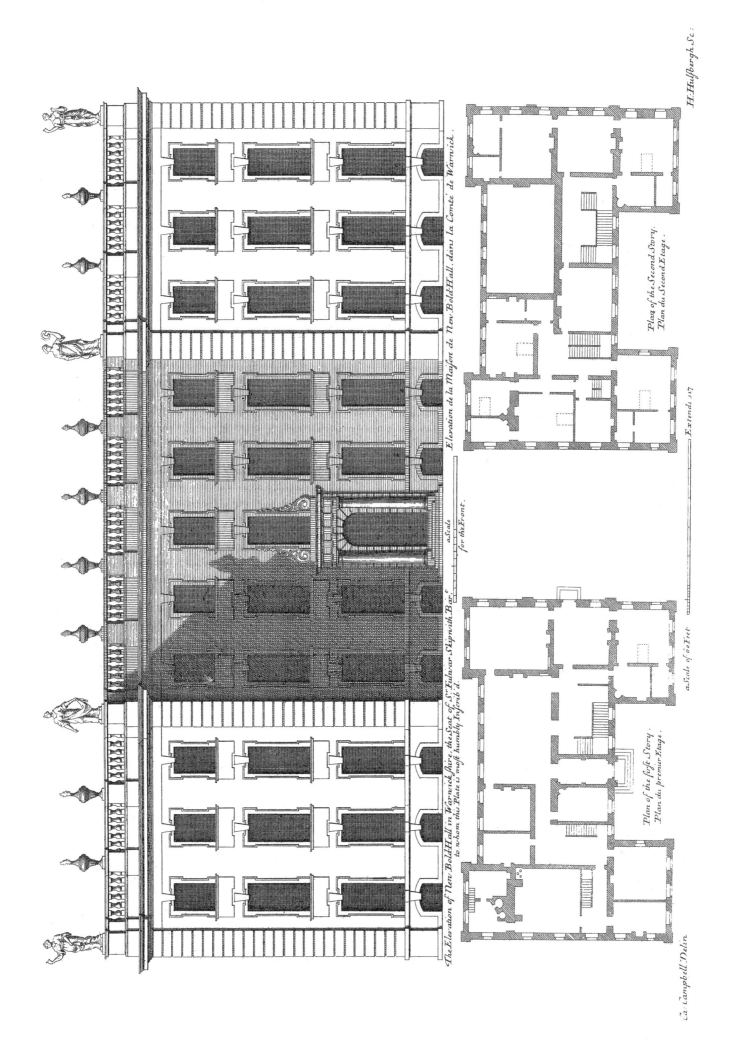

The Elevation of New Bold Hall in Warwickshire, the Seat of St Fulwar Skipwith Bart. to whom this Plate is most humbly Inscrib'd.

Elevation de la Maison de New Bold Hall, dans la Comté de Warwick.

Plan of the Second Story.
Plan du Second Etage.

Plan of the first Story.
Plan du premier Etage.

a Scale for the Front.

a Scale of 60 Feet

Extend 117

C: Campbell Delin.

H: Hulsbergh Sc:

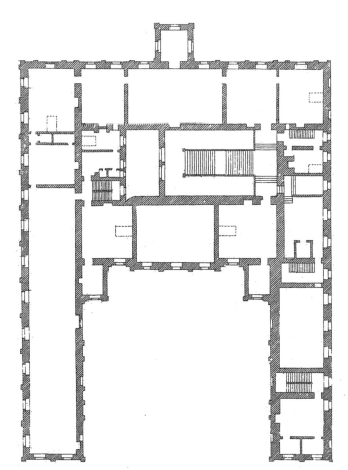

Plan of the Second Story.
Plan du Second Etage.

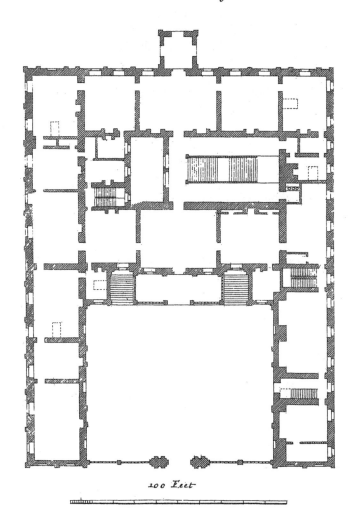

100 Feet

Plan of the first Story of Althrop.
Plan du premier Etage

Cu: Campbell Delin:

H.Hulsbergh Sc:

a Scale of 60 Feet

Extends 139 - 3 .

The Elevation of Althrop in Northampton Shire. The Seat of the R.t Hon.ble the Earl of Sunderland &c:
to whom this Plate is most humbly Inscrib'd .

Elevation de sa Maison D'Althrop dans la Comté de Northampton.

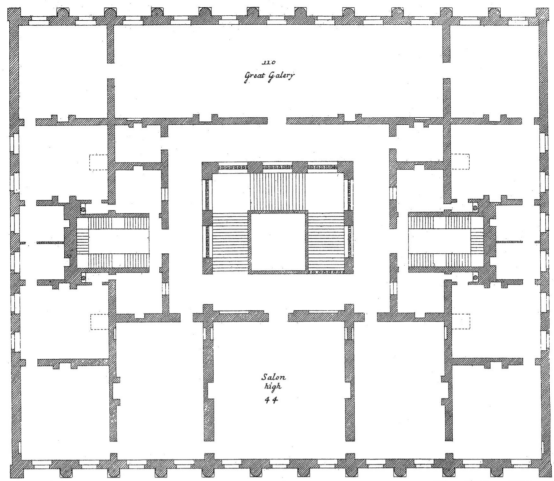

110
Great Galery

Salon
high
44

Plan of the Second Story   60 Feet   Extends 180   Plan du Second Etage.

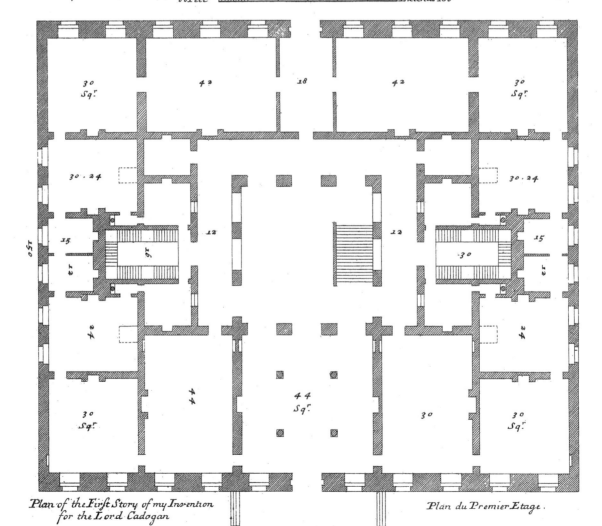

30
Sqr.   42   18   42   30
Sqr.

30 . 24   30 . 24

15   12   12   15

44
Sqr.

30
Sqr.   30   30
Sqr.

Plan of the First Story of my Invention
for the Lord Cadogan   Plan du Premier Etage.

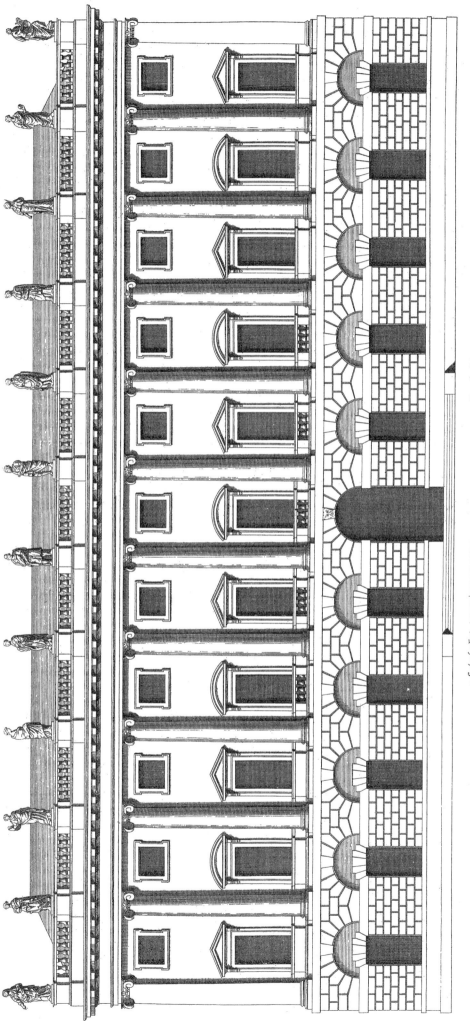

The Elevation of a New Design of my Invention in the Palatial Stile, is most humbly Inscrib'd to the R.t Hon.ble the Lord Cadogan, his Majesty's Ambassador Extraordinary to the States General, L.t Gen.ll of his Majesty's Forces, Governor of the Isle of Wight, and K.t of the most Ancient Order of the Thistle &c.

Elevation D'un Nouveau Dessein de mon Invention.

a Scale of 40 Feet   Extends 180 0

Co: Campbell Inv.r et Delin: H.Hulsbergh Sculp:

THE
THIRD VOLUME
OF
Vitruvius Britannicus :
OR, THE
BRITISH ARCHITECT.

CONTAINING

The *Geometrical PLANS* of the moſt Conſiderable
GARDENS and *PLANTATIONS*; alſo the PLANS,
ELEVATIONS, and SECTIONS of the moſt *Regular* BUILDINGS,
not Publiſhed in the *Firſt and Second Volumes*. With *Large* VIEWS,
in *Perſpective*, of the moſt Remarkable *Edifices* in *Great Britain*.

Engraven by the Beſt Hands *in* One Hundred *large Folio* PLATES.

By *COLEN CAMPBELL*, Eſquire,
Architect to His ROYAL HIGHNESS *the* PRINCE *of* WALES.

VITRUVIUS BRITANNICUS:
O U,
L' Architecte Britannique :

CONTENANT

Les *PLANS* des *JARDINS* les Plus Conſiderables,
Auſſi les PLANS, ELEVATIONS, & SECTIONS des BATIMENS *Reguliers*,
ne ſont pas encore publies dans les *Deux Premiers Tomes*. Avec quelques
VEUES, en *Perſpective*, des *Maſons* les plus *Celebres* de la *Grande Bretagne*.

Compris en 100 *grandes* Planches *gravez en taille douce par les* plus habiles Maitres.

Par Le Sieur *CAMPBELL*,
Architecte de Son ALTESSE ROYALE *Le* PRINCE *de* GALLES.

TOME III.

CUM PRIVILEGIO REGIS.

LONDON,
Printed ; And Sold by the AUTHOR, at his Houſe in *Middle Scotland-Yard*,
White-Hall ; And by JOSEPH SMITH, at the Sign of *Inigo Jones*'s Head, near
Exeter-'Change, in the *Strand*. M. DCC. XXV.

TO HIS

ROYAL HIGHNESS

GEORGE,

Prince of WALES, &c.

THE

THIRD VOLUME

OF

VITRUVIUS BRITANNICUS;

OR, THE

BRITISH ARCHITECT,

Is Moſt Humbly Inſcribed :

BY,

May it Pleaſe Your HIGHNESS,

YOUR ROYAL HIGHNESS'ſ

Moſt Faithful, Moſt Humble,

And Moſt Obedient Servant,

And ARCHITECT,

Colen Campbell.

A LIST of the SUBSCRIBERS.

Our Sovereign LORD KING GEORGE.
Their Royal Highnesses the Prince and Princess of WALES.
His Royal Highness Prince FREDERICK.
His Royal Highness the Duke of YORK.

A

DUKE of St. Albans, Captain of the Band of Pensioners 1
Duke of Ancaster, Lord Great Chamberlain of England 2
Duke of Argyle, Ld. Steward of the Houshold 2
Marquess of Annandale 2
Earl of Albemarle 2
Earl of Arran 1
Lord Ashburnham 1
Sir John Anstruther Bart. 1
Sir Jacob Astley Bart. 1
Sir Robert Adair Knt. 1
Joseph Addison Esq; 1
John Arbuthnott M. D. 2
David Anderson S. T. D. 1
James Anderson D. V. M. 1
Hon. Richard Arundel Esq; 1
Mr. Gabriel Appleby 1
James Anderson Gent. 1
Sir H. Aucher Bart. 1
John Aislabie Esq; 1
Jacob Aickworth Esq; 1
John Allen Esq; 1
Andrew Archer Esq; 1
Thomas Archer Esq; 1
Francis Annesley Esq; 1
Alexander Abercrombie Esq; 1
Richard Atherton Esq; 1
Coll. John Armstrong 1
Mr. St. Andre Chyrurgeon 1
Mr. William Ayres Carpenter 1
Mr. Francis Anderton 1
Mr. James Ayres 1
Mr. Thomas Acres Gardener 1

B

HIS Highness Prince Augustus Wilhelm, Duke of Brunswick-Lunenberg 1
Duke of Bedford 1
Duke of Beaufort 1
Duke of Buckingham 2
Duke of Bolton 2
Duke of Bridgwater 2
Dutchess of Buccleugh 2
Earl of Berkeley 1
Earl of Berkshire 1
Earl of Burlington 2
Earl of Broadalbin 1
Earl of Buchan 1
Earl of Bute 1
Late Lord Viscount Bolinbroke 1
Lord Balmerinoch 1
Lord Bruce 1
Lord Berkeley of Stretton 1
Lord Bingley 1
Lord Bathurst 1
Lord Binning 1
Lord Belhaven 1
Lord Viscount Barington Shute 1
His Excellency Count Bothmar 1
His Excellency Baron Bernstorf 1
Baron Bentenreider 1
Hon. James Brudenell Esq; 1
Sir William Bennet 1
Sir Justus Beck Bart. 1
Sir Alexand. Brand of Brandsfield 1
Sir Roger Bradshaw Bart. 1
Sir Jacob Banks Knight 1
Sir James Bateman Bart. 1
Sir Griffith Boynton Bart. 1
Hon. George Baily Esq; one of the Lords of the Treasury 5
R. Hon. William Bromley Esq; 1
R. Hon. William Blathwayt Esq; 1
William Benson Esq; 1
John Boulter, of Gawthrope-Hall, Esq; 5
Edmond Boulter Esq; 1
Nathaniel Blackerby Esq; 1
William Burnet Esq; 1
Harry Benson Esq; 1
Benjamin Benson Esq; 1

Alexander Brodie of Brodie Esq; 1
Hon. Patte Bing Esq; 1
Henry Bromley Esq; 1
Coll. Martin Bladen 1
Stephen Bisse Esq; 1
John Basket Esq; 1
Tho Baker Esq; 1
John Bligh Esq; 1
—— Baird Esq; 1
Hon. John Bylos Esq; 1
Mr. George Bincks of Covent-Garden 5
Mr. John Blackwood Merchant 1
Mr. Char. Bridgman, Gardener 1
Mr. Robert Barker Joyner 1
Mr. William Baverstock, Joyner 1
Mr. Thomas Bowls, 1
Mr. John Blake, Sen. 1
Rev. Mr. Barker 1
Dr. Brookt, M. D. 1
Mr. Daniel Brown, Bookseller 1
Mr. Boswell 1
Rev. Mr. Bowles 1
The Bodleian Library at Oxford 1
Mr. Badslade, Land Surveyor 1
Mr. Francis Bickerton 1
Mr. Burrows, Bookseller 2
Mr. Jonas Brown, Bookseller 1
Mr. Will. Brown of Shaftsbury 1
Mr. Nicholas Blake, Carpenter 1
Mr. Richard Brown 1
Mr. James Bateman 1
Mr. James Blacket, Joyner 1
Mr. Francis Bird, Statuary 1
Mr. Thomas Beale, Carpenter 1

C

LORD Carleton, President of the Council 1
Duke of Chandois 2
Earl Cowper 2
Earl of Carlisle 2
Earl of Cholmondeley 2
His Excel. the Earl Cadogan 1
Earl Coningsby 1
Earl of Cardigan 1
Earl of Coventry 1
Lord Clinton 1
Lord Cobham 1
Lord Castle-Comer 1
Lord Craven 1
Lord Colerane 1
Lord Castlemain 3
Lord Chetwynd 1
Lord Carmichael 1
Lord Carpenter 1
Lady Cairnes 1
Lady Cary 1
Hon. Coll. Charles Cadogan 1
Sir Thomas Clargis Bart. 1
Sir Nicholas Carew Bart. 1
Right Hon. Thomas Coke Esq; 1
Tho. Coke of Norfolk-street Esq; 1
Sir Archibald Campbell Knt. 1
Sir Duncan Campbell Bart. 1
Sir Hugh Campbell, of Calder, Bar. 1
Sir James Campbell, of Ardkinglass, Bart. 5
Sir James Campbell, of Achinbrake, Bart. 1
Sir Ja. Campbell, of Abruchill Bar. 1
Hon. John Campbell Esq; 1
Hon. Coll. James Campbell Esq; 1
Hon. Coll. John Campbell Esq; 1
Archibald Campbell Esq; 1
Daniel Campbell Esq; 1
Duncan Campbell Esq; 1
Capt. Matthew Campbell Esq; 1
John Campbell Esq; 1
John Campbell, of Calder, Esq; 1
Colen Campbell Esq; 1
Colen Campbell, of S. James's, Esq; 1
Sir Duncan Campbell, of Locknell, Bart. 5
Collonel Charles Churchill 1
Sir James Carmichael Bart, 1

Sir James Cuningham Bart. 1
Hon. Coll. James St. Clair 1
Hon. Thomas Cornwallis 1
Sir Thomas Cross Bart. 1
Sir Robert Child Knt. 1
Sir Alexander Cummins Knt. 1
Hon. George Clarke Esq; 1
Hon. Coll. Charles Cathcart 1
Henry Colley Esq; 1
R. Creswell Esq; 1
George Gulworth Esq; 1
Thomas Cary, Esq; 2
Henry Cuningham Esq; 1
Charles Cæsar Esq; 1
Courtney Crooker Esq; 1
Hon. Charles Cecil Esq; 1
R. Hon. Spencer Compton Esq; Speaker of the House of Commons 1
William Clayton Esq; 1
Edmund Clarke Esq; 1
—— Cholmly Esq; 1
Arthur Croft Esq; 1
Henry Cornelison Esq; 1
Edward Corbet Esq; 1
James Crooke Esq; 1
Mr. Cranenburgh 1
Mr. Chetwynd 1
John Corbett L. L. D. 1
Knightly Chetwood 1
Doctor Chamberlayn M. D. 1
Mr. Peter Courthope Merchant 1
Mr. John Churchill Carpenter 1
Mr. Thomas Churchill Bricklayer 1
Mr. Clements, Bookseller in Oxf. 1
Mr. Edward Cowper 1
Mr. William Cooper Carpenter 1
Mr. Joseph Carter of St. Albans 1
Mr. Richard Castle Gent. 1
Mr. Richard Castell 1

D

DUKE of Devonshire 2
Duke of Douglass 1
Duke of Dorset 2
Earl of Derby 1
Earl of Dartmouth 1
Earl of Denbigh 1
Lord Bishop of St. David's 1
Lord Digby 1
Lord Delawar 1
Lord Dalkeith 1
Lord Daruly 3
Sir James Dalrymple Bart. 1
Sir Matthew Decker Bart. 1
Hon. George Doddington Esq; 1
Hon. Coll. George Douglass 1
Brigadier Dormer 1
Collonel Dormer 1
Charles Delafay Esq; 1
Francis Delaval Esq; 1
Montague Gerard Drake Esq; 1
William Dashwood Esq; 1
William Dunn Esq; 1
Archibald Douglass Esq; 1
Thomas Dinely Esq; 1
George Dundass of Dundass Esq; 1
Captain N. Duboise 6
Mr. Daniel Delander 1
Mr. Dodd of Lincolns-Inn 1
Mr. William Dickinson 1
Mr. William Dissel 1
Mr. John Darby, Printer 1
Mr. Peter Dunoyer, Bookseller 1
Mrs. Dolben 1

E

JOHN Earl of Exeter 1
Earl of Essex 1
Rt. Hon. Lieut. General Erle 1
General Evans 1
Sir John Evelyn 1
Sir Gilbert Elliot of Minto, Bart. 1
Hon. R. Edgecombe Esq; 1
His Excellency Baron D'Erfe 2
John Elwick, Jun. Esq; 1
William Emmett Esq; 1

Mr. William Elliot 1
Mr. John Earle, Carpenter 1

F.

EARL of Findlater and Seafield 1
Lord Foley 1
Lord Forrester 1
Lord Fitzwilliams 1
Lord Finth 1
Sir Robert Furnese Bart. 1
Sir Thomas Frankland Bart. 1
Mr. Baron Fortescue 1
Richard Fuller L. L. D. 1
Mr. Auditor Foley 1
Hon. Collonel John Fane 1
Henry Fermor Esq; 1
John Freeman Esq; 1
William Freeman Esq; 1
Ralph Freeman Esq; 1
Thomas Frankland Esq; 1
James Fury Esq; 1
John Forbes, of Colloden, Esq; 1
Brian Fairfax Esq; 1
Mr. Alexander Fort 1
Mr. Lloyd Foley 1
Mr. Henry Fleetcroft 1
Mr. Joshua Fletcher, Mason 1

G.

DUKE of Grafton, Lord Chamberlain of the Houshold 2
Duke of Gordon 1
Earl of Godolphin 2
Earl of Grantham 1
Lord Guilford 1
Lord Viscount Gage 1
Lord Glenorchy 1
His Excel. Baron Goerts, &c. 1
Lady Elizabeth Germain 1
Sir William Gage Bart. 1
Sir Richard Grosvenar Bart. 1
Sir Robert Gordon Bart. 1
Sir William Gordon Bart. 1
Sir Samuel Garth M. D. 1
Glanville and Caius College 1
David Gansel Esq; 1
Westley Gill Esq; 1
Peter Giffard Esq; 1
Alexander Gordon of Pitburg Esq; 1
Alexander Grant Esq; Brigadier General 1
Francis Gwyn Esq; 1
William le Grand Esq; 1
William Gore Esq; 1
Richard Golf Esq; 1
Orlando Gee Esq; 1
Captain Alexander Geddes 1
Dr. Gibson. Prov. Qu. Col. Oxon. 1
Mr. Grahame 1
Robert Gray M. D. 1
Mr. Thomas Granger 1
Mr. Andrew Gelf 1
Mr. Glover, of Westminster 1
Mr. Greenway. 1

H.

DUKE of Hamilton and Brandon 1
Dutchess of Hamilton 2
Earl of Hallifax 2
Earl of Hopeton 2
Earl of Haddington 1
Lord Viscount Hatton 1
Lord How 1
Lord Haversham 1
Lord Hartington 1
Rt. Hon. Henry Lord Herbert 1
Hon. Robert Herbert Esq; 1
Bar. Hardenberg, Grand Marshal of Hanover 1
Sir Thomas Hanmer Bart. 1
Sir Roger Hill Bart. 1
Sir Joseph Hodges Bart. 1
Sir Charles Hotham Bart. 1
Sir John Harper Bart. 1
Hon. Philip Howard Esq; 1

Sir

Sir *John Hobart* Bart.   1
Sir *David Hamilton* Knt.   1
Sir *Roger Hudson* Knt.   1
John Henly of *Bristol* Esq;   1
Richard Hill of *Richmond* Esq;   1
Richard Hill of *Cleveland* Esq;   1
William Herbert Esq;   1
John Hedworth Esq;   1
John Huggins Esq;   1
Nicholas Hawksmoor Esq;   1
Francis Haws Esq;   1
Henry Hoare Esq;   1
William Heysham Esq;   1
Mrs. *Howard*   1
Thomas Heber Esq;   1
John Hallingius Esq; Envoy } from the D. of *Saxegotha*   1
John Hill Esq;   1
Mr. *Hopman*, Counsellor to } the Duke of *Holstein*   1
Baron *Hattorf*   2
Joseph Hall Esq;   1
John James Heidegger Esq;   1
William Hamilton Esq;   1
Maurice Hant Esq;   1
Brigadier *Honeywood*   1
Major *Hatley*   1
Edward Halsted Gent.   1
William Head Gent.   1
Michael Hutchinson D. D.   1
Captain *Horneck*   1
Mr. *John Hallam*   1
Mr. *Thomas Howlett*   1
Mr. *Henrichson*   1
Mr. *Richard Hill*   1
Mr. *John Hughs*, Plaisterer   1
Mr. *John Hare*   1
Mr. *Thomas Hinton*   1
Mr. *Robert Hind*   1
Mr. *Robert Halton*   1
Mr. *Henemines*   1
Mr. *John Harris*   1
Mr. *John Hulton*   1
Mr. *John Hodges* of *Derbyshire*   1
Mr. *Henry Hare* of *Docking*   1
Mr. *Thomas Hornby*   1

I.

EARL of *Islay*, Lord } Privy-Seal for *North-Britain*   2
Lord St. *John* of *Bletsoe*   1
Sir *Theodore Janssen* Kt. and Bar.   1
Sir *Henry Innes* Bart.   1
Sir *William Johnston* Bart.   1
Rt. Hon. *James Johnston* Esq;   1
Tobias Jenkins Esq;   1
Thomas Fett Esq;   1
Benjamin Jackson Esq;   1
The Rev. Mr. *Jervoys*   1
Mr. *And. Johnston* Engraver } at the *Golden Eagle* St. *Martin's* Lane.   30
Mr. *Tho. Johnson* at the *Hague*   26
Mr. *William Felks*   1
Mr. *Andrew Jelf*   1
Mr. *John James* of *Greenwich*   1
Mr. *William Jones*   1
Mr. *Henry Joines* of *Woodstock*   1
Mr. *Edward James*   1
Mr. *William Jones* F. R. S.   1

K.

DUKE of *Kingston*, Lord } Privy-Seal   5
Duke of *Kent*   2
Earl of *Kinnoul*   1
Lord Viscount *Kilsyth*   1
Lord Chief Justice *King*   1
Lord *Kingsale*   1
Robert Keck Esq;   1
John King D. D. Master of } the *Charter-House*   1
Dr. *King*, Principal of St. } *Mary-Hall*, *Oxon*.   1
Mr. *Thomas Kynaston*   1

L.

DUKE of *Leeds*   2
Earl of *Loudon*   2
Earl of *Lincoln*   1
Earl of *Litchfield*   1
Earl of *Leicester*   1
Earl of *Liesemore*   1
Lord *Lansdown*   1
Lord *Leimster*   1
Lord *Lonsdale*   1
Lord Bishop of *London*   1
Lord *Limington*   1
Lord *London Derry*   1
Right Hon. Lord *Lechmere*, } Chancellor of the Dutchy   1
Hon. *Anthony Lowther* Esq;   1
Collonel *Legonier*   1
John Law Esq;   1
Samuel Lynn Esq;   1
Audly Lynd Esq;   1
Christopher Lister Esq;   1
Henry Lawton Esq;   1

George Lockhart Esq;   1
Benjamin Lacy Esq;   1
Collonel *Leley*   1
James Lancy Esq;   1
Mr. *Leake*, of *Bath*, Bookseller   7
Mr. *John Lane*, Joyner   1
Mr. *Daniel Lock*   1
Mr. *Lockman*, St. *James's*   1
Mr. *John Leggat*   1
Mr. *William Low*   1

M.

DUKE of *Marlborough*   2
Dutchess of *Marlborough*   2
Duke of *Montague*   2
Dutchess of *Montague*   2
Duke of *Montrosse*   1
Duke of *Manchester*   1
Thomas Earl of *Macclesfield*   1
Earl of *Marchmount*   1
Late Earl of *Mareshall*   1
Late Earl of *Marr*   2
Lord *Mansell*   1
Lord *Middleton*   1
Lord *William Manors*   1
Lord *Micklethwaite*   1
Sir *William Mansell* Bart.   1
Sir *Christopher Musgrave* Bart.   1
Sir *Nicholas Morice* Bart.   1
Sir *Robert Masham* Bart.   1
Sir *Philip Meadows* Bart.   1
Rt. Hon. *Paul Methuen* Esq; } Compt. of the Houshold   1
Brigadier *Richard Munden*   1
Thomas Murray Esq;   1
John Montgommery Esq;   1
Humphrey Mildmay Esq;   1
Edward Minshoul Esq;   1
Thomas Milner Esq;   1
William Maynard Esq;   1
William Monck of *Ireland* Esq;   1
George Maddison Esq;   1
Abraham Meure Esq;   1
John Moyser of *Beverley* Esq;   1
John Mulcaster Esq;   1
John Monkton of *Hodroyd* Esq;   1
James Manley Esq;   1
Mr. Secretary *Molineux*   1
Captain *Mandell*   1
Doctor *Mead* M. D.   1
Mr. *Collet Mawhood*   1
Mr. *John Mum Moor*   1
Mr. *Arthur Manley*   1
Mr. *Georgee Montgommery*   1
Mr. *Isaac Mars*   1
The Rev. Mr. *John Maxwell*   1
Mr. *John Mount*   1
Mr. *Roger Morris*   1
Mr. *John Meards*   1
Mr. *Richard Mason* Joiner   1
Mr. *John Manley*   1
Mr. *Mahomet* of St. *James's*   1
Mr. *Mustapha*   1
Mr. *Isaac Mansfield*, Plaisterer   1

N.

DUKE of *Newcastle*, Principal Secretary of State }   2
Duke of *Norfolk*   1
Earl of *Nottingham*   1
Earl of *Northampton*   1
Lord *Newborough*   1
Grey Neville Esq;   1
Edward Nicholas Esq;   1
Michael Newton Esq;   1
Ralph Noden, Merchant   1
General *Nicholson*   1
Mr. *Nante*   1
Mr. *Newcome* of *Hackney*   1
Mr. *John Nordich*, Bricklayer   1

O.

LATE Duke of *Ormonde*   1
Earl of *Orford*   1
Earl of *Orrery*   1
Earl of *Orkney*   2
Robert Earl of *Oxford*   2
Edward Earl of *Oxford*   2
Lord *Onslow*   1
Mr. *Isaac Olley*   1
Mr. *Edward Olives*   1

P.

DUKE of *Powis*   1
Duke of *Portland*   1
Earl *Paulet*   1
Earl of *Pembroke*   2
Lord *Percival*   1
Stephen Poynton Esq; His Majesty's Envoy Extra. and } Pleni. to the K. of *Sweden*   1
Sir *Gregory Page* Bart.   1
Sir *Robert Pollock* Bart.   1
Sir *Joseph Pringle*   1
Sir *Walter Pringle*   1
Sir *John Packington* Bart.   1
Sir *Thomas Pendergrafs*   1
His Excel. Major-Gen. *Pepper*   1
His Excel. Governor *Pitts*   1

Hon. *Henry Pelham* Esq;   1
William Phipps Esq;   1
R. Hon. *William Poultney* Esq;   1
Robert Pringle Esq;   1
Blackwell Perkins Esq;   1
John Pringle of *Haining* Esq;   1
Uvedale Price Esq;   1
Collonel *Paget*   1
John Plumptre Esq;   2
Sylvester Pettyt Gent.   1
Mr. *John Price*, jun.   8
Mr. *Francis Price*   1
Mr. *Alexander Prichard*, Mason   1
Mr. *John Price* of *Richmond*   1
Mr. *James Paget*, Mason   1
Captain *Charles Pearce*   1
Mr. *Andrew Peters*, Painter   1
Mr. *Barth. Peisley* of *Ox.* Mason   1
Mr. *Thomas Paine*, Joiner   1

Q.

DUKE of *Queensbury*   1
The Library of *Queen's* } *College Oxon*   1

R.

DUKE of *Richmond*   2
Dutchess of *Richmond*   1
Duke of *Rutland*   1
Duke of *Roxburgh*, Principal Secretary of State for } *North-Britain*   2
Earl of *Rochester*   1
Earl of *Rothes*   1
Earl of *Roseberry*   1
Right Hon. the Lord *Romney*   1
Sir *William Robinson* Bart.   1
Thomas Rawlinson Esq;   1
Brigadier-General *Richards*   1
Thomas Robinson Esq;   1
Richard Rooth Esq;   1
Hugh Rose of *Kilravock* Esq;   1
John Rose Esq;   1
Benjamin Robinson Esq;   1
Samuel Ravenel Esq;   1
John Rudg Esq;   1
Rev. Mr. *Richardson*   1
Mr. *James Richards*, his Majesty's Carver }   1
Mr. *Ripley*, Clerk of the *Meuse*   1
Mr. *Alexander Read*, Painter   1
Mr. *John Richards*   1
Mr. *John Roper*   1

S.

DUKE of *Somerset*   2
Duke of *Shrewsbury*   2
Marquess of *Seaforth*   1
Earl of *Sunderland*   2
Earl of *Scarborough*   1
Earl of *Strafford*   2
Earl of *Stamford*   1
Earl of *Sutherland*   1
Earl of *Stafford*   1
Lord *Somervill*   1
Earl of *Stairs*   1
Earl *Stanhope*   2
Earl of *Sussex*   1
Lord *Somers*   1
Lord *Shelburne*   1
Count *Staremberg*   1
Lord *Stanhope*   1
Sir *Fullwar Skipwith* Bart.   1
Sir *Edmund Smith* of *Essex* Bart.   1
Sir *Thomas Seabright* Bart.   1
Lady *Seabright*   1
Sir *William Stewart* Bart.   1
Sir *John Smith* Bart.   1
Sir *Edward Seymore* Bart.   1
Sir *Edward Simeon* Bart.   1
Rt. Hon. *Edward Southwell* Esq;   1
James Stuart, of *Torrence*, Esq;   1
Sir *James Stuart*   1
Sir *Hans Sloane* M. D.   1
Sir *Edward Smith*   1
Sir *George Stuart*, of *Garrinlily* Bart. }   1
Brigadier-General *Stearne*   1
Dr. *Steygersdale*, Physician } to his Majesty   2
His Excellency Baron *Shack*   1
Sir *William Strickland*   1
Sir *Robert Sutton*, Bart.   1
Sir *Robert Stapleton* Bart.   1
Charles Stanhope Esq;   1
Collonel *Selwin*   1
David Scot Esq;   1
Thomas Strangeways Esq;   1
James Sadler Esq;   1
Thomas Smith Esq;   1
John Smith Esq;   1
Rev. Dr. *Shippen*   1
Rev. *Joseph Smith* D. D.   1
Mr. *Thomas Sayer*   1
Mr. *Sargent* of the *Tower*   1
Mr. *Henry Smart*, Mason   1
Mr. *William Sandiver*   1
Mr. *Edward Strong*, Mason   4

Mr. *John Sturget*   1
Mr. *Andrew Smith*   1
Mr. *Thomas Sadler*   1
Mr. *Thomas Suder*   1
Mr. *George Sampson*   1
Mr. *Richard Sanders*, Joiner   1
Mr. *John Sturt*, Engraver   1
Mr. *Standfast* of *Westminster Hall*   7
Mr. *Sturler*   1
Mrs. *Elizabeth Southwell*   1
Mrs. *Ann Stone*   1

T.

MARQUESS of *Tweedale*   1
Earl of *Thanet*   1
Earl of *Tankerville*   1
Earl of *Thomond*   1
Lord Visc. *Townshend*, Principal Secretary of State }   1
Lord Viscount *Tyrconnel*   1
Lord *Tarbat*   1
Collonel *Tyrel*   1
Sir *James Thornhill* Knt.   1
Hon. *Richard Tigh* Esq;   1
James Taylor Esq;   1
William Thompson Esq;   1
Joseph Thompson Esq;   1
Cholmondeley Turner Esq;   1
John Talbot Esq;   1
William Tomlins Esq;   1
John Talman Esq;   1
Samuel Thompson Esq;   1
John Turvin Esq;   1
Captain *Tusfnel* of *Westminster*   1
Mr. *Thomas Taylor*   1
Mr. *Turvin*   1
Mr. *Joseph Towtnum*   1
Mr. *Taylor* of *Stafford*   1
George Torriano, Merchant   1

V.

HIS Excel. Baron *Doiver Vorde*, Ambass. Extra. } from the States-General   1
Count *Volkra*, Imperial Envoy   1
Sir *John Vanbrugh* Knight   1
Bowater Vernon Esq;   1
Henry Vernon Esq; of *Sudbury*   1
James Vernon Esq;   1
John Upton Esq;   1
Alexander Urquhart Esq;   1
Mr. *Vaillant*, at the *Hague*   20
Mr. *Paul Vaillant*   4
Mr. *Vanderhooker*, Bookseller   7
Mr. *Vanhuls*   1

W.

DUKE of *Wharton*   1
Earl of *Weymise*   1
Earl of *Warwick*   1
Earl of *Westmoreland*   1
Lord Viscount *Weymouth*   1
Lord Bishop of *Winchester*   1
Thomas Ld. Bishop of *Waterford*   1
Lord *Walgrave*   1
Right Hon. *Robert Walpole* Esq; First Lord Commissioner of the Treasury }   1
Rt. Hon. Lord *Walpole*   1
Sir *William Wyndham* Bart.   1
Sir *John Walter* Bart.   1
Sir *Thomas Webster* Bart.   1
Sir *Robert Worsley* Bart.   1
General *Wade*   1
Sir *Anthony Wiscombe* Bart.   1
General *Wills*   1
Christopher Wren Esq;   1
John Wolf Esq;   1
Edmond Waller Esq;   1
William Wakefield Esq;   1
Thomas Woodcock Esq;   1
William Wickham, Jun. Esq;   1
Tho. Walker of the *Temple* Esq;   1
Humphrey Wild Esq;   1
Richard Wynne Esq;   1
John Warburton Esq; F. R. S.   1
Leonard Wooddison Esq;   1
David Wemys Esq;   1
Hon. *Thomas Willoughby* Esq;   1
Mr. *William West*   1
Mr. *Richard Wick*, his Majesty's Watchmaker }   1
Doctor *Welwood* M. D.   1
Mr. Serjeant *Wynne*   1
Mr. *Samuel Waters*   1
Mr. *Robert Wood*   1
Mr. *James Williams*, Mason   1
Mr. *Isaac Whood*, Painter   1
Mr. *John Woodall*   1
Mr. *William Woolvin*   1
Mr. *Thomas Wheately*, Carpenter   1
Mr. *John Williamson* of *Dublin*   1
Mr. *Wetsten* at *Amsterdam*   26
Mrs. *Margaret Weld*   1

Y.

WILLIAM Lord Archbishop of *York* }   1
Sir *Walter Yonge* Bart.   1

AN
EXPLANATION
Of ALL the PLATES
In the THIRD VOLUME.

Greenwich Hospital *in Perspective, p.* 3, *and* 4.

 Have said so much of this noble Structure in my First Volume, that I shall add nothing at present, but to assure the Readers, that the Perspective is raised from the Geometrical Plan and Elevation according to the most exact Rules of that lineary Art.

Castle Howard *in Perspective, p.* 5, *and* 6.

THIS Seat being also so fully described in the First Volume, I thought nothing could be further wanting to give a perfect Idea of the Place, but an accurate View of the same in Perspective.

Ambresbury, *p.* 7.

IS the Seat of the Right Honourable the Lord Carleton, in *Wiltshire.* This House was designed by *Inigo Jones,* and executed by Mr. *Webb.* Here is a bold rustick Basement, which supports a regular Loggio of the Composed Order. In one Plate I have given the Plans of the First and Second Story, with the principal Front. The great Staircase is remarkable here for having a little one in the Middle of it. *Anno* 1661.

Castle Ashby, *p.* 8.

IN *Northamptonshire,* the Seat of the Right Honourable the Earl of *Northampton.* The greatest Part of the Castle is very antient; but in the Reign of King *Charles* I. *Inigo Jones* was imployed to rebuild it, and finish one Front; but the Civil Wars put a Stop to all Arts, 1642. when that valiant Earl was slain at *Salt Heath* near *Stafford.* In this Plate I have also given Two Plans, and that Front by *Inigo Jones.*

Stoke Park, *p.* 9.

THE Seat of Mr. *Arundel* in *Northamptonshire.* This Building was begun by *Inigo Jones;* the Wings, and Collonades, and all the Foundations, were made by him; but the Front of the House was designed by another Architect, the Civil Wars having also interrupted this Work. In one Plate I have given both a general Plan and Front 1640.

General Wade's *House, p.* 10.

IN great *Burlington-Street, London.* This beautiful Design is the Invention of the Right Honourable the Earl of *Burlington,* who is not only a great Patron of all Arts, but the first Architect. His Lordship's learned Labours in this Art, which are now preparing for the Publick, will give a much juster Idea of his consummate Knowledge in Architecture, than any thing I am capable to say. In one Plate you have Two Plans, and the principal Front 1724.

Grimsthorpe, *p.* 11, 12, 13, *and* 14.

IN *Lincolnshire,* the Seat of his Grace the Duke of *Ancaster* and *Kesteven.* Of this I have made Four Plates, the First is the Plan of the First or principal Story, where all the Apartments are exactly figured. In the Second Plate you have the Front to the Court; in the Third, the Garden Front, adorned with a magnificent *Corinthian Portico*; and in the Fourth, you have the *West* Front the *East* Front being the same. All designed by Sir *John Vanbrugh, Anno* 1724.

Eastbury, *p.* 15, 16, 17, 18, 19.

IN *Dorsetshire,* the Seat of the Right Honourable *George Doddington,* Esquire, in Five Plates. The First contains an exact Plan of the Gardens, designed and finished by the ingenious Mr. *Charles Bridgeman.* In the Second, you have the general Plan of the House and Out-Offices, with a Table of References. In the Third Plate, an Elevation of the principal Front, with a rusticated Portico of the Dorick Order. In the Fourth, the Plan and Elevation of the great Portico, placed at the End of the Garden facing the House. The Portico is *Corinthian Hexastile.* The Columns 3 Feet Diameter, the most magnificent of its Kind in *England.* The Fifth contains the Plan and Elevation of the *Bagnio* in the Garden, fronting the Bowling Green. All designed and executed by Sir *John Vanbrugh, Anno* 1718.

Seaton Delaval, *p.* 20, 21.

IN *Northumberland,* the Seat of *Francis Delaval,* Esquire, in Two Plates. In the First, I have given the general Plan of the House and Out-Offices, with the *North* Front of the House to a larger Scale. In the Second, you have the *South* Front, where is a noble *Portico* of the *Ionick* Order Tetrastile, the Columns 3 Feet Diameter. All designed and executed by Sir *John Vanbrugh, Anno* 1720.

Burlington House *in* Piccadilly, London, *p.* 22, 23, 24, 25, 26.

THE following Designs of my Invention are contained in Two single, and one double Plate. In the First you have the general Plan of the House and Offices; the Stables were built by another Architect before I had the Honour of being called to his Lordship's Service, which obliged me to make the Offices opposite, conformable to them. The Front of the House, the Conjunction from thence to the Offices, the great Gate and Street Wall, were all designed and executed by me. In the double Plate you have the principal Front, where a bold rustick Basement supports a regular *Ionick* Collonade of ¾ Columns 2 Feet Diameter. The Line is closed with Two Towers, adorned with Two *Venetian* Windows in Front, and Two Niches

Niches in Flank, fronting each other, where the noble Patron has prepar'd the Statues of *Palladio* and *Jones*, in Honour to an Art of which he is the Support and Ornament. In the next Plate you have the great Gate, adorned with 4 ¼ Columns of the Dorick Order, 2 Feet Diameter, agreeable to the Colonade in the Court. In the laſt I have given the Plan and Elevation of the Caſina at *Chiſwick*, which is the Firſt Eſſay of his *Lordſhip*'s happy Invention, *Anno* 1717.

Houghton *from p.* 27, *to p.* 34, *incluſive*,

IN *Norfolk*, the Seat of the Right Honourable *Robert Walpole*, Eſquire, Chancellor of the *Exchequer*, and firſt Commiſſioner of his Majeſty's Treaſury, of which I have made Two double, and Four ſingle, Plates. In the Firſt you have a Plan of the Gardens and Plantations, which are very large and beautiful. In the Subſequent are all the Deſigns of my Invention; Firſt, the general Plan and Front of the Houſe and Offices, extending 450 Feet. The Firſt ſingle Plate contains the Plans of the principal and Attick Story: The great Hall is a Cube of 40 Feet, the Salon 40 by 30 Feet, and 30 Feet high, and all the other Rooms in the Four great Apartments, are 18 Feet high, the Attick Story 12 Feet, and the Ruſtick Story the ſame, all above Ground, under which is an intire Story of Cellars, all arched. In the Second Plate I have given the Front to the great Entrance, extending 166 Feet, lying open to the Park. The Baſement is ruſtick, and I have alſo ruſticated the Windows and Door-Caſe in the principal Story; the Building is finiſhed with Two Towers, dreſs'd with Two ruſtick *Venetian* Windows. In the next Plate is the Front to the Garden, with a regular *Portico Tetraſtile Ionick*, the Columns 3 Feet ½ Diameter. In this Front the Windows of the principal Story are dreſs'd without Ruſticks. The laſt Plate is the Section of the great Hall, all in Stone, the moſt beautiful in *England*; the whole Building is Stone, and, without pretending to excuſe any ſeeming, or real Defects, I believe, it will be allowed to be a Houſe of State and Conveniency, and, in ſome Degree, worthy of the great and generous Patron. *Anno* 1722.

Mereworth Caſtle, *p.* 35, 36, 37, 38.

IN *Kent*, the Seat of the Honourable *John Fane*, Eſquire, contained in One double, and Two ſingle, Plates. In the double Plate you have Three Plans of the Ground Story, the principal and Attick: The Ground Story extends 220 by 120 Feet, all arched, and 12 Feet high. In the Middle is a circular Veſtibule 34 Feet Diameter, turned with one bold Arch, illuminated by Two Windows at each End of the Traverſe Paſſage, and by Night one Lanthorn, ſuſpended from the Key Stone of this great Arch, lights into Twenty diſtinct Rooms. The Aſcent is 12 Feet high to the principal Story, being, by Two Flights of Steps, 42 Feet broad; the Square of the Houſe is 88 Feet; but including the Four *Porticoes* 120 Feet. As the Rooms of this Story are of various Extents, ſo is the Height: The Two Rooms in Front being 35 Feet by 20 Feet, and the great Gallery in the oppoſite Front 82 Feet by 20 Feet, are 22 Feet ½ high, and coved ¼: The Side Rooms, conſiſting of Two Bed-Chambers 22 Feet by 20 Feet, and Two dreſſing Rooms 14 Feet by 20 Feet, are only 15 Feet high, not coved; ſo that the Entablature of all theſe Rooms is of the ſame Height. Over the Rooms not coved, and under the Attick Story, are Mezonins for Servants, and other Conveniencies: The Circular Salon in the Center is 35 Feet Diameter, and 60 Feet high, receiving Light by Four large circular Windows in the Dome, which is finiſhed in Stucco, with Compartments much after the Manner of the Ritonda. The Ornaments are executed by *Signor Bagutti*, a moſt ingenious Artiſt. The Aſcent to the Attick Story is by Two circular Stair-Caſes, landing in a Poggio, round the great Salon, which leads into all the Apartments of this Floor, being 12 Feet high, and the Plan will ſufficiently deſcribe the reſt. The Firſt ſingle Plate contains the *North* Front: The Four *Porticoes* are all the ſame, being Hexaſtile, Euſtile: The Column *Ionick* 2 Feet ¼ Diameter; a juſt Entablature ſurrounds the whole Building, with the proper Members inriched. In the laſt Plate is the Section from *North* to *South*, extending 220 Feet. I ſhall not pretend to ſay, That I have made any Improvements in this Plan from that of *Palladio*, for *Signor Almerico*; but ſhall only obſerve the Alterations, which I humbly ſubmit to my learned Judges: The new Plan is much enlarged, and the Ground Story intirely different. In *Palladio* the Veſtibule is ſupported by Four Pires in the Middle, without any Light. In the principal Story are Four large, and Four ſmall, Rooms, but no Gallery, nor large Bed-Chambers: The Four *Porticoes* are flanked with a Wall, which are intirely open in this. In the Firſt the Stair Caſes are Triangular, which puts the Doors at unequal Diſtances. In this the Stair-Caſes, being circular, brings the Doors to anſwer the Two diagonal Lines. In the Firſt there are but Four Chimneys, which are brought up by Four Obeliſks on the Outſide Walls. The Dome is a Semi-circular Octogon covered with Red Pantiles, ſupported by Carpentry. The Columns in the *Porticoes* are Brick-work covered with Stucco. The Entablature of Wood, and all the other Ornaments are in Stucco. This Dome conſiſts of Three Shells: The Firſt is Carpentry with Stucco, which forms the Cieling of the Salon. The Outward is alſo Carpentry, covered with Lead, but of a particular Contourn: Between theſe Two Shells, there is a ſtrong Brick Arch, that brings 24 Funnels to the Lanthorn, which is finiſhed with a Copper Callot, without any Injury to the Smoke, which was not the leaſt difficult Part of the Deſign. And, if I may add the great Difference, both of Dreſs and Materials, the whole ornamental Parts being of *Portland* Stone; and as much inriched, as the Rules of our Art can admit. And here I am, in Juſtice, to acknowledge the Faults as only chargeable to me; for never Architect had a more beneficent and liberal Patron, where neither Ignorance, Caprice, or Covetouſneſs, had any Part. Here nothing was wanting for Strength, Conveniency, or Ornament. Under ſuch uncommon Encouragement, I have uſed my utmoſt Endeavours; but, *Humanum eſt labi*; It is the beſt Houſe that has feweſt Faults: And if it gives Satisfaction to the Honourable and Worthy Owner, I have my End. This Houſe was covered in *Anno* 1723.

Wanſtead, *p.* 39, 40.

IN *Eſſex*, the Seat of the Right Honourable the Lord Viſcount *Caſtlemain*. I have given the Plan, Elevation, and Section, of this great Houſe in my firſt Volume, which I ſhall not reſume here, but only give the Front with the Addition of the new Towers, which I deſigned. *Anno* 1720.

Stourhead-Caſtle, *p.* 41, 42, 43.

IN *Wiltſhire*, the Seat of *Henry Hoare*, Eſquire, in Three ſingle Plates. In the firſt I have given the Original Plan, as deſigned by me, and as altered in the Execution. The Difference lies in changing the *Portico* into 4 ¼ Columns, tranſpoſing Two back Stair-Caſes, and contracting one Front Room, and Two Side Rooms. The Second Plate gives the Front to the Court, extending 82 Feet, the
ruſtick

ruftick Bafement fupports a regular Tetraftile, Euftile, of the Compofed Order, the Columns 2 Feet Diameter, with a juft Entablature and Balluftrade round the whole Edifice. This Front gives a very beautiful and extenfive Profpect over the rich Vale of *Dorfetfhire*, *Eaft* and *South*, and is protected from the *North* by high Mountains, covered with Downs. The laft is the Garden Front *South*, extending 92 Feet, where the Windows of the principal Story are rufticated, as well as the Bafement. The whole Building is cafed with Stone, and was covered in *Anno* 1722.

The Rolls, *p.* 44, 45.

IN *Chancery Lane*, I built by a Royal Gift from our moft gracious Sovereign King GEORGE, to Sir *Jofeph Jekyll*, prefent Mafter of the *Rolls*. The Firft Plate gives the Plans of the Firft and Second Stories, extending 80 by 60 Feet. The great Caufe-Room is 42 by 30 Feet, including the Colonade, and 28 Feet high. The Second Plate gives the Front to the Court. All the Ornaments are of *Portland* Stone, and was built *Anno* 1718.

Newby, *p.* 46.

IN the *North-Riding* of *Yorkfhire*, the Seat of Sir *William Robinfon*, Baronet, in a chearful and healthy Situation. At the Diftance of 100 Yards, the *Swale* forms a perpetual Cafcade 150 Feet broad, abounding in excellent Salmon, and all Sorts of River Fifh. Of this Defign of my Invention, I have made one fingle Plate, containing the Plans of the Firft and Second Stories in a Square of 76 Feet. The Salon is a Cube of 30 Feet. The Firft Story is 15 Feet high, and the Attick 12 Feet. The Front is adorned with a Tetraftile, Euftile, *Ionick* ¾ Columns 3 Feet Diameter, with a regular Entablature and Balluftrade round the Building, which is all Stone. There are alfo Two large Wings for Offices, joined to the Houfe by an Arcade, and was covered *Anno* 1721.

Ebberton Lodge, 47.

IN *Yorkfhire*, near *Scarborough*, belonging to *William Thompfon*, Efquire, about Three Miles from his principal Seat. This fmall ruftick Edifice ftands in a fine Park well planted, with a River, which forms a Cafcade and Canal 1200 Feet long, and runs under the Loggio in the back Front.

Lord Herbert's *Houfe in* Whitehall, *p.* 48.

IN one fingle Plate I have given the Plans of the Principal and Attick Stories, with the Front next to the *Banquetting Houfe*. In the Bafement is a ruftick Arcade, and over it, an *Ionick* Loggio and Attick. The Gallery of the laft Story is moft magnificently finifhed, and gives one of the beft Profpects of the *Thames*. *Anno* 1724.

Hall-Barn, *p.* 49, 50.

NEAR *Beconsfield*, in *Bucks*, the Seat of *Edmond Waller*, Efquire, a Place for ever famous, by the Deathlefs Poems of the great *Waller*, Grandfather to this learned and worthy Gentleman. This new Building, of my Invention, ftands fronting a great Canal 200 Feet broad, and 1200 Feet long, leaving a Terras of 50 Feet between them: In Two fingle Plates. The Firft gives the Plan and Elevation of the Whole. The great Room is 30 Feet in Front, 30 Feet high, 45 Feet in Depth, coved ¼. The Side Rooms are Cubes of 12 Feet, with a Clofet to each. In the Second Plate is the Section of the great Room, expreffing the Manner of finifhing, and Form of the Ceiling. The Two Niches are to be filled with the Statues of *Homer* and *Virgil*: The Circles over them, with the Buftos

of *Milton* and *Addifon*, and Mr. *Waller* over the Chimney-Piece. I believe it will be no eafy Matter to make out fuch another Quinquevirate. This Building was begun and covered in *Anno* 1724.

Goodwood, *p.* 51, 52, 53, 54.

IN *Suffex*, the Seat of his Grace the Duke of *Richmond* and *Lenox*, Three Miles from *Chichefter*, in the moft agreeable Part of the County. I have made One double, and Two fingle Plates. The firft contains a Plan of the Park, Gardens, and Plantations, which, for the beautiful Variety and Extenfion of Profpect, fpacious Lawns, Sweetnefs of Herbage, delicate Venifon, excellent Fruit, thriving Plantations, lofty and awful Trees, is inferior to none. The great Improvements Mr. *Carné* has made in this delightful Place, will be lafting Monuments of his Art and Induftry, and *Carné's* Oaks fhall never be forgot. This Park has an eafy Defcent to the *Eaft*, *South*, and *South-weft*, with the Profpect of a rich and beautiful Landskip, bounded by the Sea for 30 Miles in Sight. The *Ifle of Wight* terminates the *South-weft* Profpect, and the famous St. *Rook's* Hill covers it from the *North*. I have given the following Defigns of my Invention in Two fingle Plates. In the Firft the general Plan of the principal Story and general Front, extending 305 Feet: The Body of the Houfe 125 by 105 Feet: The circular Salon is 40 Feet in Diameter, and 60 Feet high, illuminated by a vertical Light 10 Feet in Diameter. The Room next the *Portico* is 40 by 24 Feet: The Two Side Rooms 36 by 24 Feet: All 24 Feet high, and coved ¼. The Bed-Chambers are 24 Feet fquare, befides the Alcoves for the Beds: The Dreffing Rooms 24 by 18 Feet: The Cabinets 24 by 16 Feet: The Antichambers 24 Feet fquare: The Veftibule 32 by 24 Feet, in a Gradation of various Proportions, and all thefe are only 16 Feet high, without any Coving, with Mezonins between them and the Attick Story. The Two circular Stair-Cafes are 12 Feet in Diameter, and land in a Poggio round the Salon, that ferves all the Apartments above, which are 15 Feet high, and coved ¼. The Two Pavilions are 75 by 50 Feet, the Firft Story is 12 Feet, and the Second is 10 Feet, high, excepting the Kitchin, which takes in both. Thefe Pavilions are laid out in convenient Offices, and are joined to the Houfe by Two Colonades of the Dorick Order, with inclofed Paffages behind them. In the laft Plate is the *Weft* Front, adorned with an *Ionick Portico*, Hexaftile, Euftile. The Columns are 2 Feet ¼ in Diameter. All the Ornaments are of *Portland* Stone, and the reft of Brick-work, covered with Stucco. The fhining Qualities, and fingular Endowments, of this illuftrious Peer, is too great a Subject for me to attempt, when the moft skilful Panegyrift will find it too much. I fhall only labour, with the utmoft Zeal, as an Architect, to do fomething not unworthy fo good, fo great, and fo generous a Patron.

Mr. Plumptre's *Houfe, p.* 55.

IN *Nottingham* Town. In One fingle Plate I have given the Plan of the Firft Story and Elevation, extending 80 Feet. The Bafement is 5 Feet above Ground, which gives Light to the Offices. The Windows in the Firft Story are rufticated: In the Second they are drefs'd with Pediments, and a circular Window in the Middle. The Attick Windows are fquare, and the whole is finifhed with a regular Cornice and Balluftrade. All the Ornaments are of very good Stone, and the reft of Brickwork, covered with Stucco. The back Part of this Houfe is antient. The Front gives a Profpect of the *Trent*: But the Humanity, and Generofity

of

of this learned Gentleman, are, above all, to be recorded. It was built, *Anno* 1724.

A new Design for a Bridge at Lambeth. *p.* 56.

THE Honourable *House of Commons* having named a Committee to receive Plans and Proposals for so useful a Project, the Right Honourable *William Poultney* was chose Chairman, who was pleased to command me to prepare a Design, with the Approbation of the Earl of *Burlington.* His Lordship was not only pleased to countenance my Architectonical Labours, but out of his superabundant Goodness, did procure the Judgment and Approbation of our ablest Mathematicians. Dr. *Hally,* Dr. *Arbuthnot,* and several others, were unanimously of Opinion, that this Plan would be no Obstruction to the Navigation of the River, nor any Prejudice to the adjacent Property, which were the pretended Objections of some who were no Well wishers to the Bridge, for other Reasons. And to put this in a true Light, I shall give the Dimensions of the old and new Bridge. The Extent of *London-Bridge* is 850 Feet, of which 450 Feet for the Watercourse above the Starlings in the 19 Arches, and 200 Feet Water-course below the Starlings: The 18 Solids make 400 Feet. The new Bridge is 770 Feet long: The present Channel 727 Feet, to be inlarged 43 Feet: The Water-courses by 7 Arches 650 Feet above the Starlings, and 608 Feet below them: The 6 Solids 120 Feet, from which subtract 43 Feet added to the River, the Remainder is 77 Feet, being $\frac{1}{10}$ of 770 Feet. The Watercourse in the old Bridge above the Starlings, is as 9 to 8 Feet, being 450 to 400 Feet Solid. The Water-course below the Starlings, as 4 to 13 Feet, being 200 to 650 Feet Solid; so that the greatest Water-course in the old Bridge, is 450 Feet, in the new 650 Feet. In the old Bridge below the Starlings 200 Feet, in the new Bridge 608 Feet. In this new Plan I have made 5 Arches, each 100 Feet Diameter, and the Two extream Arches have 75 Feet, the Radius being $\frac{1}{2}$ of the same, the Pires have 20 Feet, each being $\frac{1}{5}$. The Breadth of this Bridge is 50 Feet, besides the Triangular Butments. The Middle Cause-way is 30 Feet broad, for Coaches and Carriages. Of each Side is a good Pavement, raised 1 Foot higher for Foot-People, and 10 Feet broad. including the Parapet. The Ornaments are rustick and strong, with Two Towers at each End. This Subject is intirely omitted by our Father *Vitruvius:* And *Leon Baptist Albert* is the First Architect to whom we are indebted for any Instruction, in the Eighth Book of his Architecture. In the Works of Antiquity, we find a great Diversity in the Proportion of these Pires and Arches. In that at *Rimini,* by *Augustus,* the Arches are Semi circular 25 Feet Diameter, and the Pires 11 Feet: That at *Vicenza,* over the *Bachiglione,* has Three Arches, the Middle one is 30 Feet in Diameter, the Radius $\frac{1}{2}$: The Side Arches are 22 Feet $\frac{1}{2}$, and the Pires are 5 Feet, being $\frac{1}{5}$. That at *Vicenza,* over the *Rorone,* has also 3 Arches, the Middle is 29 Feet, and the Side Arches 25 Feet, and the Pires 5 Feet. In the *Pons Senatorius* at *Rome,* the Arches are Semi-circular, the Pires $\frac{1}{4}$, without any Impost at springing the Arch. That of St. *Angelo,* formerly the *Pons Ælius,* the most magnificent in all *Rome,* whose very Ruins raise Veneration; the Pire is $\frac{1}{4}$ of the Arch, which is Semi-circular. In that *de Quatro Capi,* anciently the *Pons Tarpeius,* the Pire is $\frac{1}{4}$ of the Arch also Semi-circular. The last is a few Miles above *Rome,* formerly the *Pons Milvius,* now called *Ponte Mole,* the Pire is $\frac{1}{4}$ of the Arch, which is Semi-circular. After this Variety in the Works of Antiquity, I shall mention but one of *Palladio,*

Lib. 3. *Cap.* 14. with Three Arches; that in the Middle has 60 Feet in Diameter, the Sides 48 Feet, their Rise is $\frac{1}{3}$: The Pires have 12 Feet, being $\frac{1}{5}$ of the great Arch. Upon this Proportion I have formed my Design, and I think I can conclude with no greater Authority.

Wilton, *p.* 57, 58, 59, 60.

IN *Wiltshire,* the Seat of the Right Honourable the Earl of *Pembroke* and *Montgomery.* I have made Two double Plates in Perspective, and having said so much in the Second Volume, with Respect to the Building, I shall add nothing here.

Apple Dorecombe, *p.* 61.

IN the *Isle of Wight,* in the County of *Southampton,* the Seat of Sir *Robert Worsley,* Baronet. I have made One Plate in Perspective of this House, which is adorned with a *Corinthian* Pillastrade; the Wings have Pediments, and the middle Part is finished with an Attick. The whole is cased with *Portland* Stone, and was built, *Anno* 1710.

High Meadow, *p.* 62.

IN *Gloucestershire,* the Seat of the Right Honourable the Lord Viscount *Gage.* Having published the Plans and Elevation of this House to the Court, in my Second Volume, I have in this Plate given the Garden Front in Perspective.

Long Leate, *p.* 63, 64, 65, 66.

IN *Wiltshire,* the Seat of the Right Honourable the Lord Viscount *Weymouth.* In my Second Volume I have represented the Plans and Elevation, and in this are Two double Plates. The First gives the Geometrical Plans of the Gardens and Plantations, which were executed with great Expence by the late Lord. They are of large Extent, adorned with Statues, Fountains, Cascades, and many other Decorations. The Gardens were laid out by the late Mr. *London.* The Second double Plate is a Representation in Perspective of the Principal and Garden Front.

Chatsworth, *p.* 67, 68.

IN *Derbyshire,* the Seat of his Grace the Duke of *Devonshire.* In my First Volume I have given Three Plans, and Two Elevations of this magnificent Palace, and in this I have given these Two Fronts in Perspective in One double Plate.

Belton, *p.* 69, 70.

IN *Lincolnshire,* the Seat of the Right Honourable the Lord Viscount *Tyrconnel.* In my Second Volume I published the Plan and Elevation of this House, and in this I have made Two Plates. In the First, the Geometrical Plan of the Gardens and Plantations, which are very beautiful and improving. In the Second Plate is the House in Perspective.

Woodstock Park, *p.* 71, 72.

IN *Oxfordshire,* the Seat of her Grace the Dutchess of *Marlborough.* Having given the various Plans and Elevations of this stupendious Fabrick in my First Volume, I have here given an exact Geometrical Plan of the Park, Gardens, and Plantations, which are of very great Extent. The Table of References will explain the whole.

Boughton, *p.* 73, 74.

IN *Northamptonshire,* the Seat of his Grace the Duke of *Montagu.* The Geometrical Plan of the Gardens and Plantations are expressed in One double Plate. They were formed by the late Duke, and improved by his present Grace, with so many Additions, that they are esteemed now, the largest in *England.* The Particulars are to be taken from the Plan and Scale.

Hampton-

Hampton-Court, p. 75.

IN *Herefordſhire*, the Seat of the Right Honourable the Earl of *Coningsby*. In my Second Volume I have given the Plan and Elevation of this
ancient Edifice, and in this, a Geometrical Plan of
his Lordſhip's Gardens and Plantations, which are
eſteemed very curious, and the large Decoy is remarkable.

Lowther-Hall, p. 76.

IN *Weſtmoreland*, the Seat of the Right Honourable the Lord Viſcount *Lonſdale*. Having publiſhed the Plans and Elevation of this Houſe in my
Second Volume, I have here made a Geometrical
Plan of the Gardens and Plantations.

Claremont, p. 77, 78.

IN *Surrey*, one of the Seats of his Grace the Duke
of *Newcaſtle*. In One double Plate is a Geometrical Plan of the Gardens and Plantations, with
ſeveral large Pieces of Water, which his Grace has
finiſhed at a very great Expence. The Situation
being ſingularly romantick, and from the high
Tower has a moſt prodigious fine Proſpect of the
Thames and the adjacent Villas.

Cholmondley, p. 79, 80.

IN *Cheſhire*, the Seat of the Right Honourable
the Earl *Cholmondley*. In my Second Volume
I have publiſhed the Plan and Three Fronts of this
Houſe. Here in One double Plate I have given
the Geometrical Plan of the Gardens and Plantations, which are very large and beautiful. This
Noble Lord has ſpared no Expence to render them
worthy of his Lordſhip's Name.

Thorsby, p. 81, 82.

IN *Nottinghamſhire*, the Seat of his Grace the
Duke of *Kingſton*. In my firſt Volume I have
alſo given the Plan and Elevation of this Houſe,
and in this Plate you have a Plan of the Gardens
and Plantations. Here is a fine Parterre, a Canal,
Caſcade, and Lake, formed by a River. The
Park is of great Extent, being about Ten Miles
round, with all manner of Conveniencies worthy
of ſo Noble a Patron.

Althrop, p. 83, 84.

IN *Northamptonſhire*, the Seat of the Right Honourable the Earl of *Sunderland*. In my Second
Volume I gave the Plan and Elevation of this Houſe,
and in this, I have given a View in Perſpective of
the ſame, in One double Plate.

Duncomb-Park, p. 85, 86, 87, 88.

IN *Yorkſhire*, the Seat of *Thomas Duncomb*, Eſquire.
Of this I have made Two double Plates: In the
Firſt is a General Plan, and General Front of the
Houſe and Offices, extending 460 Feet, of which
the Houſe is 150 Feet. The Baſement is plain,
10 Feet high, which ſupports a *Tuſcan Portico Tetraſtile* 4 Feet in Diameter, finiſhed with a Pedement,
with an Entablature and Parapet round the whole
Building. The Windows in the principal Story
are Semi-circular, with Key Stones, without any
Architraves: In the Attick Story they are ſquare.
The Apartments are ſpacious, and the great Hall is
very Noble. The whole Building is Stone. In
the Second Plate is a large View in Perſpective of
the ſame. All deſigned by *William Wakefield*, Eſq;
Anno 1713.

Atherton, p. 89.

IN the County of *Lancaſter*, the Seat of *Richard
Atherton*, Eſquire. In One ſingle Plate I have
given the Plan of the principal Story and Front,
extending 102 Feet. The ruſtick Baſement, 10 Feet
high, ſupports, an *Ionick, Tetraſtile*, ⅓ Columns, 3
Feet ½ in Diameter, with Two Pillaſters at the
Corners. The Windows in the Principal and At-

tick Story, are dreſſed with an Architrave; and
an Entablature and Parapet ſurrounds the whole
Building. The Great Hall is very large, being 36
by 45 Feet, beſides ſeveral good Apartments. It
was deſigned by *William Wakefield*, Eſq; *Anno* 1723.

Rookby Park, p. 90.

IN the County of *York*, the Seat of *Thomas Robin-
ſon*, Eſquire. In one ſingle Plate, I have given
the Plan of the Principal and Attick Story, with
the Front, extending 96 Feet; the Ruſtick Baſement is 10 Feet high, and ſupports a *Corinthian*
Ordonance, conſiſting of 4 ¾ Columns, and 2 Pillaſters ¾ Feet in Diameter. The Door and
Windows in the principal Story are Semi-circular;
the Attick is only over the middle Part of the
Building, and has ſquare Windows, and concludes
with an Entablature and Balluſtrade. The Apartments are convenient, as the Plan more fully ex-
preſſeth. It is deſigned by *William Wakefield*, Eſq;
Anno 1724.

Horſe-Heath Hall, p. 91, 92.

IN *Cambridgſhire*, the Seat of *Henry Bromley*, Eſq;
In one double Plate, you have the general
Plan of the principal Story, and general Front, ex-
tending 600 Feet, whereof the Houſe is 140. The
Baſement is 9 Feet high, and the great Hall is
40 Feet in Front, and 48 deep, being in Height
equal to the Firſt and Second Story, with a noble
Gallery for Communication at the farther End.
All the Apartments are very good, the Offices very
ſpacious and commodious, the Windows in Two
Stories are dreſſed with Architrave, Frize and
Cornice. The whole was deſigned by Mr. *Webb*,
about the Year 1669.

A New Houſe at Twickenham, p. 93.

IN *Middleſex*. This Houſe is ſituated very near
the *Thames*, and has a good Proſpect of that
beautiful River. In one ſingle Plate you have the
Plans of the Firſt, Second, and Attick Story, with
Two Fronts. All the Apartments in the different
Stories, are diſtinctly figured in the Plans. The
Salon is a Cube of 24 Feet, the Ornaments are of
Portland Stone, and the reſt covered with Stucco.
The Entablature goes round the whole Edifice,
and the Roof is formed after the *Palladian* Manner.
It was built *Anno* 1724.

Leyton-Grange, p. 94.

IN *Eſſex*, the Seat of *David Ganſel*, Eſq; deſigned
and built by himſelf, with convenient Offices,
Gardens and Plantations, of his own Invention.
The Houſe is ſituated on a riſing Ground, with
good Proſpects, in the Middle of a ſmall but plea-
ſant Park, well water'd. It was built *Anno* 1720.

Narford, p. 95.

IN *Norfolk*, the Seat of Sir *Andrew Fountain*. In
One Plate I have given a Geometrical Plan of
the Gardens and Plantations: This Learned and
Ingenious Gentleman, as he is diſtinguiſhed by his
univerſal Knowledge in all the Polite Arts, has given
Marks of his good Taſte and Affection for Architecture, in ſeveral Pieces lately erected there.

Caverſham, p. 96, 97.

IN *Oxfordſhire*, the Seat of the Right Honourable
the Earl of *Cadogan*. In One double Plate I
have given a Geometrical Plan of the Park, Gardens, and Plantations of this magnificent Place.
The Situation is very high, but the Aſcent ſo eaſy
and gradual, that you riſe inſenſibly to it; where
the Eye is entertained with moſt beautiful Proſpects; particularly that from the grand Terras,
1200 Feet long, towards *Reading* and the *Thames*.
The Deſcent from this Terras to the Bottom of the
Parterre, is 50 Feet perpendicular, by Two double
Flights of Steps, all of *Portland*-Stone. The Parterre

terre is nobly adorned with Fountains, Vafes and Statues, particularly Four Originals in Statuary Marble, of King WILLIAM, King GEORGE, Duke of MARLBOROUGH, and Prince EUGENE, all fo very like, that they are known at Sight; befides many valuable ones, caft from the beft Antiques. Of each Side of the Parterre, are Two great Canals 900 Feet long, with a *Dorick* Portico at each End. From the great Iron Gates, to the End of the Park Pale, are Four beautiful Lawns, divided by Three Walks of very lofty Trees, 2200 Feet long, and the whole Park is well Wooded, Watered, and Plenty of Deer, a Pheafantry, Menagerie, and all manner of Conveniencies. This Noble Lord, from a Place that could pretend to nothing but a Situation capable of Improvement, with vaft Labour and Expence, has now rendered it one of the nobleft Seats in the Kingdom. Thefe Gardens were form'd by Mr. *Acres*, where he has left lafting Monuments of his Capacity. *Anno* 1723.

P. 98, 99, 100.

OF this Defign of my Invention, I have made one double and one fingle Plate: The Firft contains a general Plan of the principal Story and general Front, extending 250 Feet; That is 100 for the Houfe, 50 to each Side, and 25 Feet to each Wing, whereof one contains the Kitchin and all proper Offices, with a covered Communication to the Houfe, and a large Arch in the Middle for a Coach to land in rainy Weather. The other Wing makes one large Gallery 20 Feet broad, and 20 high, and 100 long; but the Two Ends are reduced to Cubes of 20 Feet, by introducing fome Columns. The Ground Story is all arched, and is 3 Feet under Ground. The Bafement is 9 Feet high, which fupports an *Ionick Octaftrle*, having 6 ¾ Columns, and 2 Corner Pillafters 4 Feet in Diameter, finifhed with a regular Entablature, and bold Pedement, which covers the whole Houfe. The Great Hall is a Cube of 40 Feet; The Salon is 40 by 24 Feet; The 4 Corner Rooms are Cubes of 24 Feet, and coved ¼. Two Side-Rooms are 24 by 18, and Two are 20 by 18, all 16 Feet high, without coving, with *Mezonins* over them. The Attick Story is 15 Feet high, and coved ¼; The Stair-cafes are lighted from the Top, and are only divided by Rails, without any Partition, which makes the Opening very noble above. The laft fingle Plate is a Section of the Hall, dreffed with ¾ Columns of the *Compofed* Order, and great Variety of proper Decorations, all in Stone, defigned *A.* 1724.

Umberflade, p. 101.

THE Seat of *Andrew Archer*, Efquire, in the County of *Warwick*.

A TABLE of what is contained in the THIRD VOLUME.

Ca: Campbell Delin:

The prospect of the Royall Hospital at Greenwich to the River Thames

H. Hulsbergh Sculp:

C. 3, PL. 3-4

Ca: Campbell Delin:

Castle Howard in Yorkshire the Seat of the E

Honourable the Earl of Carlisle &c :

H:Hulsbergh Sculp:

40 Feet ————————— 10   20   30   40 Extends 80.

Ambresbury in Wiltshire the Seat of the Right Honourable the Lord Carlton president of Council

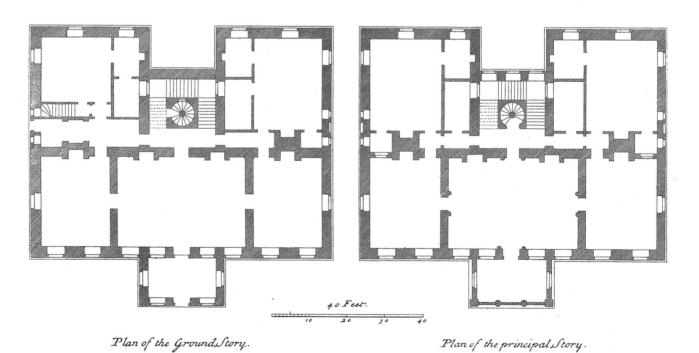

40 Feet ————— 10   20   30   40

Plan of the Ground Story.   Plan of the principal Story.

Inigo Iones Invt: Ca: Campbell Delin: H: Hulsbergh Sculp:

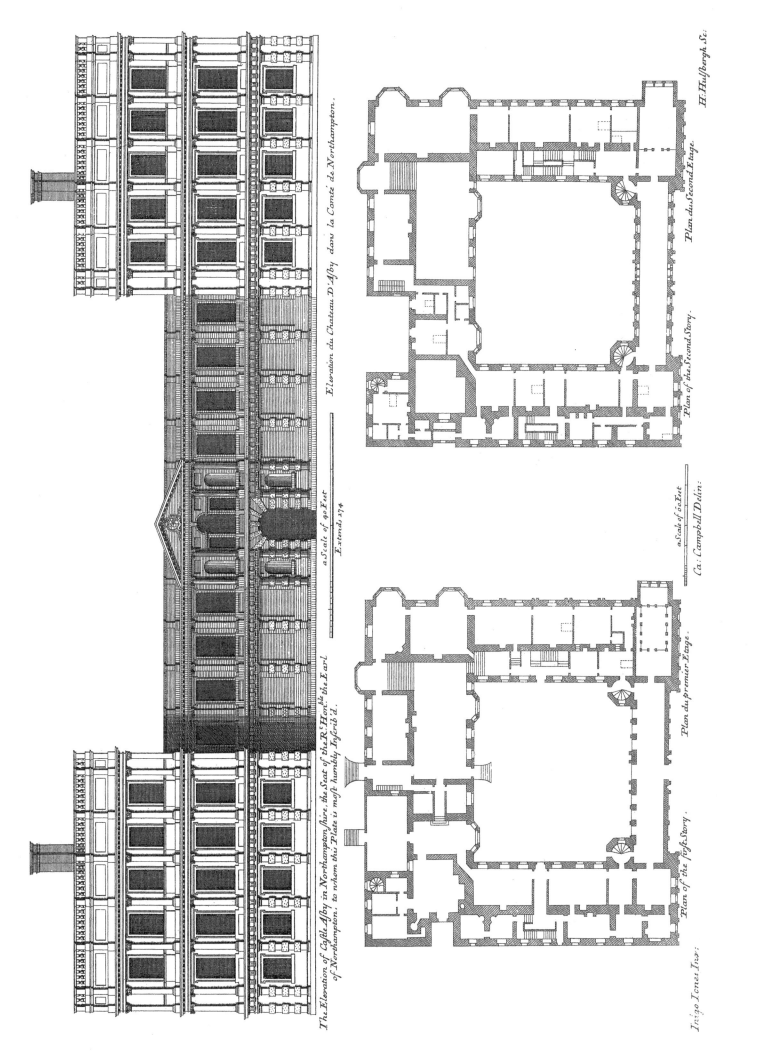

The Elevation of Castle Asby in Northamptonshire, the Seat of the Rt Honble the Earl of Northampton. to whom this Plate is most humbly Inscrib'd.

Elevation du Chateau D'Asby dans la Comté de Northampton.

a Scale of 40 Feet

Extends 174

Plan of the first Story.

Plan du premier Etage.

Plan of the Second Story.

Plan du Second Etage.

a Scale of 60 Feet

Inigo Jones Inv:

Ca: Campbell Delin:

H: Hulsbergh Sc:

C. 3, PL. 8

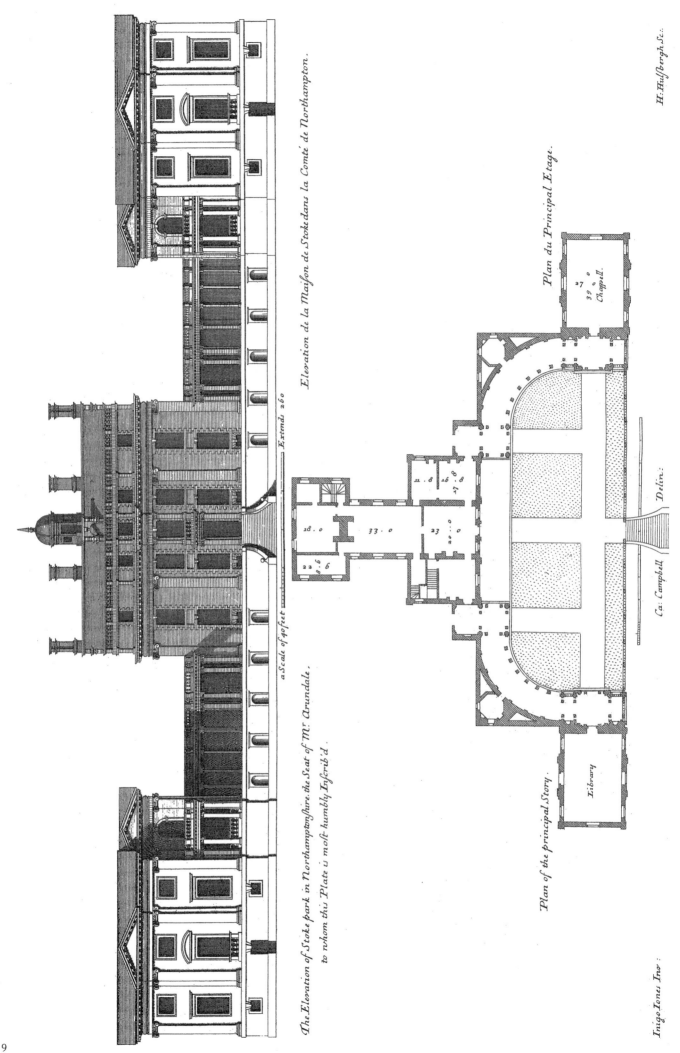

The Elevation of Stoke park in Northamptonshire, the Seat of Mr. Arundale.
to whom this Plate is most humbly Inscrib'd.

Elevation de la Maison de Stoke dans la Comté de Northampton.

a Scale of 40 feet

Extends 260

Plan of the principal Story.

Plan du Principal Etage.

Library

33.0

18.0

22.6

23

20.0

11.8

16.8

17.8

37.0
39.0
Chappell

Inigo Iones Inv:

Ca: Campbell Delin:

H: Hulsbergh Sc:

C. 3, PL. 9

a Scale of 40 feet

10   20   30   40

The Elevation of General Wade his house in great Burlington-Street ,
Defign'd by the R.t Honourable Richard Earl of Burlington and Cork &c. 1723 .

10   20   30   40   50   60 feet

Plan of the first Story   Plan of the principal Story

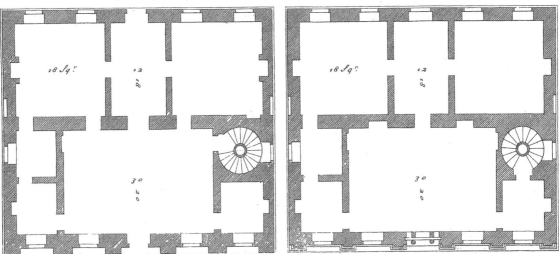

Ca: Campbell delin: H: Hulfbergh Sculp:

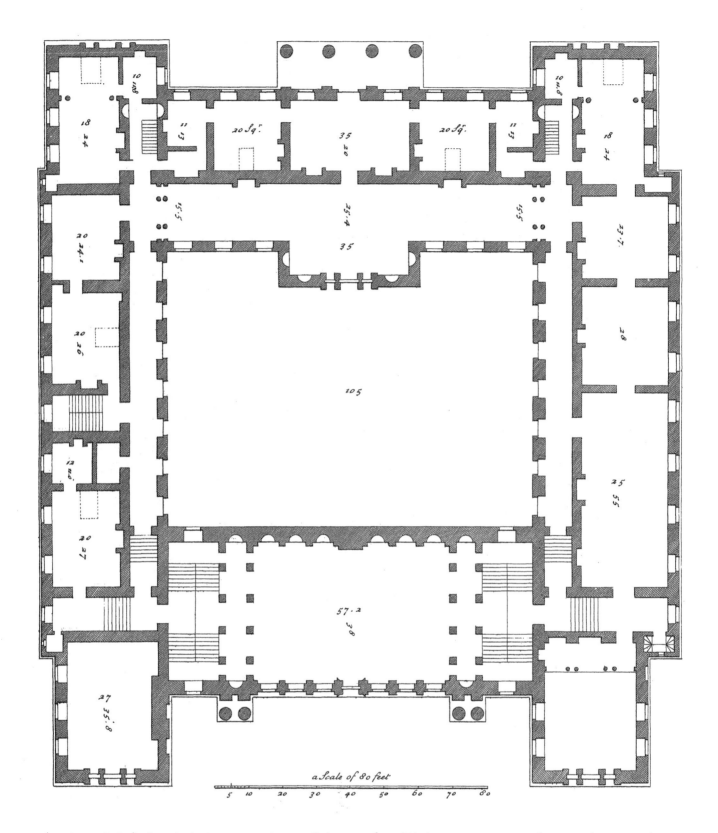

10
108

18
34

13
17

20 Sq.

35
20

20 Sq.

11
13

10
108

18
34

5.5.
55

35.4

13.7

35

20
14.1

28

20
26

105

12
11.0

25
55

20
17.1

57.2
38

27
35.8

a Scale of 80 feet

5   10   20   30   40   50   60   70   80

Plan of the Principall Floor of Grimsthorp in the County of Lincoln the Seat of his Grace the Duke of Ancaster and Kesteven Hereditary
Lord great Chamberlain of England. Design'd by Sʳ Iohn Vanbrugh Kᵗ 1723.

Ca: Campbell delin:

H: Hulsbergh Sculp:

The North front of Grimsthorp in the County of Lincoln the Seat of his Grace the Duke of Ancaster and Kesteeran Hereditary Lord great Chamberlain of England. Designd by Sir John Vanbrugh Kt. 1723.

Ca: Campbell delin:

H: Hulsbergh Sculp:

C. Campbell delin:

The Garden front of Grimsthorp in the County of Lincoln the Seat of his Grace the Duke of Ancaster and Kesteven Hereditary Lord great Chamberlain of England. Design'd by S.r John Vanbrugh K.t 1723

H. Hulsbergh Sculp:

10 20 30 40 50 60 feet

Cu: Campbell delin:

The West front of Grimsthorp in the County of Lincoln the Seat of his Grace the Duke of Ancaster and Kesteven Hereditary Lord great Chamberlain of England. Design'd by
Sr. John Vanbrugh Kt. 1723.

5 10 20 30 40 50 60 70 80 90 100 feet

H: Hulsbergh Sculp:

C. 3, PL. 14

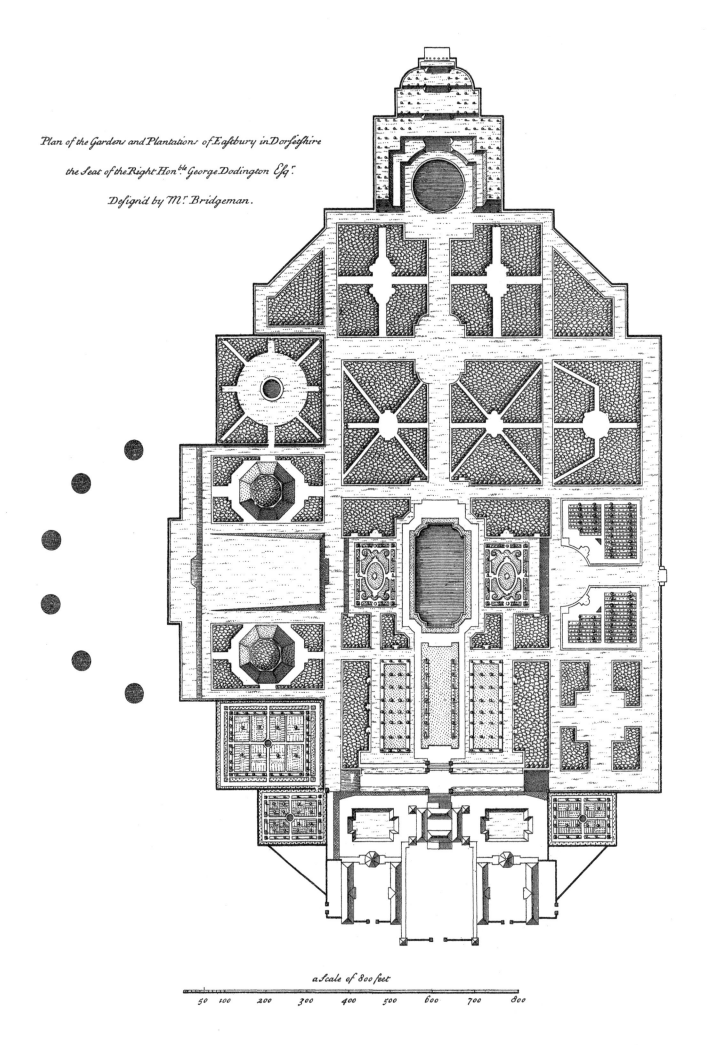

Plan of the Gardens and Plantations of Eastbury in Dorsetshire

the Seat of the Right Honble George Dodington Esqr.

Design'd by Mr. Bridgeman.

a Scale of 800 feet

50 100   200   300   400   500   600   700   800

Ca: Campbell delin:

H: Hulsbergh Sculp

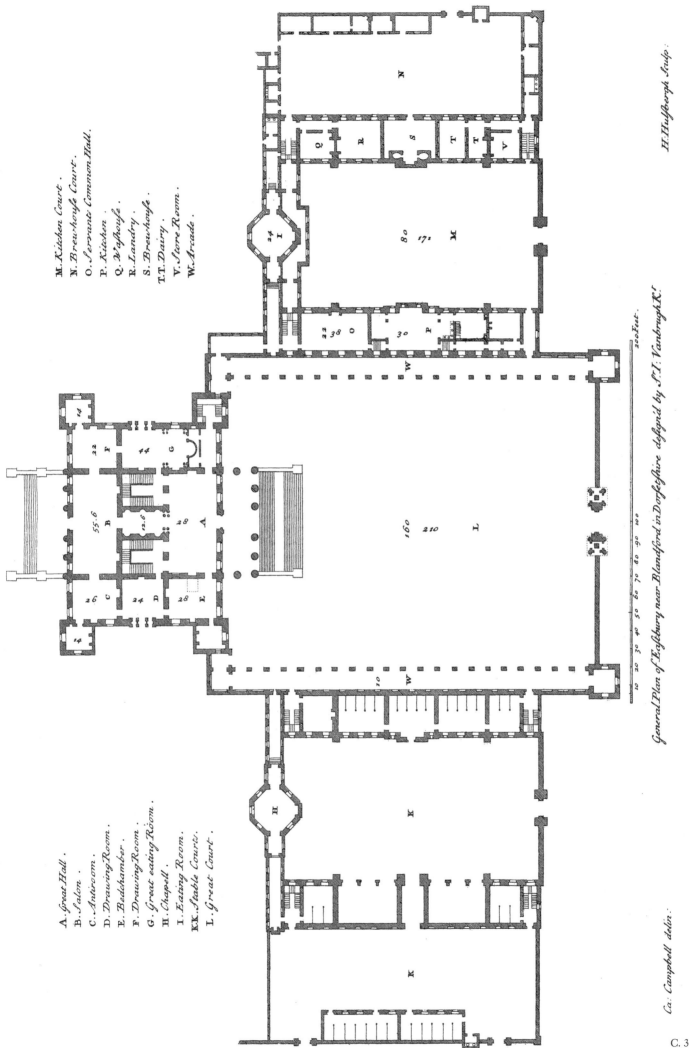

A. Great Hall.
B. Salon.
C. Antiroom.
D. Drawing Room.
E. Bedchamber.
F. Drawing Room.
G. Great eating Room.
H. Chapell.
I. Eating Room.
KK. Stable Court.
L. Great Court.

M. Kitchen Court.
N. Brewhouse Court.
O. Servants Common Hall.
P. Kitchen.
Q. Washouse.
R. Laundry.
S. Brewhouse.
T.T. Dairy.
V. Store Room.
W. Arcade.

Ca: Campbell delin:

General Plan of Eastbury near Blandford in Dorsetshire design'd by Sr I. Vanbrugh Kt.

H. Hulsbergh Sculp:

C. 3, PL. 16

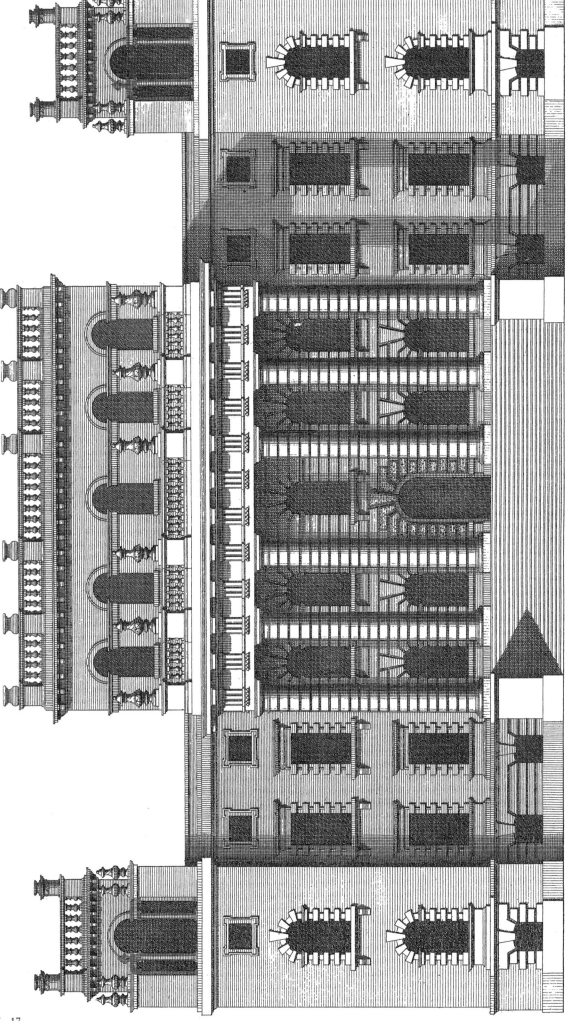

Co: Campbell delin:

H: Hulsbergh Sculp:

Elevation of Eastbury in Dorsetshire the Seat of the Right Honble George Dodington Esqr.
Designd by Sr John Vanbrugh Kt.

10   20   30   40   50   60 feet

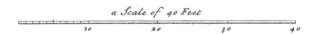

a Scale of 40 Feet

10   20   30   40

Plan and Elevation of the great Temple in the Garden at Eastbury, design'd by Sr T. Vanbrugh Kt.

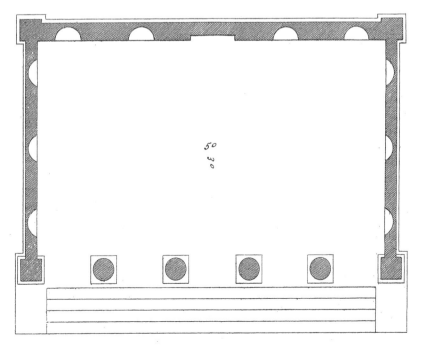

a Scale of 40 feet

10   20   30   40

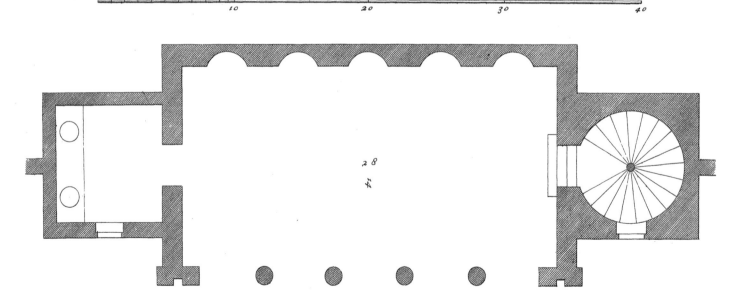

Plan and Elevation of the Bagnio in the Garden at Eastbury in Dorsetshire the
Seat of the Right Honourable George Dodington Esq: Design'd by Sr. Iohn Vanbrugh Kt.

Ca: Campbell delin:

C. 3, PL. 19

H. Hulsbergh Sculp:

The North front of Seaton Delaval in the County of Northumberland the Seat of Francis Delaval Esq.ʳ.   design'd by S.ʳ Iohn Vanbrugh K.ᵗ. 1721.

10   20   30   40   50   60 feet

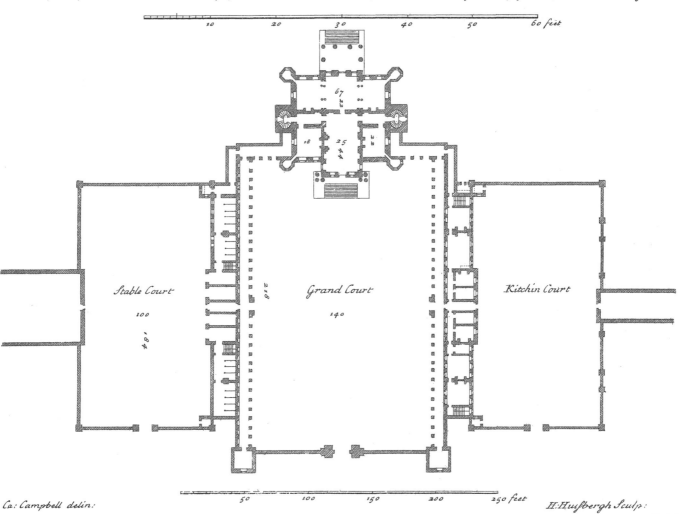

Stable Court

100

Grand Court

140

Kitchin Court

Ca: Campbell delin: H: Hulfbergh Sculp:

50   100   150   200   250 feet

C. 3, PL. 20

The South front of Seaton Delaval in the County of Northumberland the Seat of Francis Delaval Esq.: design'd by Sr. John Vanbrugh Kt. 1721.

Ca: Campbell delin:

H: Hulfbergh Sculp:

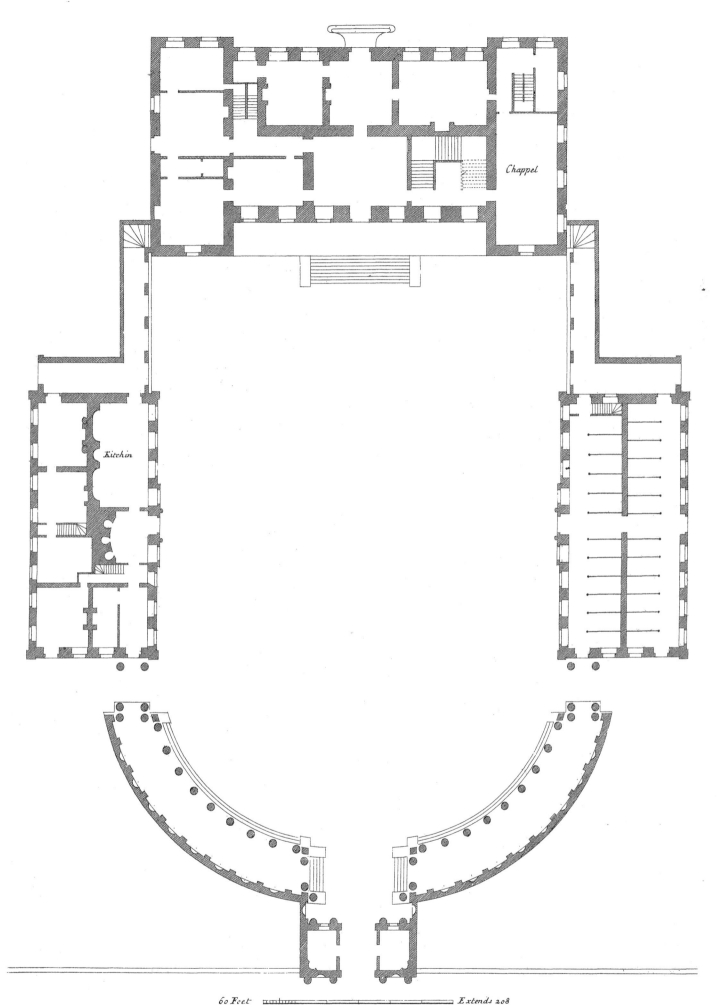

Kitchin

Chappel

60 Feet   Extends 208

General Plan of Burlington House and Offices in Pickadilly.

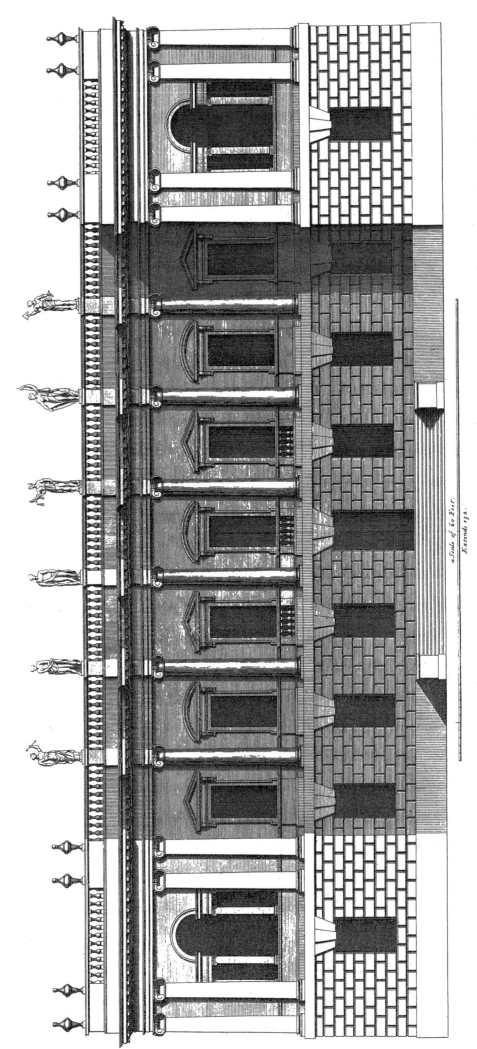

Burlington houſe in Pickadilly London. Erected by the Rt. Honourable Richard Boyle. Earl of Burlington and Cork. Lord High Treaſurer of the Kingdom of Ireland &c: Deſigned by Colen Campbell Anno 1717

H. Huſſbergh Sculp:

C. Campbell Invt: et Delin:

a Scale of 60 Feet.

Extends 132.

40 Feet

The great Gate at Burlington house in Picadilly. Erected by the Rt: Honble: Richard Boyle Earl of Burlington and Cork. Lord High Treasurer of the Kingdom of Ireland &c: Designed by Colen Campbell 1718.

H. Hulsbergh. Sculp.

The New Bagnio in the Gardens at Chiswick in the County of Midlesex Erected by the R.t Hon.ble Richard Boyle Earl of Burlington and Cork.
Lord High Treasurer of the Kingdom of Ireland &c: in the Year 1717.

20 Feet.   Extends 37

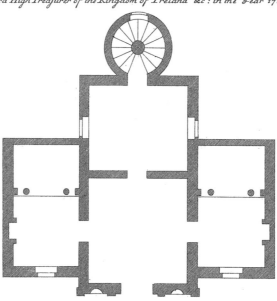

Ca: Campbell Delin:

H: Hulsbergh Sculp:

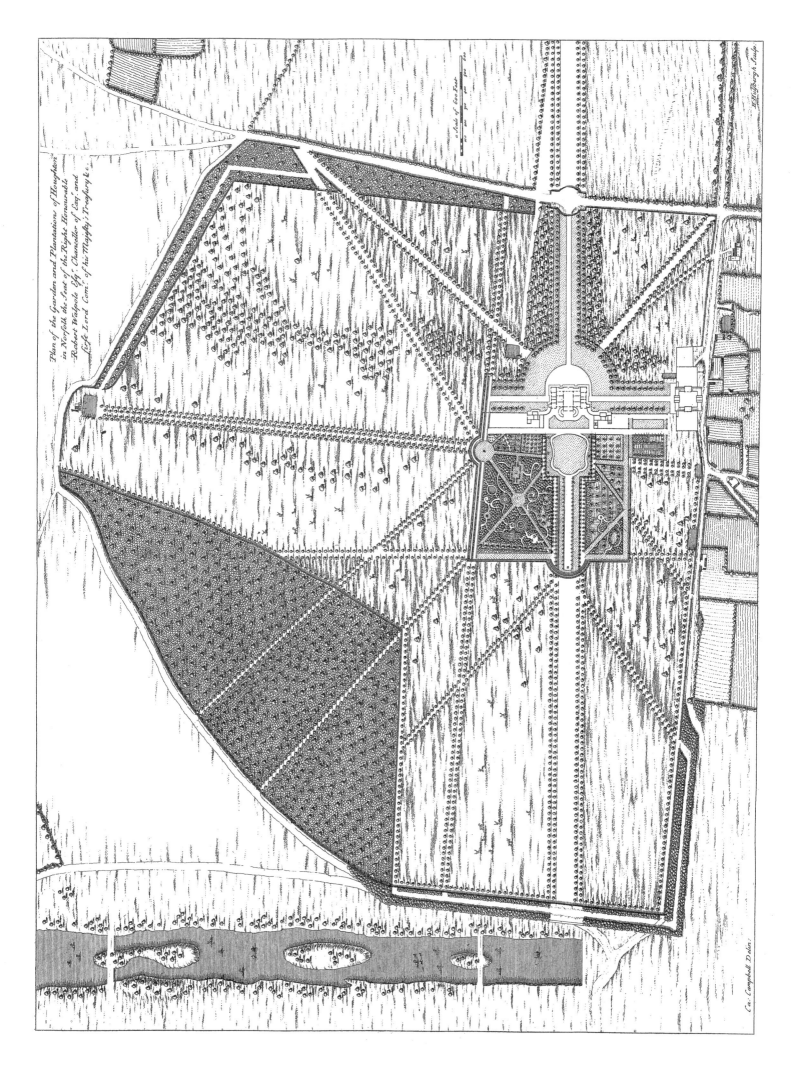

Plan of the Garden and Plantations of Houghton
in Norfolk the Seat of the Right Honourable
Robert Walpole Esq.: Chancellor of Exc: and
First Lord Com: of his Majesty; Treasury &c.

Scale of 600 Feet

Ca: Campbell D.elin:

H.Hulsbergh Sculp.

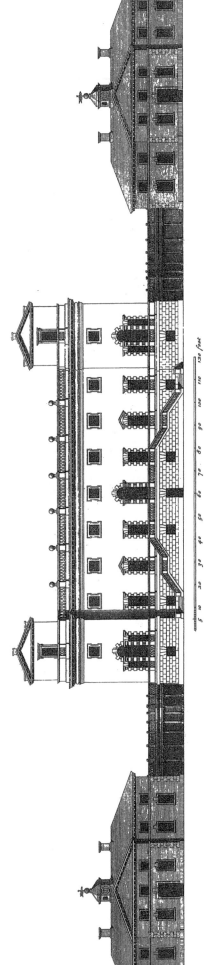

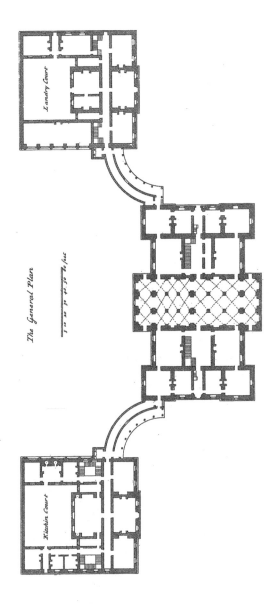

The General front of Houghton in Norfolk the Seat of the Right Honourable Robert Walpole Esq; Chancellor of Exq; and first Lord Com.r of his Majesty's Treasury, &c.: design'd by Colen Campbell Esq.r 1723

The General Plan

H: Hulsbergh Sculp:

Co: Campbell Architect:

Plan of the principal Story of Houghton in Norfolk the Seat of the Right Honourable Robert Walpole Esq.r:
Chancellor of Exq.r and first Lord Com. of his Maje(ty's Treafury. Erected Anno 1723 Defigned by Colen Campbell Efq.r:

Plan of the Attik Story.

a Cube of 40 feet

4 . 30

3 . 24

3 . 24

22 fq.s:

2 . 25

2 . 9

20 . 25

22 fq.s:

a Scale of 80 feet

Extend 166 feet

10   20   30   40   50   60   70   80

Co: Campbell Architectus

H: Huffbergh Sculp.:

C. 3, PL. 31

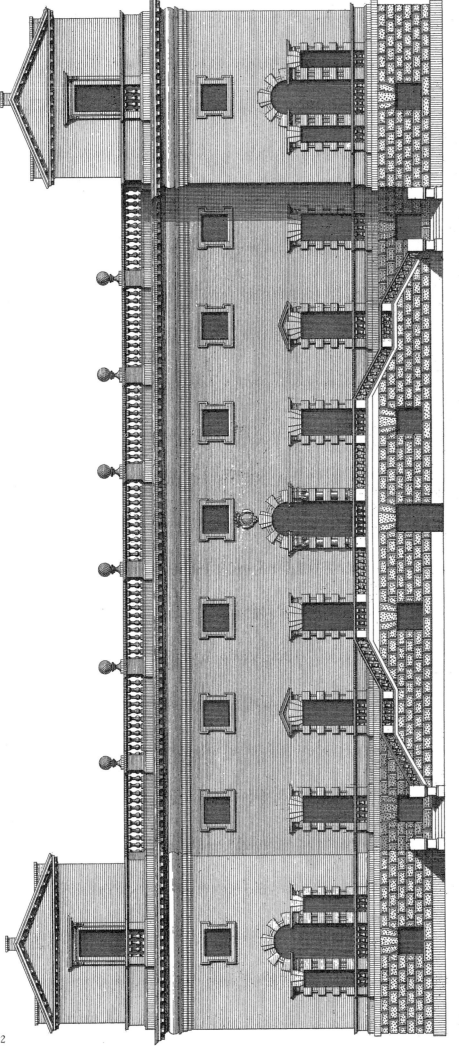

Elevation of the North front of Houghton in Norfolk the Seat of the Right Honourable Robert Walpole Esq.ʳ Chancellor of Exq.ʳ and
first Lord Com.ʳ of his Majesty's Treasury. &c.: Erected Anno 1723. designed by Colen Campbell Esq.ʳ

a Scale of 80 feet

Extends 166

H. Hulsbergh Sculp.

Co: Campbell Architect.

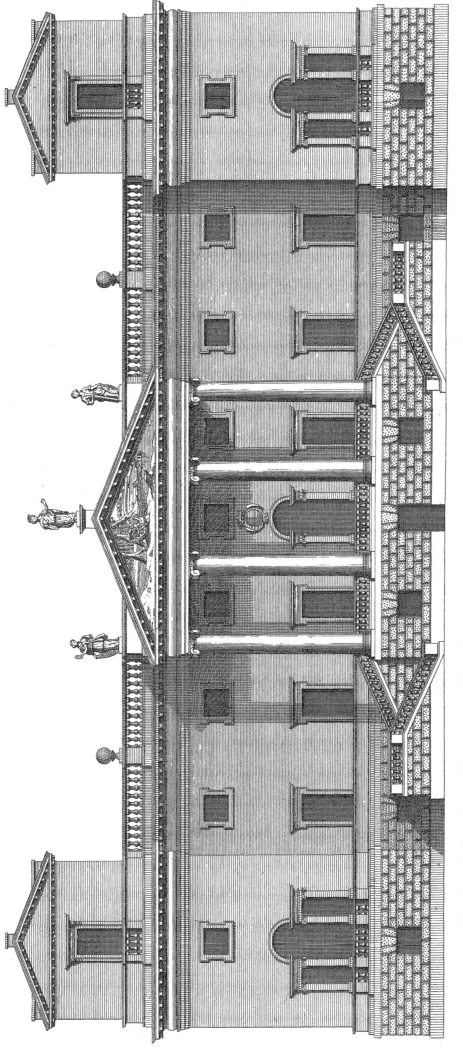

Elevation of the South front of Houghton in Norfolk, the Seat of the Right Honourable Robert Walpole Esqʳ Chancellor of Exchʳ and first Lord Comʳ of his Majesty's Treasury, &c.

Erected Anno 1723. Designed by Colen Campbell Esqʳ.

a Scale of 60 feet.

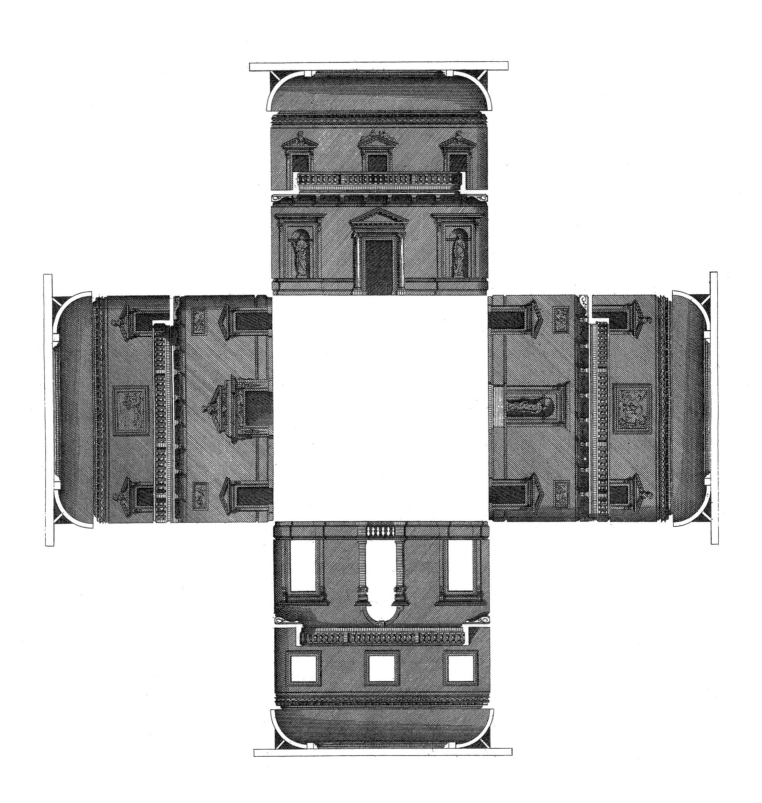

a Scale of 40 feet

10 20 30 40

Section of the great Hall of Houghton in Norfolk. the Seat of the Right Honourable Robert Walpole Esq.

Chancellor of Excq: and first Lord Com. of his Majesty's Treasury. &c:

Ca: Campbell Architectus .

H: Hulsbergh Sculp:

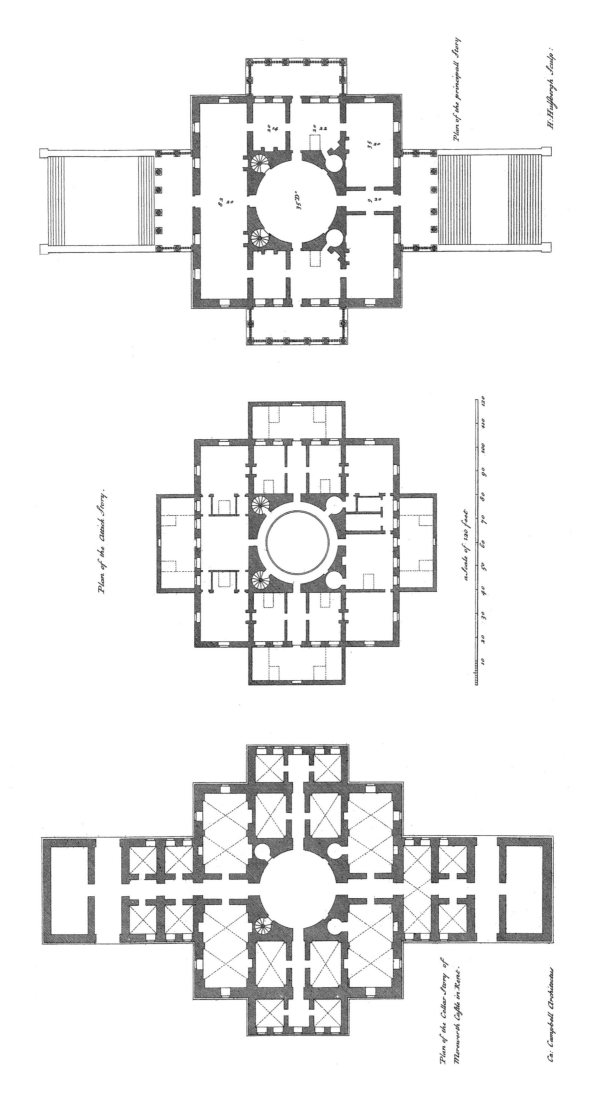

Plan of the Attick Story.

Plan of the principall Story

H: Hulsbergh Sculp:

Plan of the Cellar Story of Mereworth Castle in Kent.

Co: Campbell Architect:

a Scale of 120 feet

35:"D"

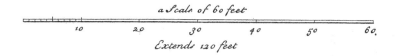

a Scale of 60 feet

10   20   30   40   50   60

Extends 120 feet

The Elevation of Merewrth Castle near Maidstone in Kent
the Seat of the Honourable Iohn Fane Esqr.

Ca: Campbell Architectus.

H. Hulsbergh Sculp:

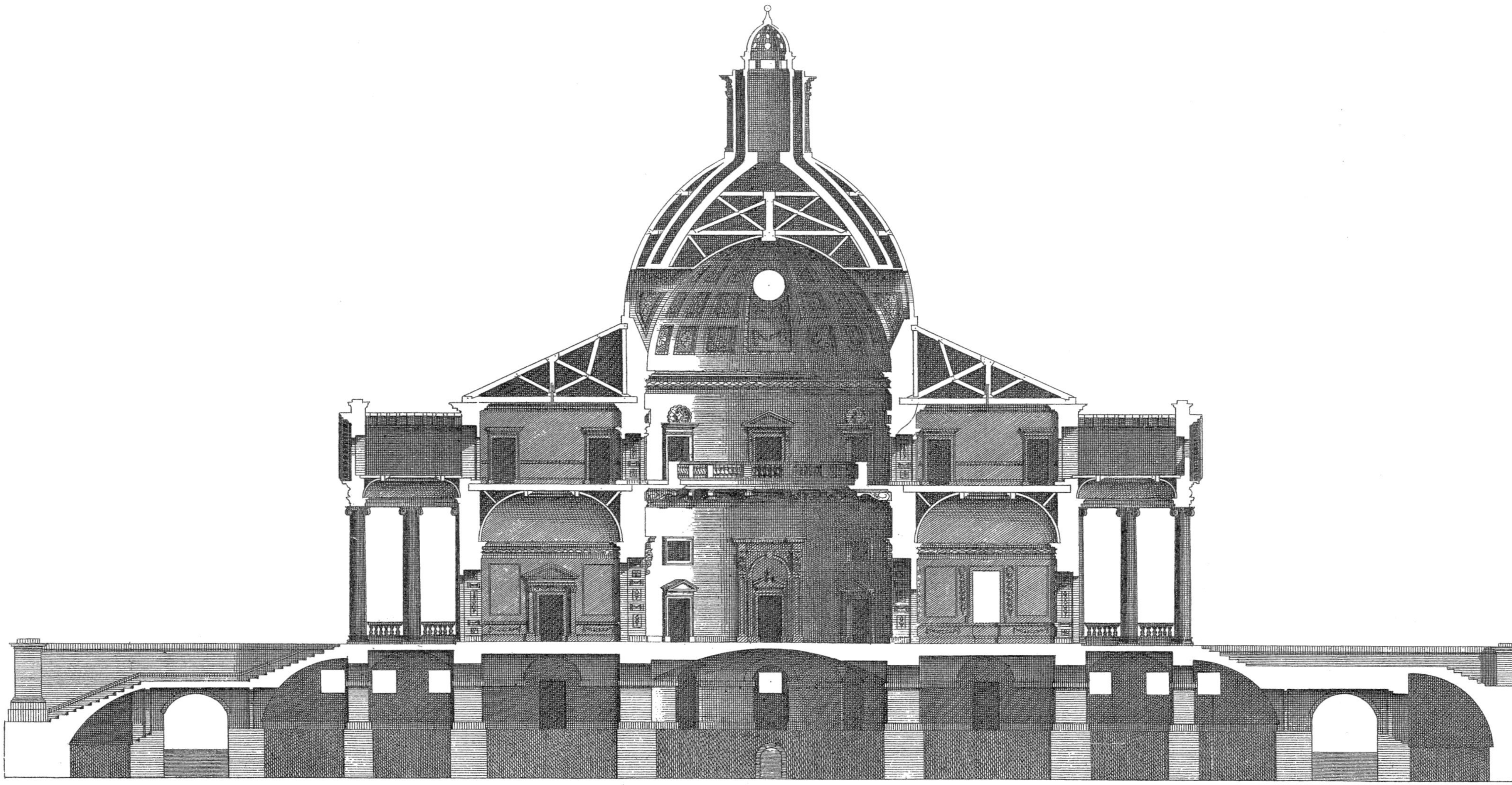

a Scale of 60 feet
10 20 30 40 50 60

Section of Mereworth Castle in Kent.

Ca: Campbell Architectus. H: Hulsbergh Sculp:

The West front of Wanstead in Essex with the four new Towers, the Seat of the Right Hon.ble the Lord Vicount Castlemaun. designd by Colen Campbell Esq.r 1721.

a Scale of 60 feet

5 10 20 30 40 50 60

H.Hulfbergh Sculp:

Co: Campbell Architect.

H: Hulßbergh Sculp.

- *Plan of the principal Story of Stourhead as Executed by Mr. Hoare.*

a Scale of 40 Feet.

10 20 30 40

Ca: Campbell Inven.t

Plan of the principal Story of Stourhead in Wiltshire as designed by Mr. Campbell.

Chapell 30.

20 Sq.r

12

20 Sq.r

20 + 0

25 + 0

20 Sq.r

a Cube 30.

30 + 0

20 + 0

C. 3, PL. 41

C. 3, PL. 42

Ca: Campbell Invent.

H: Hulsbergh Sculp:

The East front of Stourhead in Wiltshire the Seat of Henry Hoare Esqr.

40 Feet   10   20   30   40

Extent: 82.

Ca: Campbell Invent.

H. Hulfbergh Sculp.

The Garden or South front of Stourhead in Wiltshire

40 Feet   10   20   30   40 Extend 92.

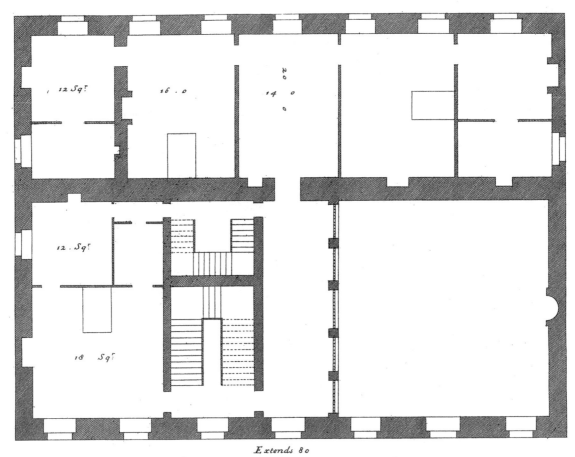

12 Sq.̃ 16.0 20 14.0 0

12 . Sq.̃

18 Sq.̃

Extends 80

The Second Story.

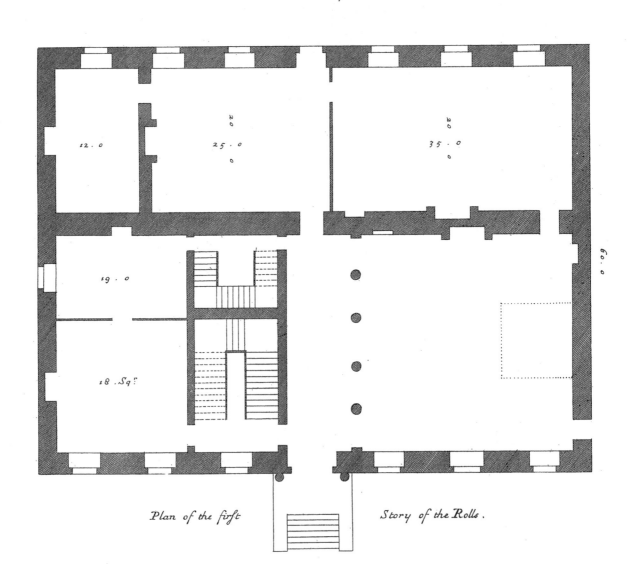

12.0 20 25.0 0 20 35.0 0

19.0

18 . Sq.̃

60.0

Plan of the first Story of the Rolls.

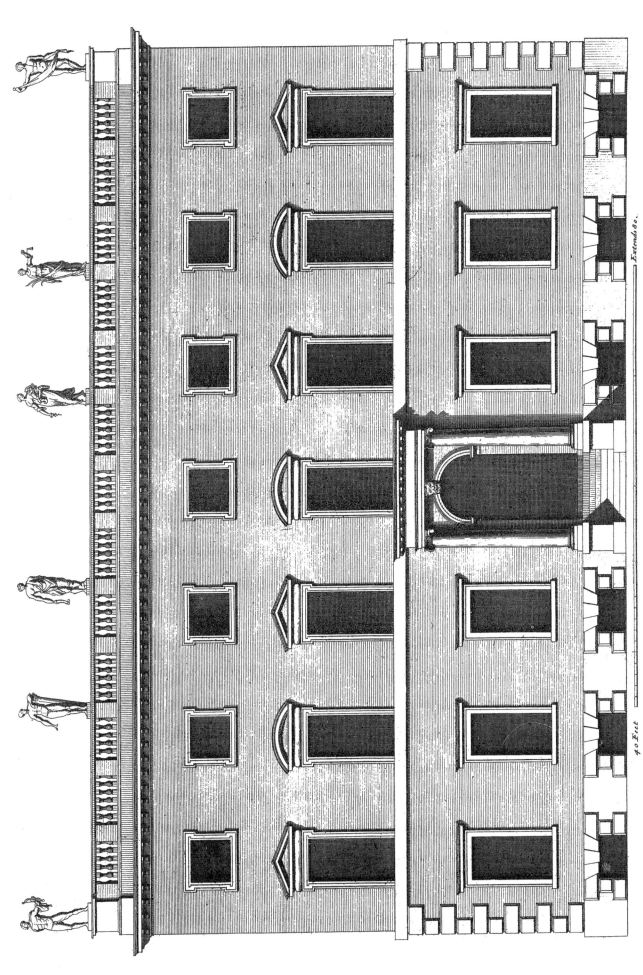

The West front of the Rolls in Chancery Lane, Erected by His most Sacred Majesty King George, is most humbly Inscrib'd to the Rt: Honourable Sr: Joseph Jekyll Master of the Rolls, Designed by Collen Campbell

Ca: Campbell Inv: et Delin:

H. Hulsbergh Sculp:

1718.

40 Feet

Extends 80.

Elevation of Newby upon Swale in the North Riding of Yorkshire the Seat of S.ᵣ William Robinson Bar.ᵗ design'd by Co: Campbell 1720

a Scale of 40 feet   *Extend 76 feet*
5   10   20   30   40

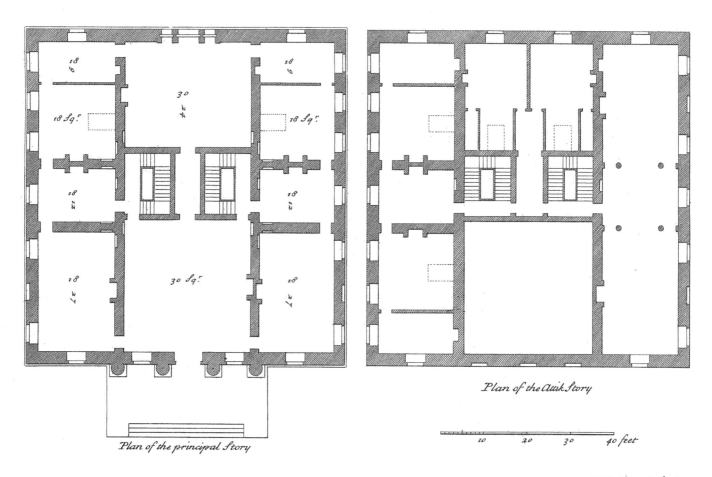

Plan of the principal Story

Plan of the Attik Story

10   20   30   40 feet

Ca: Campbell Architectus   *H. Hulsbergh Sculp:*

The Elevation of Ebberston Lodge near Scarborough in Yorkshire, belonging to William Thompson Esq. Design'd by

Colen Campbell Esq. Anno 1718.

a Scale of 30 feet   Extend 48 feet

5   10   20   30

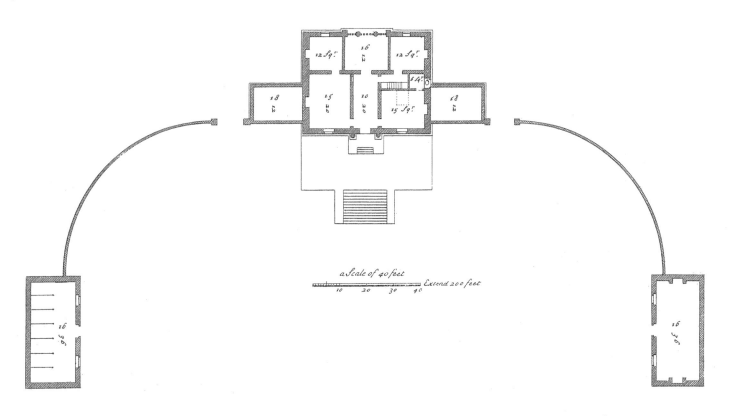

a Scale of 40 feet

10 20 30 40 Extend 200 feet

Ca: Campbell Architectus.   H. Hulsbergh Sculp: C. 3, PL. 47

Elevation of the Right Honourable the Lord Herbert his House in Whitehall.

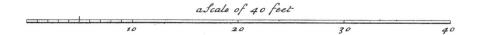

a Scale of 40 feet

10   20   30   40

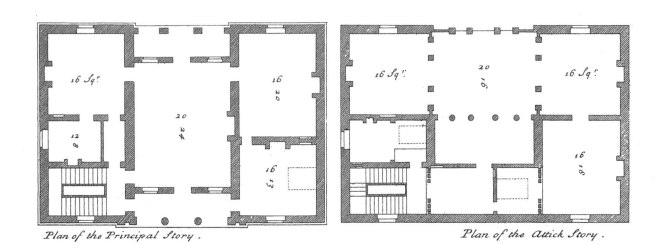

Plan of the Principal Story.

Plan of the Attick Story.

10   20   30   40 feet.

Ca: Campbell Architectus.

H: Hulsbergh Sculp.

A new Garden Room at Hall Barn near Beacons field in the County of Bucks, the Seat of Edmond Waller Esq.r Defign'd by
Colen Campbell Esq.r 1724.

5   10   20   30   40 feet

5   10   20   30   40 feet

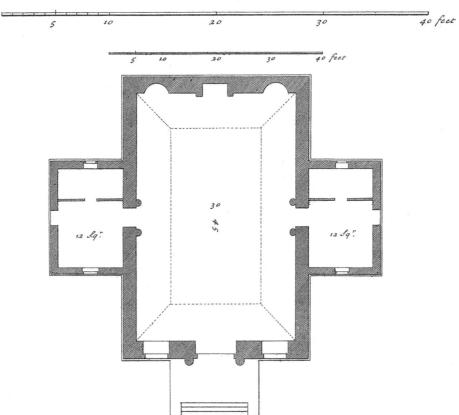

30
45

12 Sq.r   12 Sq.r

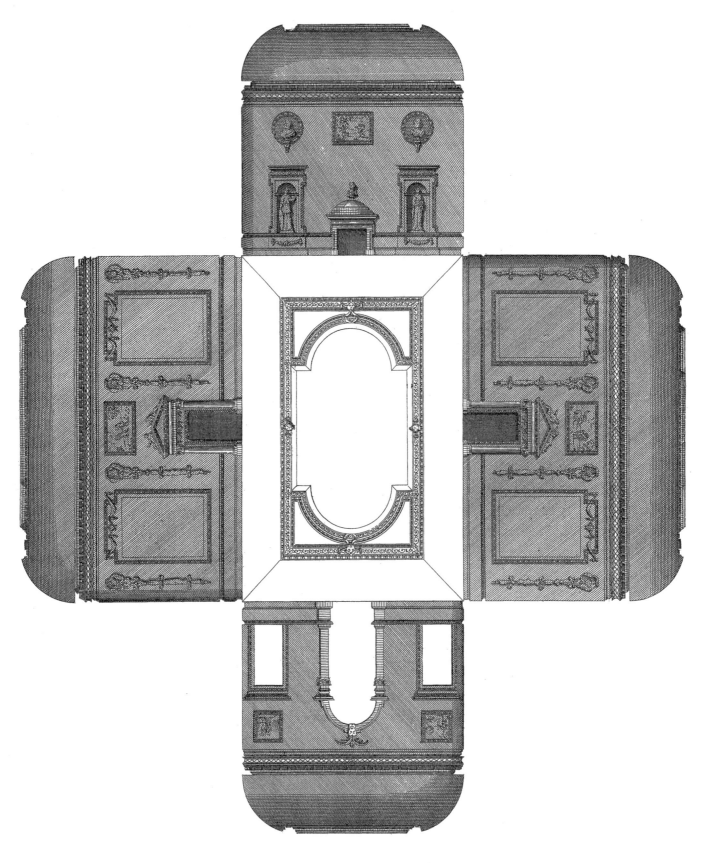

Section of a New Garden Room at Hall Barn near Beaconsfield in the County of Bucks the Seat of Edmond Waller Esqr.
Design'd by Colen Campbell Esqr. 1724

5   10   20   30   40   50   60 feet

Ca: Campbell Architectus.

H: Hulsbergh Sculp:

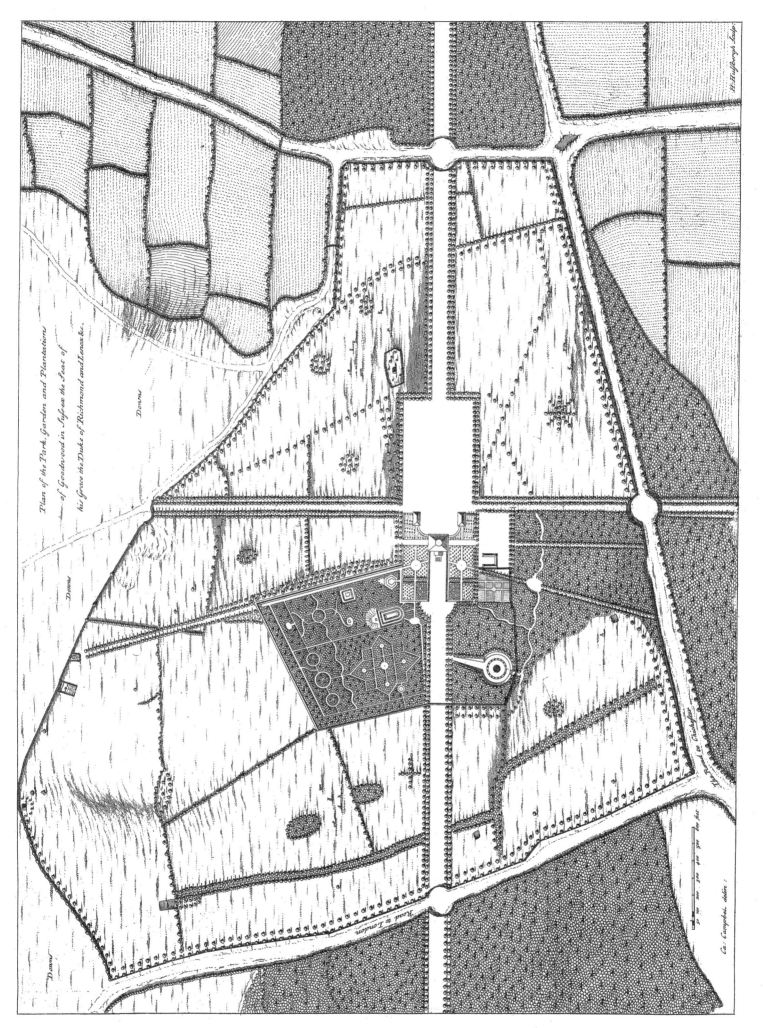

Plan of the Park, Garden and Plantations
of Goodwood in Sussex the Seat of
his Grace the Duke of Richmond and Lenox &c.

Downs

Downs

Downs

Downs

Road to London

The Road to Chichester

Ca: Campbell. delin:

H. Hulsbergh Sculp.

Elevation of the General front Eastward of Goodwood in Sussex the Seat of his Grace the Duke of Richmond and Lenox. ────

Design'd by Colen Campbell Esq: 1724.

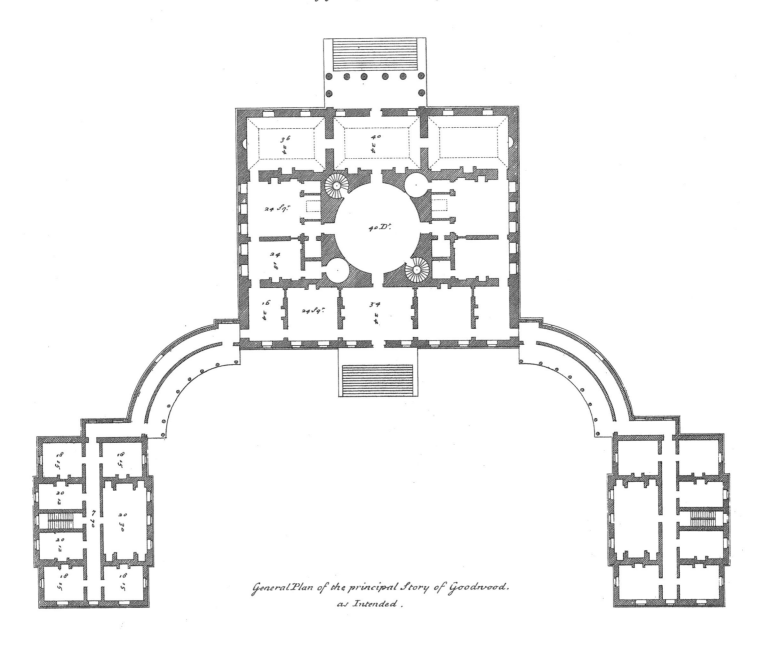

General Plan of the principal Story of Goodwood.

as Intended.

a Scale of 100 feet

5 10   20   30   40   50   60   70   80   90   100

Ca: Campbell Architectus.

H: Hulsbergh Sculp:

Ca: Campbell Architect.

Elevation of the West Front of Goodwood in Sussex the Seat of his Grace the Duke of Richmond and Lenox. design'd by Colen Campbell Esq: Anno 1724.

H.Hulsbergh Sculp :

10   20   30   40   50   60 feet

The Elevation of Iohn Plumptre Esq.r his House in the Town of Nottingham.

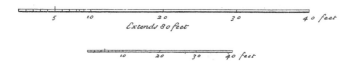

Extends 80 feet

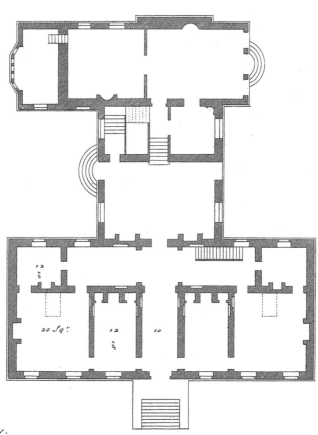

Ca: Campbell Architectus.

H: Hulsbergh Sculp:

This new Design for a Bridge over the River Thames at London near Lambeth
is most humbly Inscrib'd to the Right Honourable William Pulteney Esq.

a Scale of 400 Feet

10 20 30 40 50   100   200   300   400

75 . 0   100 . 0   100.0   100.0   50.0   100.0   100.0   75 . 0

Ca: Campbell Inv: et del:

H:Hulsbergh Sculp:

C. 3, PL. 56

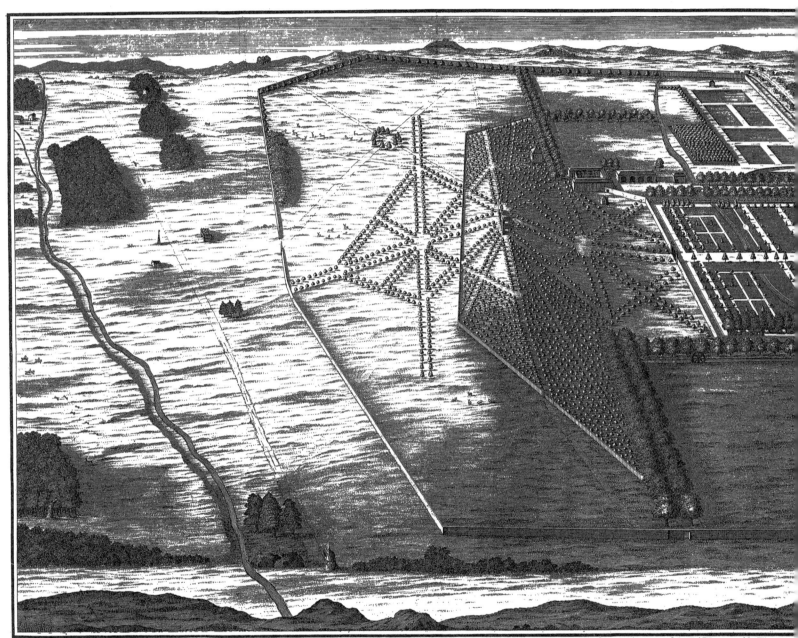

Wilton in Wiltshire, The Seat of the R.ᵗ Honourable The Ea...

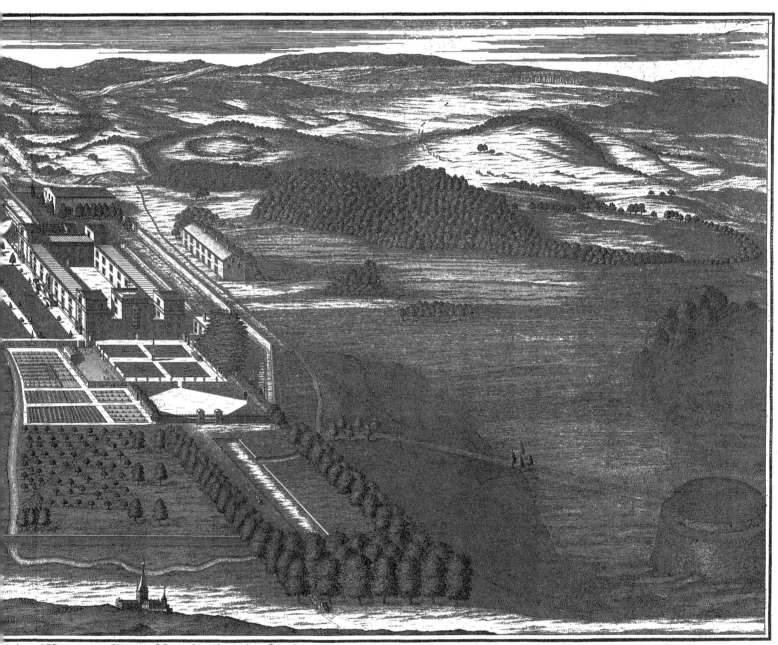

roke *ard Montgomery, Knight of the most Noble Order of the Garter &c:*

H.Hulsbergh Sculp:

Ca: Campbell Delin:

Appledorecombe in the Ifle of Wight, in the County of Southampton, the Seat of Sr. Robert Worſley, Bart: rebuilt Anno 1710.

H: Huſbergh Sculp:

High Meadow in Glocestershire, the Seat of the Right-Honourable
Thomas Lord Vyscount Gage.

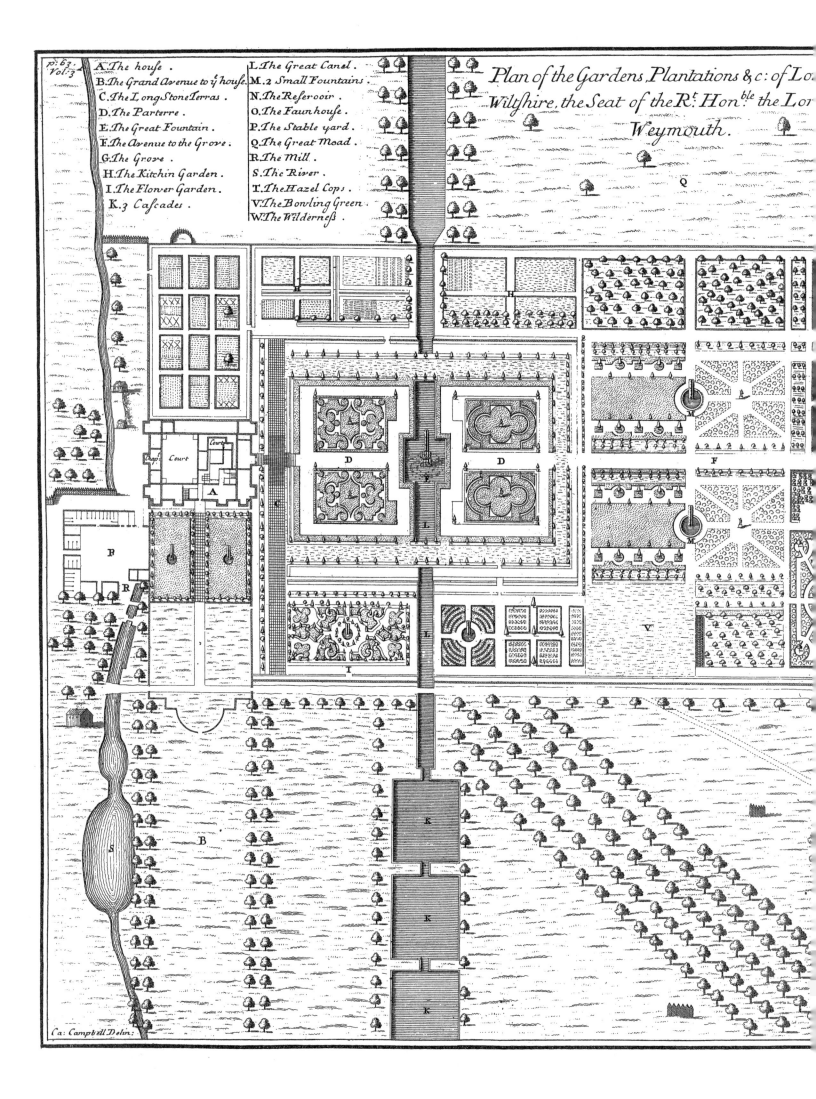

A. The house .
B. The Grand Avenue to y^e house.
C. The Long Stone Terras .
D. The Parterre .
E. The Great Fountain .
F. The Avenue to the Grove .
G. The Grove .
H. The Kitchin Garden .
I. The Flower Garden .
K. 3 Cascades .

L. The Great Canal .
M. 2 Small Fountains
N. The Reſervoir .
O. The Faun house .
P. The Stable yard .
Q. The Great Mead .
R. The Mill .
S. The River .
T. The Hazel Cops .
V. The Bowling Green .
W. The Wilderneß .

Plan of the Gardens, Plantations &c: of Lo[ng]
Wiltſhire, the Seat of the R^t Honble the Lor[d]
Weymouth.

Ca: Campbell Delin:

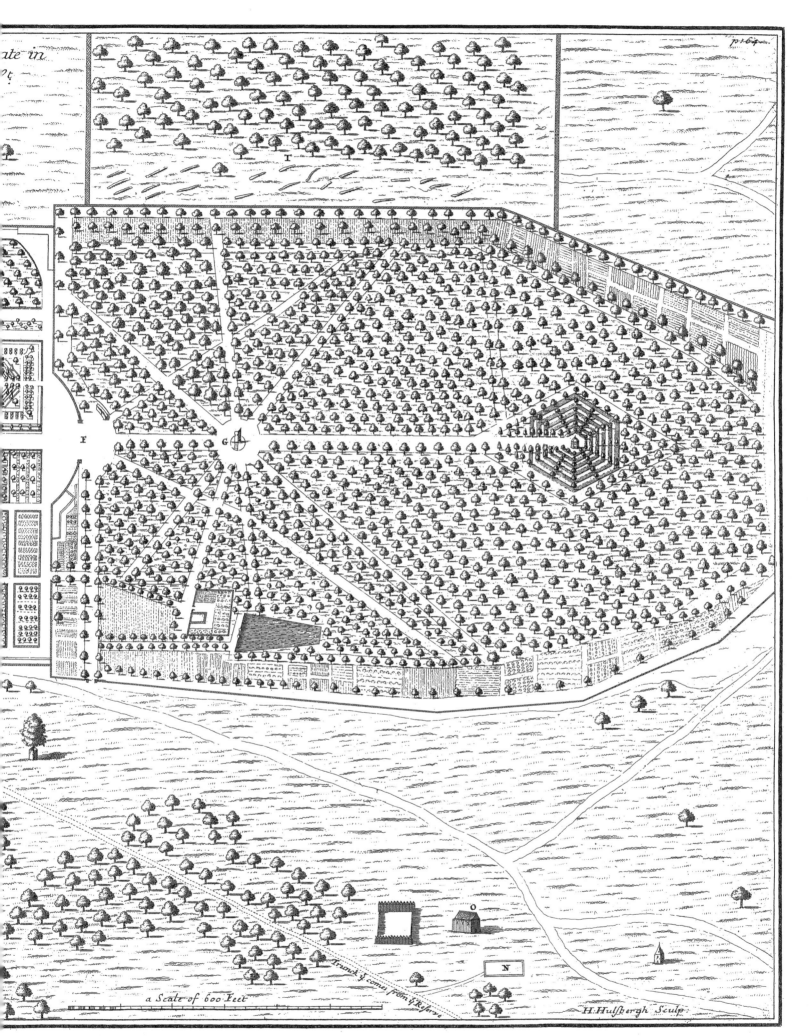

T

F

G

O

N

a Scale of 600 Feet

Trunck y comes from y Reserve

H. Hulsbergh Sculp.

Ca: Campbell Delin:

Long Leate in Wiltshire, The Seat of the Right

nourable the Lord Viscount Weymouth &c:

H: Hulsbergh Sculp:

Chatsworth in Derbyshire. The Seat of his Grace the Duke of Devonshire &c:

Ca: Campbell Delin:

H. Hulsbergh Sculp:

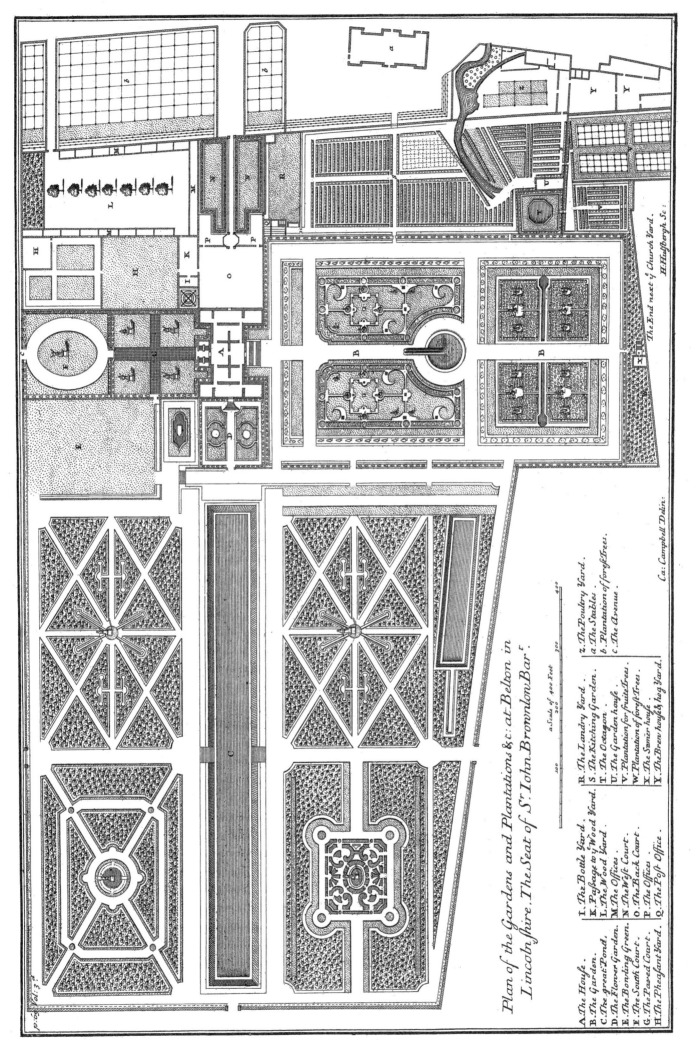

Plan of the Gardens and Plantations &c: at Belton in
Lincolnshire. The Seat of S.r Iohn Brownlow Bar.t

A Scale of 400 Feet

A. The House.
B. The Garden.
C. The great Pond.
D. The Flower Garden.
E. The Bowling Green.
F. The South Court.
G. The Paved Court.
H. The Pheasant Yard.
I. The Bottle Yard.
K. Passage to y.e Wood Yard.
L. The Wood Yard.
M. The Offices.
N. The West Court.
O. The Back Court.
P. The Offices.
Q. The Post Office.
R. The Laudry Yard.
S. The Kitching Garden.
T. The Octagon.
U. The Garden house.
V. Plantation for fruit-Trees.
W. Plantation of forest-Trees.
X. The Somer house.
Y. The Brew house & hog Yard.
z. The Poultry Yard.
a. The Stables.
b. Plantation of forest-Trees.
c. The Avenue.

Ca: Campbell Delin:

H. Hulfbergh Sc:

The End next y.e Church Yard.

C. 3, PL. 70

Ca. Campbell Delin:

Belton in Lincolnshire, the Seat of S.r Iohn Brownlow Bar

H. Hulsbergh Sculp:

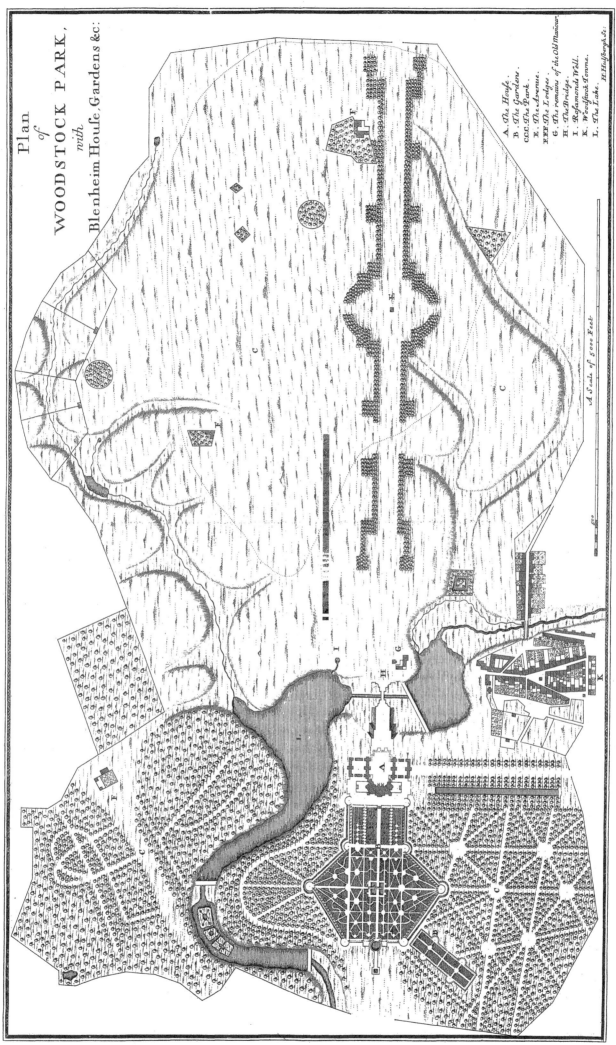

Plan
of
WOODSTOCK PARK,
with
Blenheim Houſe, Gardens &c:

A. The Houſe.
B. The Garden.
C.C.C. The Park.
E. The Avenue.
F.F.F. The Lodge.
G. The remains of the Old Manour.
H. The Bridge.
I. Roſamonds Well.
K. Woodſtock Towne.
L. The Lake.

H. Huſbergh Sc:

A Scale of 5000 Feet

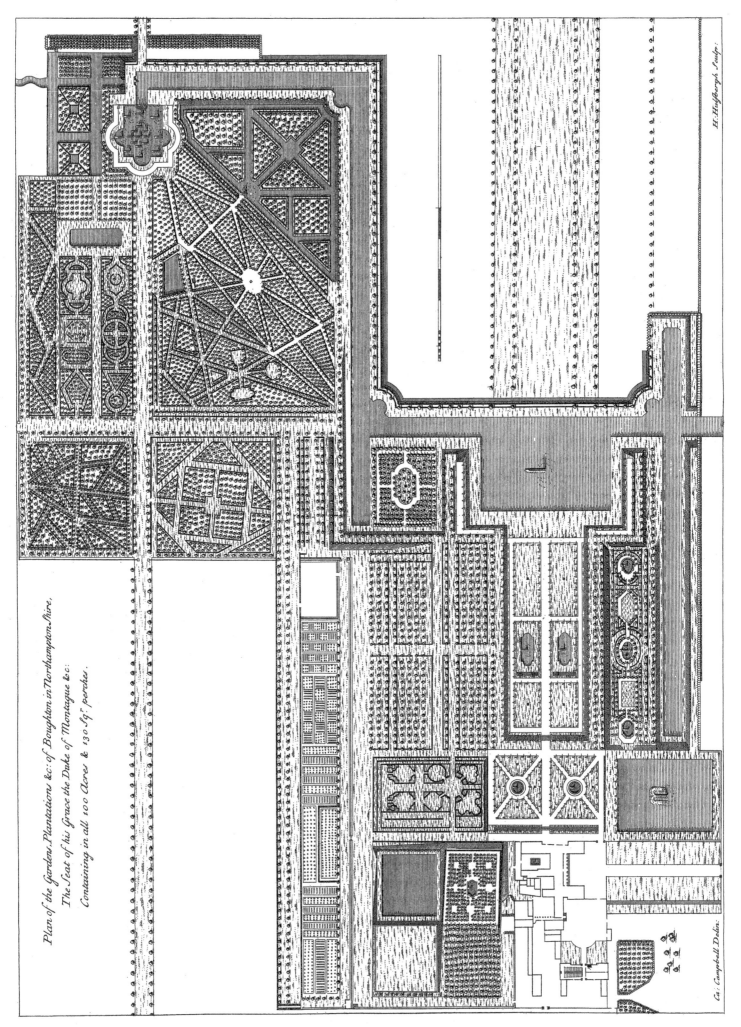

Plan of the Gardens, Plantations &c: of Boughton in Northampton Shire,
The Seat of his Grace the Duke of Montague &c:
Containing in all 100 Acres & 130 Sq: perches.

Co: Campbell Delin:

H: Hulsbergh Sculp:

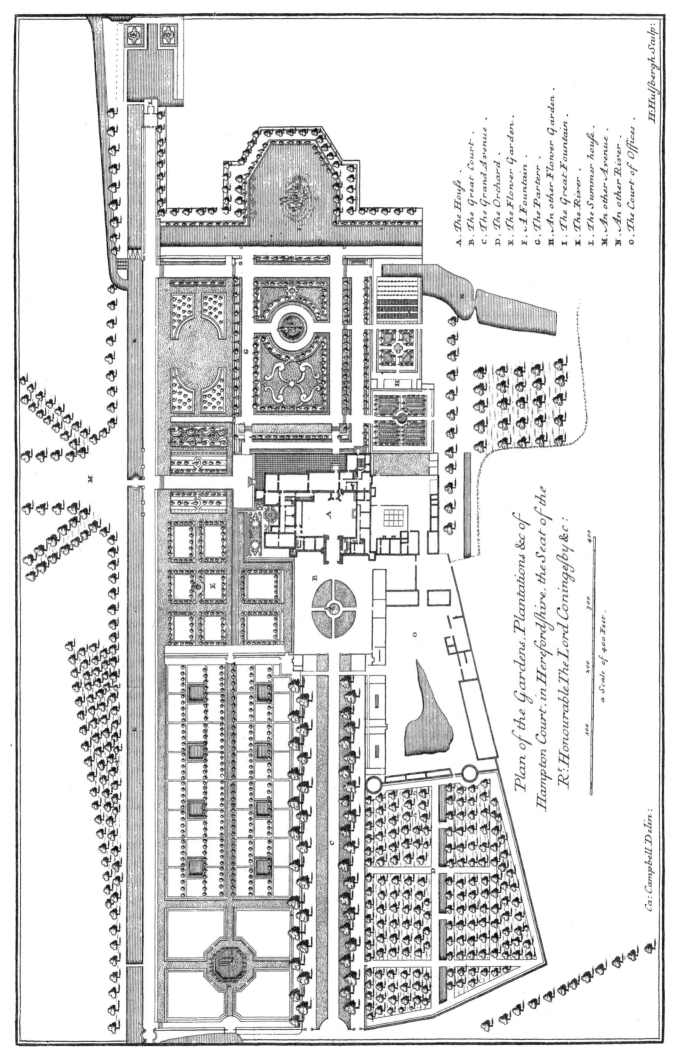

Ca: Campbell Delin:

H:Hulssbergh Sculp:

Plan of the Gardens, Plantations &c of
Hampton Court, in Herefordshire, the Seat of the
Rt: Honourable The Lord Coningesby &c:

A . The Houfe .
B . The Great Court .
C . The Grand Avenue .
D . The Orchard .
E . The Flower Garden .
F . A Fountain .
G . The Parterr .
H . An other Flower Garden .
I . The Great Fountain .
K . The River .
L . The Summer houfe .
M . An other Avenue .
N . An other River .
O . The Court of Offices .

100   200   300   400

a Scale of 400 Feet .

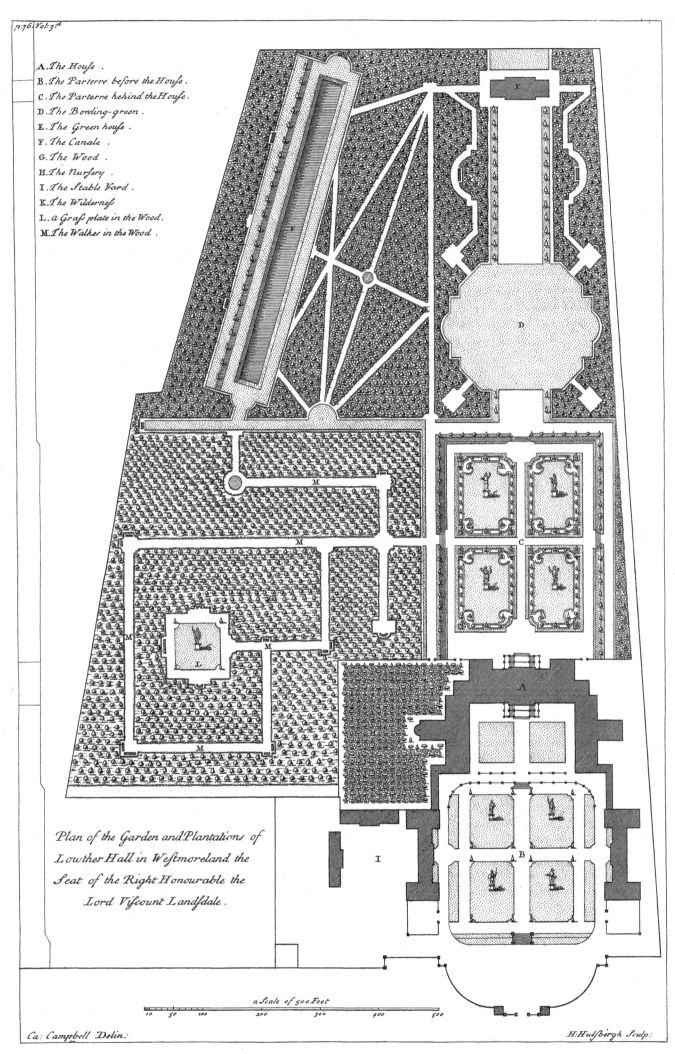

A. The House .
B. The Parterre before the House .
C. The Parterre behind the House .
D. The Bowling-green .
E. The Green house .
F. The Canale .
G. The Wood .
H. The Nursery .
I. The Stable Yard .
K. The Wilderness
L. a Grass plate in the Wood .
M. The Walkes in the Wood .

Plan of the Garden and Plantations of
Lowther Hall in Westmoreland the
Seat of the Right Honourable the
Lord Viscount Landsdale .

a Scale of 500 Feet
10 50 100   200   300   400   500

Ca: Campbell Delin:

H: Hulsbergh Sculp:

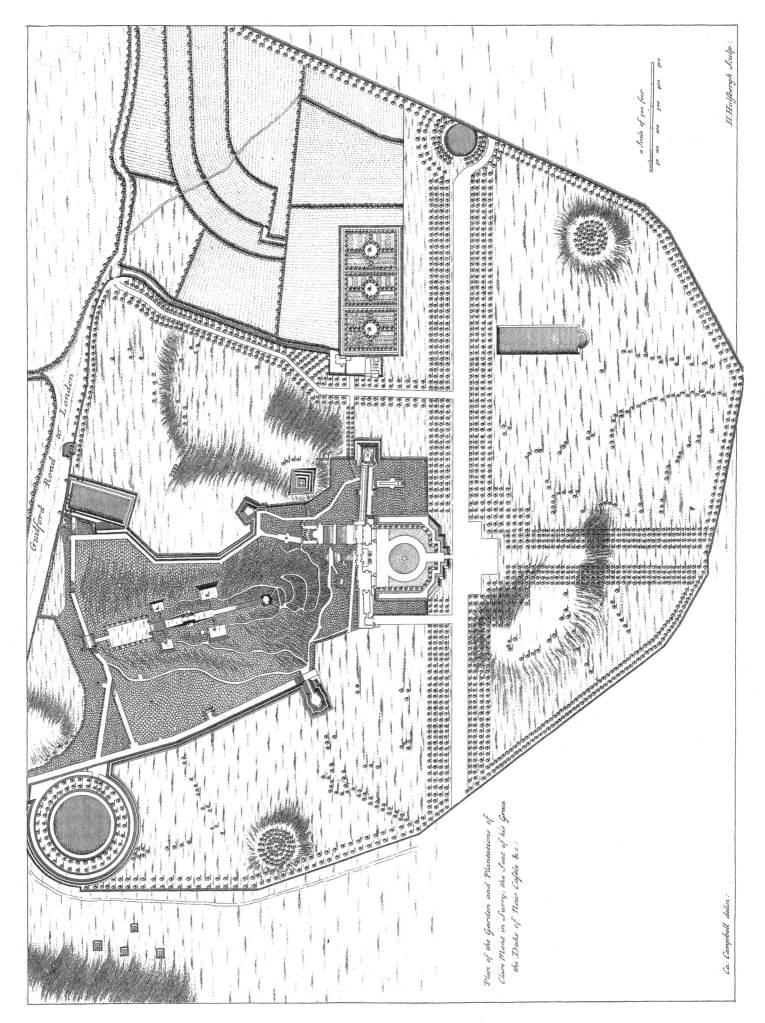

Guilford Road to London

a Scale of 500 feet

H. Hulsbergh Sculp:

Plan of the Garden and Plantations of
Clare Mont in Surry, the Seat of his Grace
the Duke of New Castle &c:

Co: Campbell delin:

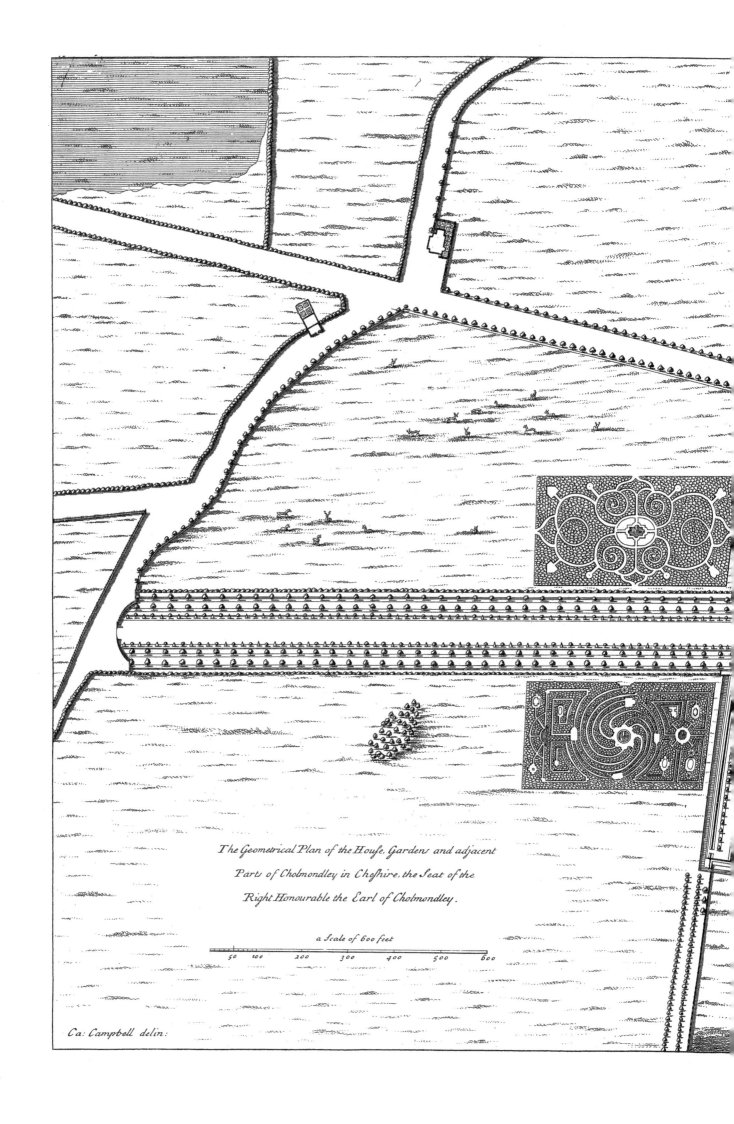

The Geometrical Plan of the House, Gardens and adjacent
Parts of Cholmondley in Cheshire, the Seat of the
Right Honourable the Earl of Cholmondley.

a Scale of 600 feet

50   100   200   300   400   500   600

Ca: Campbell delin:

H. Hulsbergh Sculp:

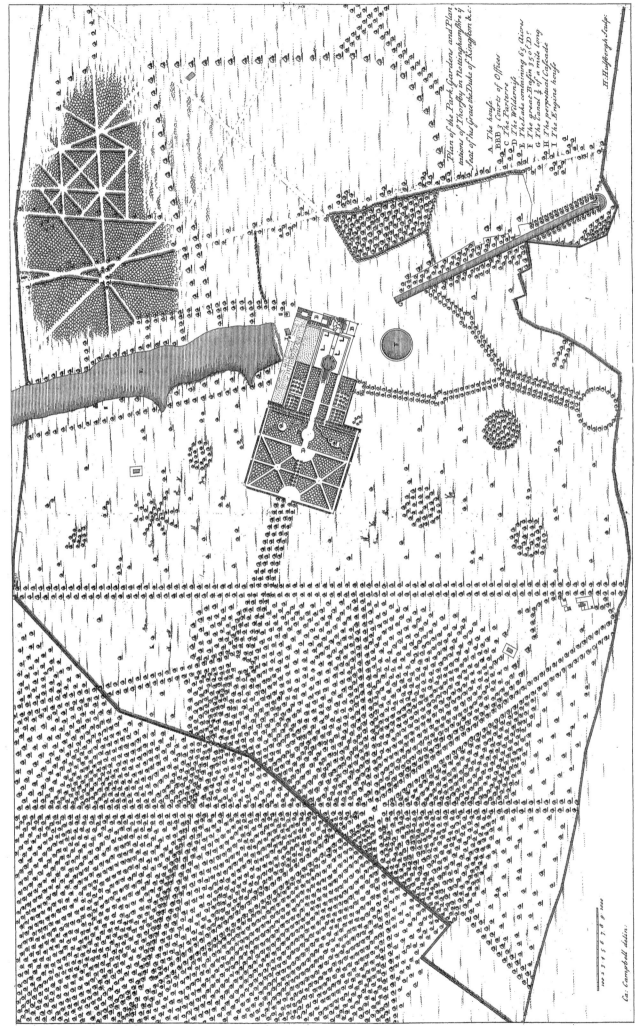

Plan of the Park, Gardens and Plantations of Thorsby in Nottinghamshire ye
Seat of his Grace the Duke of Kingston &c.

A. The house
BBB 3 Courts of Offices
C The Parterre
D The Wilderness
E The Lake containing 65 Acres
F The great Bason 350 D.
G The Canal ¾ of a mile long
H The perpetual Cascade
I The Engine house

Ca: Campbell delin:

H. Hulsbergh Sculp:

Ca: Campbell Delin:

Althrop in Northamptonshire, The Seat of the Rt: Honourable the Earl of Sunderland &c:

H: Hulsbergh Sculp:

Elevation of Duncomb Park in Yorkshire, the Seat of Thomas Duncomb Esq. Designed by William Wakefield Esq. 1713.

a Scale of 100 Feet

Plan of the Principal Story of Duncomb Park.

Ca. Campbell Delin.

H. Hulsbergh Sculp.

C.Campbell Delin:

Duncomb Park in Yorkshire, the Seat of Thomas Duncomb Esq: Designed by William Wakefield Esq: 1713.

H.Hulfbergh Sculp:

Elevation of Atherton in the County of Lancaster the Seat of Richard Atherton Esq.: Design'd by W.m Wakefield Esq.: 1723

5 10 20 30 40 50 60 feet

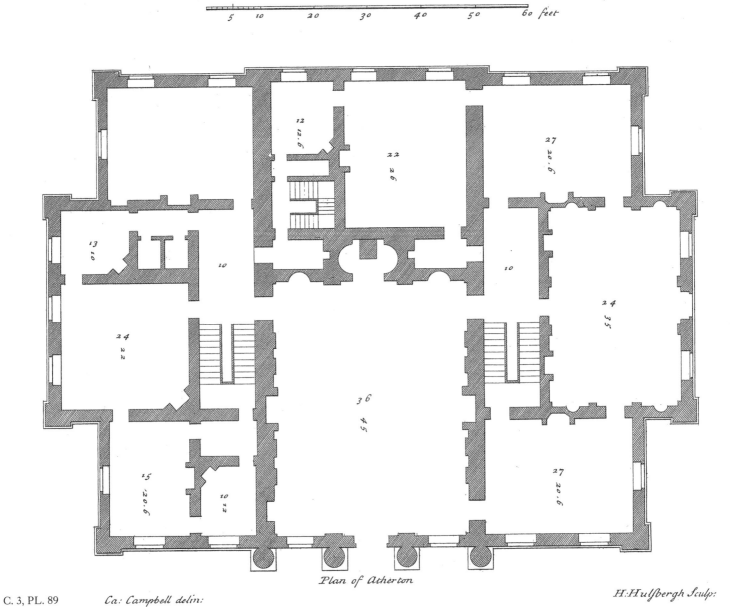

Plan of Atherton

Ca: Campbell delin: *H: Hulsbergh Sculp:*

Rookby Park in the County of York, the Seat of Thomas Robinson Esq.r Designed by William Wakefield Esq.r

Extend 96 feet

10   20   30   40   50   60 feet

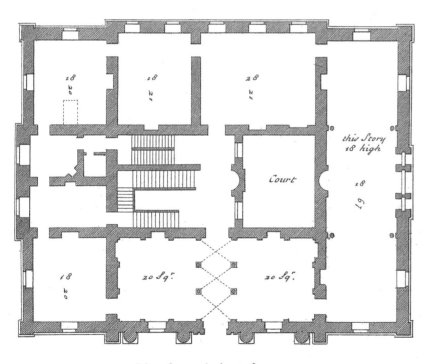

this Story
18 high

Court

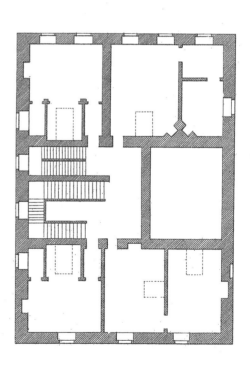

Plan of the principal Story   Plan of the Attik Story

10   20   30   40   50   60 feet

Ca: Campbell delin: H: Hulsbergh Sculp:

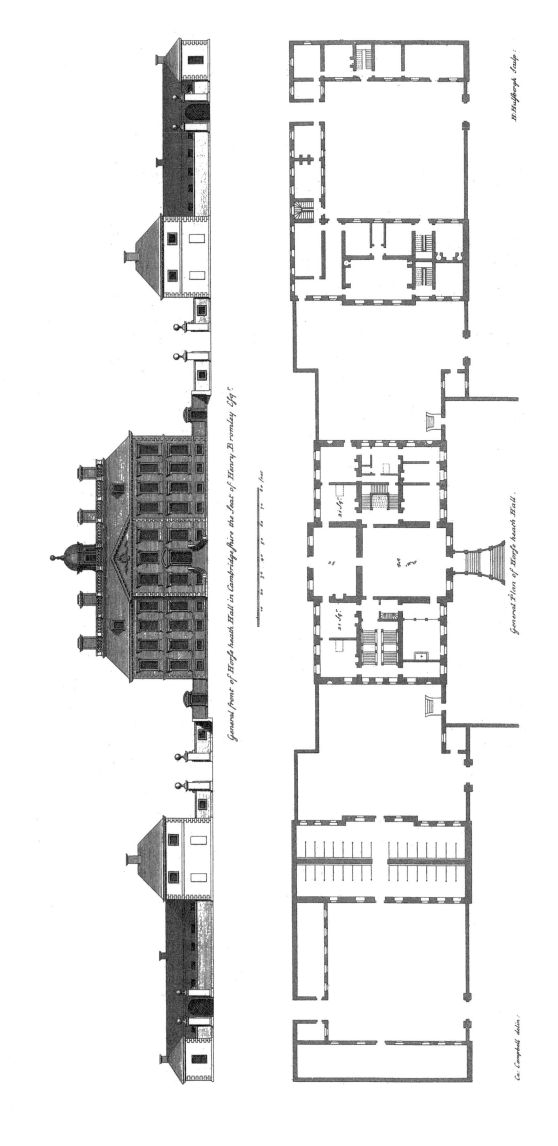

General front of Horse heath Hall in Cambridgeshire the Seat of Henry Bromley Esqr.

General Plan of Horse heath Hall.

H. Hulsbergh Sculp:

Ca: Campbell delin:

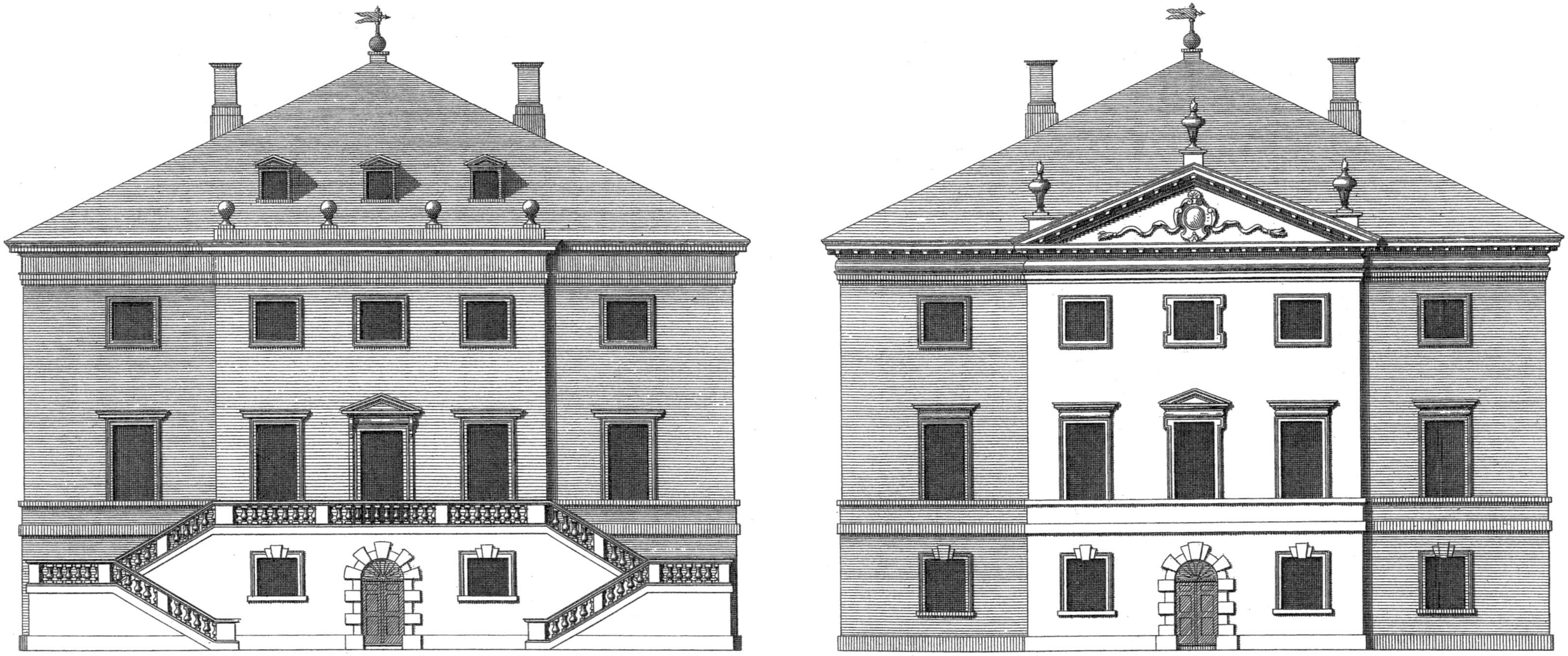

front to Twittenham park

A house in Twittenham midlesex near the River Thames.

Front to the River.

24 Sq.r
Ground Story
Attick Story
5 10 20 30 40 f.
5 10 20 30 40 f
15 Sq.r
a Cube of 24
15 25
15 Sq.r
15 Sq.r
Principall Story

Ca: Campbell delin:

H: Hulsbergh Sculp:

C. 3, PL. 93

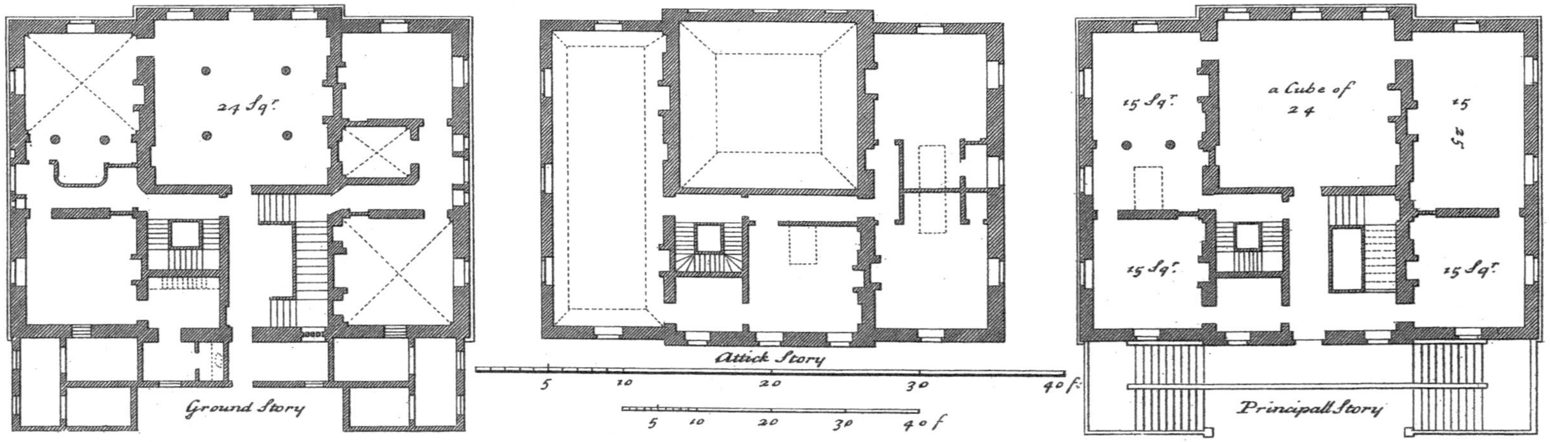

Elevation of Leyton Grange in Essex, the house of David Gansel Esqr.

Designd and built by him Self. 1720.

5   10   20   30   40 feet

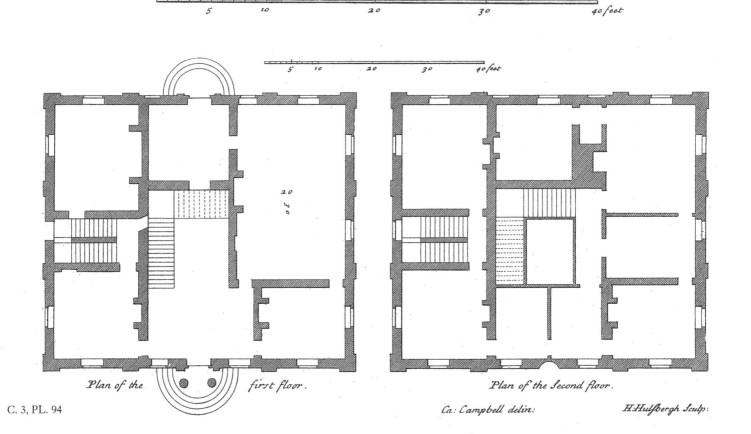

Plan of the first floor.

Plan of the Second floor.

Ca: Campbell delin: *H. Hulsbergh Sculp:*

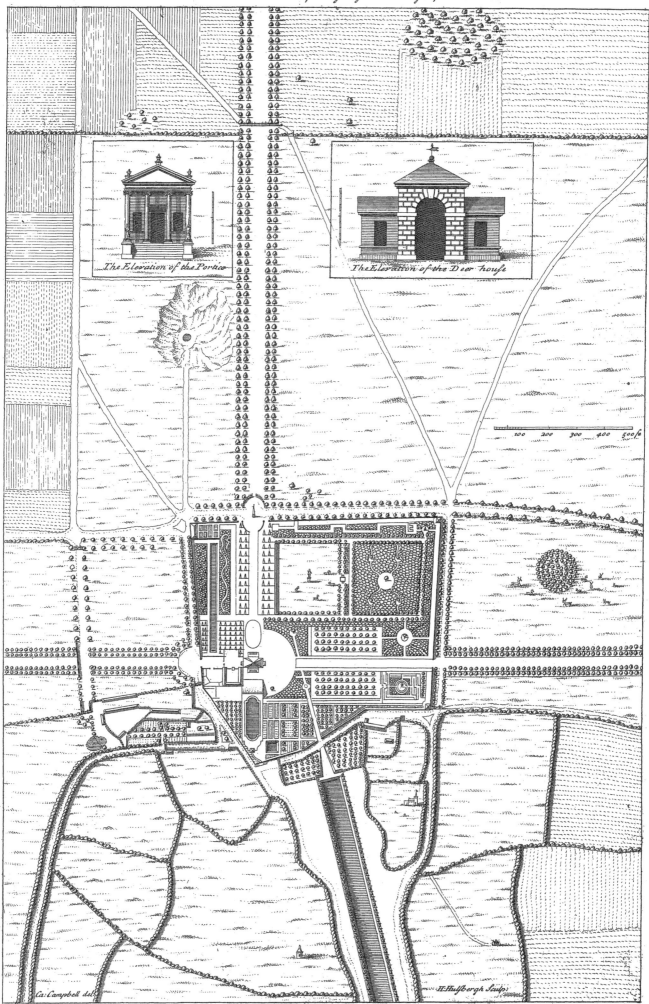

Plan of the Garden and Plantations of Narford in the County of Norfolk, the Seat of the Honourable S.ᵗ Andrew Fountain Vice Chamberlain to her Royal Highness the Princess of Wales. &c.

The Elevation of the Portico

The Elevation of the Deer house

Ca: Campbell delin.

H. Hulsbergh Sculp.

100   200   300   400   500 ft

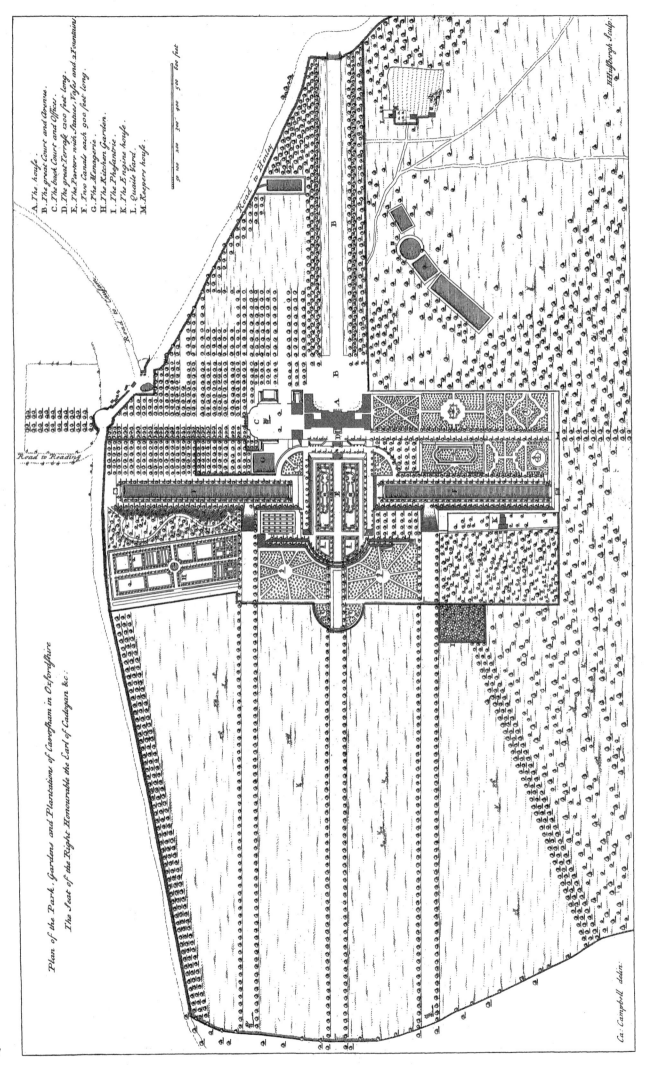

Plan of the Park, Gardens and Plantations of Caversham in Oxfordshire

The Seat of the Right Honourable the Earl of Cadogan &c.

A. The house.
B. The great Court and Avenue.
C. The back Court and Offices.
D. The great Terrass 1200 feet long.
E. The Parterre with Statues, Vases and 12 Fountains.
F. Two Canals each 900 feet long.
G. The Menagerie.
H. The Kitchen Garden.
I. The Pheasantrie.
K. The Engine house.
L. Quaile Yard.
M. Keepers house.

Road to Henley

Road to Reading

Ca: Campbell delin:

H.Hulßbergh Sculp:

C. 3, PL. 96-97

Co: Campbell Architect.

General Front of a New Design of my Invention extending 250.

General Plan of the Principall Story.

H. Hulsbergh Sculp:

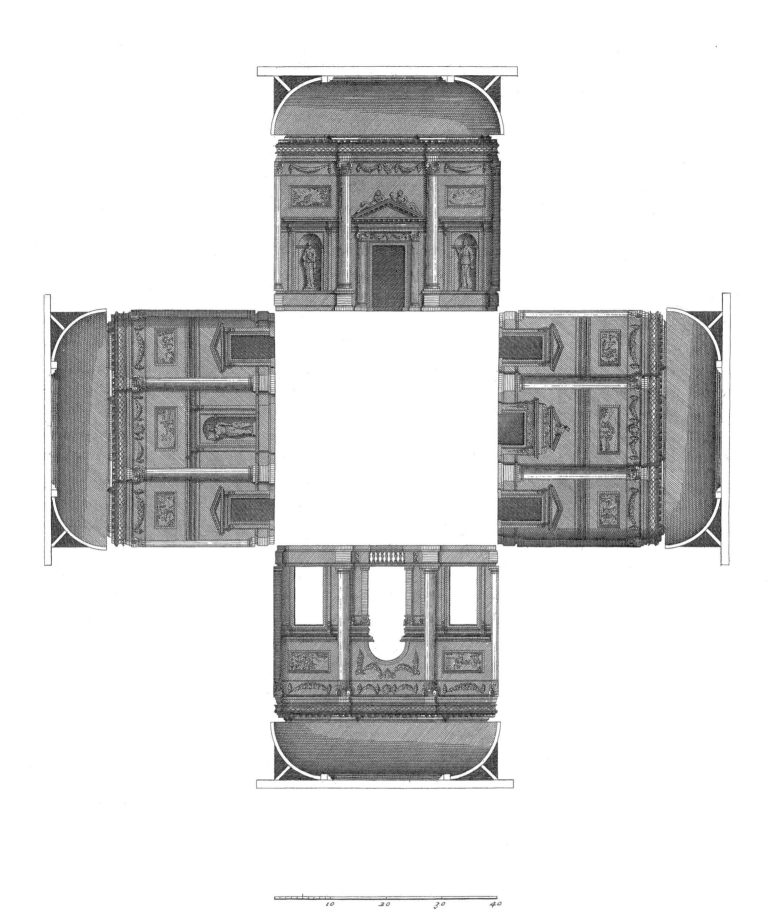

Section of the Great Hall of my Invention being a Cube of 40 feet.

Ca: Campbell Architectus

H.Hulßbergh Sculp:

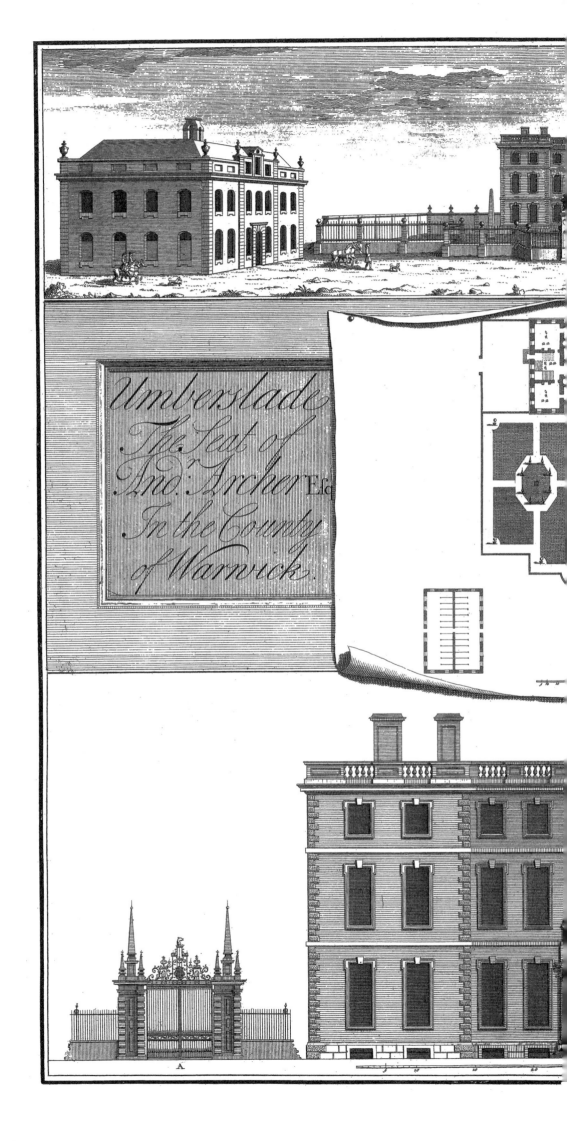

Umberslade
The Seat of
Andᵣ Archer Eſqᵣ
In the County
of Warwick.

A

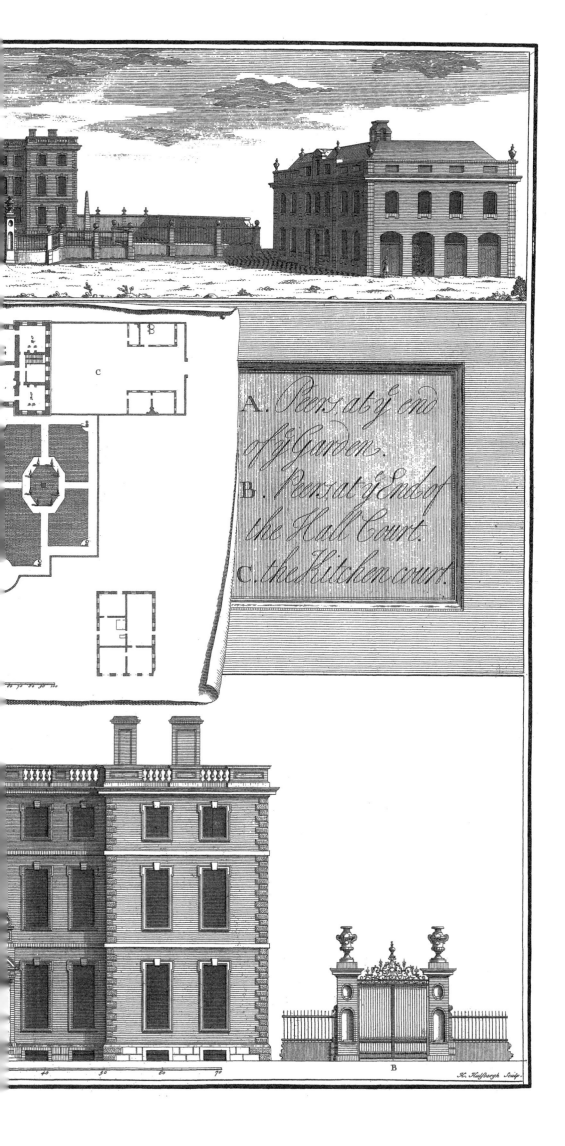

A. Piers at ye end
of ye Garden.

B. Piers at ye End of
the Hall Court.

C. the Kitchen court

B

H. Hulsbergh Sculp.